MW00814889

AN EXTRAORDINARY ORDINARY MAN

AN EXTRAORDINARY
ORDINARY MAN
The Life Story of Edgar House

DOUG HOUSE AND ADRIAN HOUSE

With a Foreword by BOB COLE

ISER

**Institute of Social and
Economic Research**

© 2015 by Doug House and Adrian House

All rights reserved. The use of any part of this publication reproduced, transmitted in any form or by any means, electronic, mechanical, recording, or otherwise, or stored in a retrieval system, without the prior written consent of the publisher is an infringement of copyright law.

Library and Archives Canada Cataloguing in Publication
House, Doug, 1944-, author
    An extraordinary ordinary man : the life story of Edgar House / Doug House and Adrian House ; with a foreword by Bob Cole.

(Social and economic studies ; 78)

Includes bibliographical references and index.
ISBN 978-1-894725-26-2 (paperback)

    1. House, Edgar, 1911-. 2. St. John's (N.L.)--Biography. 3. Newfoundland and Labrador--History--20th century. 4. Newfoundland and Labrador--Social conditions--20th century. I. House, Adrian, 1978-, author II. Title. III. Series: Social and economic studies (St. John's, N.L.) ; 78

FC2196.26.H68H68 2015   971.8'104092   C2015-906836-3

Cover photographs: Edgar House. (Courtesy of House family). Land grant to James Winter from Governor Molineux Shuldham, 1774. (Courtesy St. John's City Archives)
Design and typesetting: Alison Carr
Copy editing: Richard Tallman

Published by ISER Books — Faculty of Arts Publications
Institute of Social and Economic Research
Memorial University of Newfoundland
297 Mount Scio Road
St. John's, NL A1C 5S7
www.arts.mun.ca/iserbooks/

Printed and bound in Canada

Dedication

We are pleased to dedicate this book to the other members of our extended family: Edgar and Margie's daughter, Jan, married to George (Jordy) Squires; their daughter-in-law, Jeannie House; their granddaughter, Lynn, married to John Cadigan; their granddaughter, Vanessa, married to Cory Milley; their granddaughter, Meg, married to Steve Doherty; their grandson, Matthew, married to Daphne Dumbrille; their grandson, Greg; and their great-grandchildren, Erin, Ben, Katie, Michael, Claire, Olivia, Sadie, Sophie, Maeve, and Lola.

Contents

Acknowledgements 9

Foreword by Bob Cole 12

Maps

    Map 1. The island of Newfoundland 15

    Map 2: St. John's in the 1950s 16

Preface 17

General Introduction: Edgar House

    and Twentieth-Century Newfoundland 19

Introduction to the Text 69

The Life Story of Edgar House in His Own Words 73

1. Family. 75

2. Margie 88

3. Jerry and Georgie 103

4. War and a War Hero 114

5. Old St. John's 123

6. Sports and Recreation 142

7. Trinity: The Early Years 161

8. Trinity: The Later Years 180

9. Education 189

10. Teaching Career at Feild and Buchans 209

11. Headmaster, 1944–52 225

12. Politics and Joe Smallwood 248

13. TB and the Lung Association 257

14. Rotary and the Rotarians. 268

    Conclusion 278

Bibliography 285

Index 303

Acknowledgements

This is Edgar's story, told in his own words in 18 recorded conversations with his son, Doug. But it has taken a lot of work to piece the material together from many different conversations into a narrative that flows well and is organized into discernible topics. Adrian was mainly responsible for making this happen. We are also grateful to Andrea Nurse (now Andrea Nolan), who did much of the early sorting and organizing of the interview material. Andrea also conducted the final, nineteenth, interview with Edgar, and was successful in encouraging him to talk about certain topics, notably Confederation, about which he was somewhat reticent in talking to his son.

We are grateful to the J.R. Smallwood Centre for Newfoundland Studies of Memorial University for providing a research grant in support of this project and to Memorial's Department of Folklore and its Folklore and Language Archive for providing a recording machine and tapes. Big thanks are due to Barbara Reddy for professionally transcribing the tapes. Copies of all the tapes and transcriptions are available to other researchers and interested parties in the Memorial University of Newfoundland Folklore and Language Archive.

We would like to acknowledge the support of Memorial University's Publications Subvention Program for providing financial assistance towards the costs of publishing this book.

Annotating this manuscript has required a wide-ranging survey of people, places, and events in Newfoundland. We have made extensive use of the excellent five-volume *Encyclopedia of Newfoundland and Labrador*, available online, and the *Dictionary of Newfoundland Biography*. Definitions of Newfoundland words come mostly from the *Dictionary of Newfoundland English*. Other sources have been accessed primarily at the Centre for Newfoundland Studies in the Queen Elizabeth II Library of Memorial University, which houses a vast collection of material on Newfoundland and Labrador.

The staff at the Centre for Newfoundland Studies were invaluable in helping Adrian research the explanatory notes for the people, places, and events in Edgar's reminiscences. Huge thanks to director Joan Ritcey and staff — Jackie Hillier, Colleen Field, Debby Andrews, Carl White, Glenda Dawe, Donna Doucette, Sharon Thompson, Jane Deal, and Deanna Matthews — for their patience and perseverance.

Charlie Conway of Memorial University's Department of Geography did a great job of designing and producing the maps for this book. And we are grateful to Sandra Clarke for her insights on the section about Edgar's English. We also acknowledge the assistance of Assistant Deputy Minister Alton Hollett, Robert Reid, and Ashley Davis of the Economics and Statistics Branch of the Department of Finance, Government of Newfoundland and Labrador, in locating some of the historical statistics we have cited.

We would also like to thank Janet Squires, Edgar's daughter, for her helpful comments on an early draft of the manuscript, as well for her help in putting together the collection of photographs reproduced in the book. We are also grateful to Edgar's daughter-in-law, Jeannie House, for her comments and help in editing the manuscript and to Matthew and Vanessa House for their reviews of the text.

We are grateful to Larry Dohey of The Rooms Archives, to Jim Miller, Project Co-ordinator of the Trinity Historical Society, and to Bernard Davis, archivist for the Church Lads' Brigade, for their help in choosing the photographs we have included.

The following people also deserve our thanks for reviewing and commenting on specific parts of the text: Judith Adler, Bob Cole, Sandra Clarke, John Crosbie, Kim Hong, Bill Rompkey, and Gary Wilansky. A special thanks to Bob Cole for writing the heartfelt Foreword to this book.

We are grateful to Sharon Roseman, Alison Carr, and two anonymous reviewers at ISER Books for their insightful and challenging comments on earlier drafts of this manuscript. Finally, we express our appreciation to Richard Tallman for his careful and thorough copy-editing.

Foreword
Bob Cole

The year 1944 turned out to be very significant for me and 40 of my friends, 10- to 11-year-olds getting ready to face the world ahead. We were the Grade 4 class of Bishop Feild College, an all-boys school on Bond Street in St. John's.

Some extraordinarily studious young boys were in this class and, then, the other group — of which I was a part — always was striving to be a part of a winning sports team. Something happened in 1944 that would help both sides. At the final morning assembly of June, I remember that we were called together for this special assembly to say goodbye to our Headmaster, Mr. R.E. Tanner, who was leaving Newfoundland and returning to his home in England to enjoy his retirement. It was a very emotional meeting for everybody. Mr. Tanner was a great educator. He demanded strict discipline at all times, and surely would be missed. The school produced successful graduates under his watch.

Intercollegiate sporting activities, however, seemed to need a shot in the arm. We won nothing as a school. We needed something to happen. Classes started for the new school year, 1944, which was the centennial year of the founding of Bishop Feild College. Many of the teaching staff were back and as we awaited the announcement of the name of our new Headmaster there was a buzz in the air. He had been Principal of the high school in Buchans, Newfoundland, for the past five years, but was from St. John's. More importantly, he was a former student and teacher at Bishop Feild, as was his father, George House. The word spread quickly through the student body that this new Headmaster, Edgar House, had been a great football player (what they call "soccer" today) — one of the very best at his game. He was the MVP of his league. The whole school felt it — We have found a winner!

That centennial year of Bishop Feild College was amazing. The discipline was unchanged. The dress code was the same — shirt and tie, shoes shined, everything neat and tidy — and always right on time, just like our new Headmaster. The junior intercollegiate team won the football championship; the senior intercollegiate team won the football championship. From here on, things were surely looking up.

He was our teacher for English grammar, English literature, and chemistry. We always enjoyed his classes, and he seemed to be a part of everything Bishop Feild College had to offer. I vividly recall one September day when our football team was working out on the Feildian Grounds, a beautiful property not far from the College. Practice was usually from 4:30 to 6:00 p.m. On this day, we were working on corner kicks. The Headmaster was there watching. None of us was doing a very good job. A shout came from the sidelines: "Kick that ball over here, please." Someone drove the ball over to Mr. House. He said a few words to us and then booted three in a row — perfectly placed corner kicks. He was wearing a tweed suit and black, highly shined shoes but made three perfect corner kicks! Nobody said a word. We just stared at each other. This man had been reading from Shakespeare's *Hamlet* an hour before, had stopped on his way home to watch our football team practice, and had skilfully demonstrated how to make corner kicks. He participated with us inside or outside the classroom. That's the way he was. He was part of us.

On game day for intercollegiate football, the team was excused from the final class of the afternoon so that they could get to the field and prepare. I recall one game day when the team was leaving class and Mr. House singled me out as he was wishing the team well. "Don't forget, Cole, boots and all!" Yes, everyone got a lift from that. What he said and did seemed to be the right thing for everybody. I wish every high school could be as fortunate as our 40-strong class of '51 in having a Headmaster just like our Mr. Edgar G. House.

I am delighted that Edgar's son Doug recorded several long conversations with his father during the later years of his life; and that he and Edgar's grandson, Adrian, have compiled this fascinating book about the life of a great Newfoundlander.

Map 1. The island of Newfoundland.

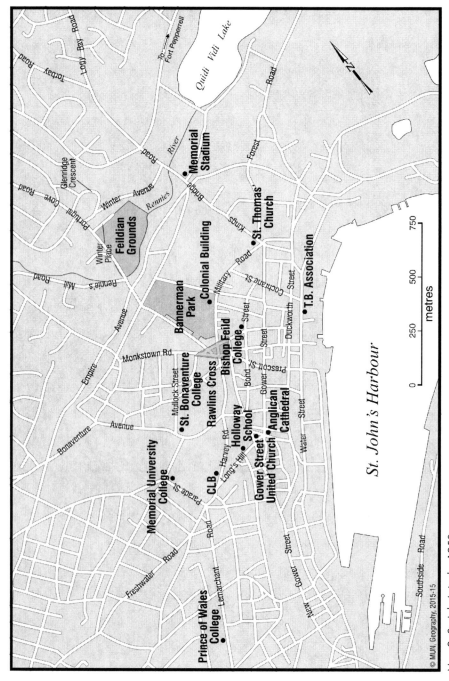

Map 2. St. John's in the 1950s.

Preface
Doug House

As my parents were growing older, several of my contemporaries, whose parents had died, expressed their regret at never having recorded their life stories. I resolved that would not be the case for me and my family. Sadly, my mother, Margaret House, had already contracted Alzheimer's disease when I made this resolution, so I could not record her story. It would indeed have been an interesting one, including her years at Memorial University College and Mount Allison University, where she became one of the very few women from Newfoundland in the early 1930s to earn a B.Sc. degree. She does feature prominently in this collection of reminiscences of her husband of 60 years.

Fortunately, my father, Edgar House, was still healthy at 89, his mind sharp and his memory amazing, particularly for the early years of his life. He agreed to sit with me in his living room to reminisce about his interesting and fulfilling life. This book is based on some 19 hours of conversation recorded with my father. Although I asked questions from time to time, for the most part I just let Dad talk and lose himself in his memories, most of them happy, about his life and times. In his words, "They were good times." For samples of these interviews, please visit www.edgarhouse.ca.

Edgar was a very dedicated citizen of Newfoundland and, later, of Canada. He was much involved in education as a teacher, at Bishop Feild in St. John's, as Headmaster at both Feild and Buchans in central Newfoundland, as President of the Newfoundland Teachers' Association, and as a member of Memorial University's Board of Regents. In his second career, beginning in the 1950s, he worked diligently for the

Newfoundland Tuberculosis Association (now the Newfoundland and Labrador Lung Association), first as Director of Rehabilitation and later as Executive Director. He was involved in much volunteer service, mainly through the St. John's Rotary Club, of which he was a proud member for over 50 years.

Edgar House was also a fine athlete. He played hockey and tennis. He loved rugby, and was disappointed when it died out in Newfoundland and delighted at its recent successful revival. As an athlete, he was best known for his prowess in soccer and was honoured to be selected as a member of both the St. John's and the provincial soccer halls of fame in 1999. Edgar also coached several school teams and emphasized sports and sportsmanship as fundamental to a sound education.

We knew him mainly as a dedicated family man, as father and grandfather. In recognition of how much he and his wife Margie meant to his family we have dedicated this book to his children and their spouses, his grandchildren and their spouses, and his 10 great-grandchildren.

Edgar House and Twentieth-Century Newfoundland
Doug House

In their seminal book, *Character and Social Structure*, Hans Gerth and C. Wright Mills show that a person's character or personality is moulded by the social institutions and culture of his or her place and time. The aim in this introduction is to locate the life and times of Edgar House within the historical development of New-foundland society and culture in the twentieth century, and in terms of his particular place within that society.[1] The categories to be con-sidered are: family and kinship, place and community types, religion and education, social stratification, gender, voluntary associations, and self-identity.

While his position and experience within these social institutions helped mould Edgar's character, we want to avoid a simply determin-istic point of view. While Edgar was heavily influenced by his social and cultural environment, he was a distinct personality with his own passions and points of view, which were not merely reflections of

---

1   Although the official name of the province was changed to Newfoundland and
     Labrador in 2001, Edgar's formative experiences all were on the island of New-
     foundland. During his lifetime, Newfoundland was, first, an independent domin-
     ion, then, a kind of British protectorate under a Commission of Government from
     1934 to 1949, and, after 1949, the tenth province of Canada. Edgar continued to
     refer to Newfoundland as a "country" throughout his life.

external social and cultural forces. As we shall see, some of his attitudes and values were at odds with what one might expect from his
social location, for example, his attitudes towards women and gender
relations, his liberal views about different ethnic groups, and his
heartfelt opinions about Confederation with Canada.[2]

Edgar lived through the major historical events of the twentieth
century. Some of these were international in scope: World War I, the
Great Depression of the 1930s, and World War II. Each of these im-
pacted Newfoundland profoundly. Edgar was too young to fight in
World War I and, for reasons to be explained in his own terms, was
not directly involved in World War II, either. Nevertheless, because
these two wars were pivotal to understanding the history of Newfoundland and Labrador in the twentieth century, I will discuss them
briefly here. They set the context for much of Edgar's life story. The
War of 1914–1918 was disastrous for the Dominion of Newfoundland.
Some 1,419 of its young men were killed. At the Battle of Beaumont
Hamel, on the fatal day of 1 July 1916, of the 801 Newfoundlanders
who fought, 710 were killed, wounded, or missing ("Dominion of Newfoundland," 2014).[3] Nearly every family in the country was directly or
indirectly affected by these losses. The social, economic, and political
effects of that war, compounded a decade later by the beginning of the

---

2   In this regard, we concur with a social action theoretical approach, along the
     lines established by Max Weber and George Herbert Mead. Weber argued that
     action occurs when human beings attach subjective meanings to their behaviour,
     and that sociological analysis involves "the interpretation of action in terms of its
     subjective meaning" (Weber 8). Mead focused more on how social interaction
     gives rise to one's sense of self, which is primarily a social product: "The unity
     and structure of the complete self reflects the unity and structure of the social
     process as a whole." (Mead 144).

3   For a detailed account of the Royal Newfoundland Regiment during World War I,
     see Colonel G.W.L. Nicholson, The Fighting Newfoundlander, n.d. [1964?]. For an
     analysis of how this battle became mythologized into Newfoundland's Great War
     myth, and how this cultural memory changed after Confederation with Canada in
     1949, see Robert James Allen Harding, "Glorious Tragedy: Newfoundland's Cul-
     tural Memory of the Battle of Beaumont Hamel, 1916–1949," 2004.

Great Depression, led to the surrendering of sovereignty and the loss of democratic government for 15 years.

World War II, 1939–1945, also was disastrous in terms of casualties, with another 1,000 young Newfoundlanders and Labradorians killed (Chen 2014). Because of Newfoundland's strategic position as the nearest point in North America to Europe, however, the economic, social, and political effects of this war were dramatically different. The establishment of strategic naval and air force bases with an influx of thousands of Canadian and American military personnel created new employment opportunities for civilian Newfoundlanders and new revenues for government. Ironically, although World War I had created conditions that contributed to the loss of democracy in the 1930s and 1940s, World War II created the conditions for a return to democracy in 1949.[4]

These two major wars and the Depression were international in scope. In addition, three major developments specific to Newfoundland characterized its history during the first half of the twentieth century: its financial crisis in the early 1930s that led to its relinquishing responsible government in favour of a non-elected Commission of Government from 1934 to 1949; the National Convention, which was elected to advise Great Britain on the appropriate form of government for Newfoundland after World War II; and the Confederation of Newfoundland as the tenth province of Canada in 1949. To varying degrees, the conversations that I recorded with my father touch on each of these topics from his point of view.

Edgar was strongly committed to his family and his community. Although not a mover and shaker in the political and economic life of Newfoundland, he was widely respected for his contributions to the educational and social development of his country/province.

Recent years have brought a proliferation of memoirs, biographies, and reflections written by and about people who grew up in pre- and post-Confederation Newfoundland and Labrador. Academic

---

4   For an analysis of Newfoundland's role in World War II and its aftermath, see, for example, David Mackenzie, *Inside the Atlantic Triangle*, 1986.

interest in the province has yielded much writing by historians, geographers, anthropologists, sociologists, and folklorists. One of our purposes here is to indicate how this life story of Edgar House contributes new information and perspectives to that larger literature.

Oral History, Life Stories, and Memory

First, I will outline some of the methodological issues and strengths and weaknesses of the approach we have taken to record, collate, analyze, and present Edgar House's life story.

"Oral history" refers to historical accounts of past events and processes based on the spoken words of people who have been directly involved at the time or, less reliably, their spoken reports about others who were directly involved. For non-literate societies, oral accounts are the main source of information about the past for social and cultural anthropologists, who depend on such accounts in writing ethnographies to describe the present but also, either explicitly or implicitly, to reconstruct the past to analyze patterns of culture and social organization. Folklorists also depend on people's verbal accounts of past practices in documenting the customs and mores of different cultures and subcultures.[5] Historians depend mainly on written documents, but some complement these sources by using oral history, which adds another dimension to their research, particularly for events that occurred in the recent past.

The oral historian focuses mainly on significant events that took place within living memory. A good example of oral history is *Occupied St. John's*, a recent social history of St. John's during World War II.[6] The book is based mainly on 50 interviews with people who lived

---

5   The Folklore Department of Memorial University of Newfoundland maintains a rich archive of such material. Copies of the tapes used to record the conversations with Edgar House on which this book is based are stored in the Memorial University Folklore and Language Archive.

6   Steven High, ed., *Occupied St. John's*, 2010. See also Bill Rompkey, ed., *St. John's and the Battle of the Atlantic*, 2009.

in St. John's during those years. The oral accounts not only add new information to historical understanding about the period, but also offer an important corrective to the claims of some historians that American servicemen were loved but Canadians despised.

> Our in-depth interviews with fifty men and women do not support this position. To the contrary, almost everyone warmly remembered the courage and sacrifice of the Canadian sailors who were fighting and dying in the North Atlantic. We heard about a harbour crowded with warships, battle damaged vessels, exhausted survivors, the blackout, the hostels, and about families having Canadian servicemen over for supper. In fact, the Canadians were often at the centre of the war stories being told. The Americans were well liked, but so too were the Canadians. (High 14–15)

This analysis relates to Edgar's views about Confederation, discussed below.

Edgar's memoirs do not constitute an oral history as such, because they do not focus on just one historical period or event. Some of his accounts do, however, contribute new material and perspectives on Newfoundland history during the twentieth century, notably the section on World War I hero Tommy Ricketts, the comments about the first President of Memorial University College, John Lewis Paton, various anecdotes about Joseph Smallwood, and descriptions of boys in school who were later to become prominent Canadians, such as National Hockey League announcer Bob Cole and politician John Crosbie.

The approach that I took in the conversations that I recorded with my father approximates more what has come to be known as the "life history" or "life story" approach to research. We prefer the term "life story" because it seems less portentous. Our approach accords with Robert Atkinson's description that "the aspect that most distinguishes the approach described here from others is that it keeps the presentation of the life story in the words of the person telling the story. The finished product is entirely a first-person narrative, with the researcher removed as much as possible from the text" (Atkinson 1).

The text that comprises the main part of this work expresses our attempt to allow Edgar to tell his own life story in his own words. Or perhaps "life stories" would be more accurate.[7] As will be seen, Edgar took a storytelling approach to talking about his life and times. The text is largely a series of stories and anecdotes about his life growing up, working, and living in Newfoundland during the twentieth century. The various stories do, however, have common themes that fit into a pattern that can be said to constitute Edgar's life story.[8] Although the conversations with him were free-flowing and comprehensive, we cannot claim to have done more than touch on aspects of what must have constituted the whole story of Edgar's life. The best that we can claim is that we did touch on all of the topics that he felt were most important as he reflected on his life during his late eighties.

Although I was mainly non-directive in my approach, there were nevertheless some topics that I wanted to be sure to cover, and I did guide the conversations in those directions. As Gluck and Patai point out, oral history "involves at least two subjectivities, that of the narrator and that of the interviewer" (Gluck and Patai 2). The same applies to life stories. In addition to the narrator Edgar House and interviewer Doug House, other subjectivities involved in the creation of this text of Edgar's life story include research assistant, Andrea Nurse (now Nolan), who did some of the early collating; Adrian House, who did

---

7   In referring to one of her main informants in her article about Galician Death Narratives, Sharon Roseman uses the plural term "Celia's life stories" (Roseman "Going" 442).

8   In Roseman's term, there is a "storytelling thread" that "refers to a series of linked stories told about the same or different incidents over a period of time" (Roseman "Hai que" 199).

most of the collating and editing; and the editors and readers for ISER Books whose suggestions contributed to the final text. Finally, we should note that the final subjectivity is that of the various readers who will interpret the text differently depending on their own backgrounds and perspectives, from Old Feildians and Rotarians to nationalist historians. Although its focus is the life story of one individual, this book is very much a social product.

Edgar's stories and anecdotes (brief stories) were drawn from his well of personal memories. But memory itself is a complex matter. Teski and Chimo argue that "Memory is not recall. Rather, it is a continuous process based on rumination by individuals and groups on the content and meaning of the recent and more distant past" (Teski and Chimo 2). Given the difficulties in determining the truth of anyone's memories, some scholars argue that the focus should be mainly on what memories reveal about meaning and identity, on personal truth rather than factual accuracy.[9] Edgar's memories are presented as they are meaningful to him and his self-identification, but we nevertheless believe it has been incumbent on us as researchers to check the facts he cites as thoroughly as possible. We have done that mainly by checking Edgar's claims against the written record where one could be identified, and against other people's memories (including my own) of various events. To take one example, in one of his stories Edgar identifies the Headmaster of Bishop Feild College at the time as Ralph R. Wood, but we know from the historical record that the Headmaster actually was R.E. Tanner. We have been able to run some of the stories by people mentioned in them to check them for accuracy and sensitivities. The final text is as factually accurate as we could make it. It probably includes some small inaccuracies on some minor details, but we can take comfort in the text as a whole being true to our appreciation of Edgar's "personal truth." I will return to the matter of Edgar's self-identity later, after locating this book within the large body of published works about twentieth-century Newfoundland and Labrador

---

9   See Jacob J. Climo and Marian G. Cattell, eds., *Social Memory and History*, 2002. In
     their view, "Coherence and meaning are what matter" (16).

and analyzing his life experiences within the major social institutions in which he lived and worked.

Edgar's Life Story and the Literature on Newfoundland Society and Culture

Edgar lived his formative years and up to age 37 in pre-Confederation Newfoundland and his subsequent 57 years as a Canadian living in the province of Newfoundland and Labrador. Other than the two years (1931–33) he spent completing his B.Sc. degree at King's College and Dalhousie University in Halifax, Nova Scotia, he spent his whole life in Newfoundland.

Many excellent historical accounts of nineteenth- and twentieth-century Newfoundland and Labrador are available.[10] Although Edgar was not born until 1911, the kind of society and culture he was born into was largely shaped during the second half of the nineteenth century, after Newfoundland was granted responsible government in 1855. We found Patrick O'Flaherty's year-by-year narrative history particularly useful for our purposes. Although writing from a Newfoundland nationalist perspective, O'Flaherty is fair in presenting both sides of the story on such important issues as the loss of sovereignty and the campaigns for and against Confederation with Canada. He expresses puzzlement at how easily most Newfoundlanders acquiesced in giving up their democratic government in 1934 (O'Flaherty *Leaving* 133). As will be shown below, this is easier to understand from Edgar's point of view than it would be from O'Flaherty's.

For St. John's in particular, Paul O'Neill's popular two-volume history has been helpful for understanding the main locale of Edgar's

---

10   See, for example, James Hiller and Peter Neary, *Newfoundland in the Nineteenth and Twentieth Centuries*, 1980; Peter Neary, *Newfoundland in the North American World 1929–1949*, 1988; and the last two volumes of Patrick O'Flaherty's three-volume history of Newfoundland: *Lost Country*, 2005, and *Leaving the Past Behind*, 2011.

upbringing and working life.[11] Again, Edgar's English/Anglican perspective would undoubtedly cause him to question some of O'Neill's
preoccupations. With respect to his alma mater, O'Neill claims: "No
school in Newfoundland seemed able to compete with St. Bonaventure's College for all-round excellence. It was outstanding in academics, athletics, debating, theatricals, and music" (*Seaport Legacy* 767).
While he had respect for St. Bon's, Edgar would no doubt have made
a similar claim for Bishop Feild College.

Confederation ushered in a rapid era of change throughout Newfoundland and Labrador. In recent years there has been a proliferation
of memoirs and biographies by and about people whose lives were
transformed in the process. Most of these have been written by people
who grew up in rural communities, especially in "outports," the many
small fishing villages that dot the coastlines of the island and mainland
parts of the province.[12] Informative memoirs have been written by or
about a few of Newfoundland and Labrador's Aboriginal people.[13]

Comparatively few memoirs have been written by the "townies"
of St. John's. There are a couple by "corner boys" from working-class
backgrounds about growing up in downtown St. John's.[14] *Corner Boys*
by Robert Hunt paints a compelling verbal picture of working-class

11   Paul O'Neill, *The Oldest City*, 1975, and *A Seaport Legacy*, 1976. The history was
     published in a single-volume revised edition in 2003. See also the two-volume
     pictorial history by former St. John's mayor Fred Adams, *Fred Adams' St. John's*,
     1986, and *St. John's—The Last 100 Years*, 1988; Frank Galgay and Michael McCar-
     thy, *Olde St. John's*, 2001.

12   Examples include: Gerald W. Andrews, *Heritage of a Newfoundland Outport*, 2006;
     Maurice Burke, *Memoirs of Outport Life*, 1985; George W. Clarke, *Can Any Good
     Thing Come Out of Crocker's Cove?*, 1992; Doug Cole, *Elliston*, 1997; Victor Kendall
     and Victor G. Kendall, *Out of the Sea*, 1991; Dennis Knight, *The Place*, 2010; Wil-
     fred B.W. Martin (with the assistance of Eileen Martin), *Random Island Pioneers*,
     1990; Willis P. Martin, *Two Outports*, 2006; Cle Newhook, *Mostly in Rodneys*, 1985.

13   See Paulus Maggo, *Remembering the Years of My Life*, 1999; Louie Montague, *I
     Never Knowed It Was Hard*, 2013.

14   See Wallace Furlong, *Georgestown*, 2004; Frank Kennedy, *A Corner Boy Remem-
     bers*, 2006; Robert Hunt, *Corner Boys*, 2011.

life in the Brazil Street area of downtown St. John's, and of the joys and hazards of being an underprivileged boy subject to the whims of the Irish Christian Brothers who taught at Holy Cross School at the time (82–94). Although poor and underprivileged as compared to middle-class families like the Houses, Hunt and his family managed to carve out satisfying lives. The author's father, who was born in 1912, a year later than Edgar, could afford only a Grade 5 education because "education was a luxury back then" (35). He served in the Canadian Merchant Navy during World War II and was on a ship that was torpedoed near Dover, England. He moved to St. John's from Harbour Breton after the war, when he changed from working on the coastal boats to a porter's job on the trains. He enjoyed a happy marriage and family life and had many friends. He did not complain of his lot in life. In his son's words, "Being poor never bothered him in the least. He knew who he was and where he had come from, and he never forgot" (36).

Accounts of growing up in other parts of St. John's are even rarer. Notable exceptions have been written by two of Newfoundland and Labrador's most distinguished writers.[15] Harold Horwood was born in 1923 "on Campbell Avenue, a large, gracious-looking bungalow built by my grandfather," a sea captain (Horwood A Walk 1). At the time, this would have been a suburban area to the west of what was then "a small city of some 30,000 or 40,000" (1). In reminiscing about his boyhood, Horwood remembers a stable background. His father was the manager of a department in a merchant's business, a level above a clerk. Horwood remembers a life of elegance, but: "In no sense were we wealthy or affluent people. Like most of those we knew, we lived from payday to payday" (9). He attended Holloway School, which he describes as "the 'upper-class' school of the United Church Board of Education where the fees charged to parents were much higher than those at the lower-class schools on Bond Street and Parade Street" (87). Horwood liked his teachers, who were "marvellously understanding and kind" (86), but he had difficulty adjusting to his fellow

---

15   Harold Horwood, A Walk in the Dream Time, 1997; Helen Fogwill Porter, Below the Bridge, 2011.

students: "the real shock of starting school was the sudden plunge into the barbarian society of the playroom and the schoolyard" (87).

During the Great Depression of the 1930s, Horwood remembers that, although he and his own family managed well, there was a great deal of poverty and hardship in both St. John's and the outports:

> There was little begging on the streets, but a lot from door to door, where endless slices of bread were handed out by housewives. People "on the dole" were close to starvation. A family of five could qualify for a food order worth, as a rule, $2.10 a week, but this couldn't possibly provide even minimum sub-sistence. (84)

As we shall see, Harold Horwood's memories of the Depression were similar in many ways to Edgar House's, although Edgar had more hands-on experience in his work on the playground in inner-city St. John's and in visiting his outport cousins. Horwood's impressions of the Depression help explain why, in 1946, he became a supporter of Joseph Smallwood and his campaign for Confederation with Canada.

> I was one of the first to be wooed. He struck me in-stantly as a winner. I was converted to Smallwood himself first, and only later to his cause, not because of any political or idealistic considerations, but solely because of the economic good that would accrue to Newfoundlanders through their political union with Canada. (158)

After Confederation, Horwood served initially in Smallwood's first cabinet, but later became disillusioned with his autocratic style and went on to be one of his fiercest critics.

Helen Fogwill Porter's book, *Below the Bridge*, is about her grow-ing up on the southside of St. John's harbour, a unique and distinct part of the city to this day. Born in 1930, she too remembers the Depression, but muses: "The Depression. Is there any way to express, I wonder,

what it was really like then so that people who weren't around at the
time will understand?" (20). "We were all poor during the Depression,
or almost all, but some were poorer than others" (19). Her family was
better off than some because her father had a steady job, although his
salary was cut from $105 to $90 a month, and they were able to save
money by living with her grandparents. Southsiders considered themselves to be distinct, and this continued to be an important part of
Porter's self-identity. Like Harold Horwood, she attended Holloway
School and Prince of Wales College, but she felt she was looked down
upon by more affluent students from the north side of town:

> I was not unhappy throughout all my schooldays;
> there are good memories here and there, but I did
> not feel at all privileged to attend one of the schools
> where the grand ones sent their children, at least un-
> til they were old enough to continue their education
> outside Newfoundland, as most of them inevitably
> did. (28–29)

In Porter's experience, there was a real snobbishness about this practice of the more affluent class ("the grand ones") sending their children
to school in England or mainland Canada. She remembers asking one
of her classmates whether she would be going to school at Edgehill (in
Nova Scotia). The girl's response: "'No,' she said, and paused a moment
before continuing. 'I'm going to Ontario Ladies College. Mummy says
there are too many Newfoundlanders at Edgehill'" (29).

   Although her family was United Church, most of the residents on
the southside were Church of England, and St. Mary's Church was a
key institution for the neighbourhood. There were some Roman
Catholic families as well, who were distinguishable from Protestants
by various customs and speech patterns.

> The pronunciation of the word "was" had proved
> almost foolproof as a means of telling Catholics
> from Protestants. They said "waws" and we said
> "wuz." There were other things, too; their r's were

> much broader than ours, and they used expressions
> like "Oh, my Sacred Heart of God" or "Jesus, Mary
> and Joseph." (42)

Porter's book concludes with the sad story of the destruction of much of the southside in the 1950s and early 1960s for the cause of harbour renewal and expansion, with many of the residents being resettled to the north side of the harbour. The process culminated with the bull-dozing of the 102-year-old St. Mary's Church and the grave of Shawnadithit, the last of the Beothuk Indians in Newfoundland. While the term "resettlement" is generally thought of as applying to the controversial government-sponsored resettlement of hundreds of rural outports and their families in post-Confederation Newfoundland and Labrador, Porter's account shows that there was an equally poignant urban dimension to this as well.

As we shall see, Edgar House's reflections in this book about his early years growing up on Winter Place,[16] which at the time was a privileged suburban area of pre-Confederation St. John's, add another dimension that complements these other memories about growing up in the old city.[17]

The focus on rural versus urban communities in the popular literature about Newfoundland and Labrador is to be found as well in the scholarly work of social anthropologists, sociologists, folklorists, and linguists. Confederation engendered much interest among American, British, and Norwegian social scientists, who saw the new province as one of the last frontiers for researching communities on

---

16 The Winter Place/Winter Avenue area, with the subsequent addition of Glenridge Crescent, which was to become the neighbourhood where Edgar's children grew up, is still considered a prime residential part of the city, but it is now closer to downtown than it is to the new outlying suburbs of contemporary St. John's.

17 Glenn David Colton has recently published a book about another prominent Anglican and Feildian, Frederick R. Emerson, who grew up in the same neighbourhood as Edgar. It does not tell Emerson's life story in his own words, but rather relies on secondary sources and interviews with key informants, in particular Emerson's daughter, Carla Emerson Furlong. See Colton, *Newfoundland Rhapsody*, 2014.

the verge of modernization. Memorial University established an Institute of Social and Economic Research that contributed greatly to research and writing about rural communities and social change in the 1960s and 1970s.[18]

The richness of the sociological record on post-Confederation rural Newfoundland and Labrador contrasts sharply with the paucity of material about St. John's and the other urban centres and large towns.[19] One of the purposes of this book, for Edgar's life story and in this introduction, is to contribute to the sociological understanding of the city of St. John's and its relations with the outports as they played out in Edgar's life. We begin by considering the institutional sphere closest to home: family and kinship.

Family, Kinship, and Friendship

As far as we can tell, the patrilineal line of the House family in Newfoundland originated in Poole, Dorset. There is a medium-sized merchant business named George House in Dorset to this day. In his efforts to trace the family tree, the earliest reference that Edgar could find was to a George House, a fisherman in Trinity who married Elizabeth Honor in 1832. They had four children, William, Mary Ann, Stephen, and George. George, Edgar's grandfather, became the captain of the mail packet (small vessel) that operated in Trinity Bay for many years, carrying mail from Trinity on the northwest side to New Perlican on the

---

18   See the ISER Books website for a list of the works currently in print. Some of the most notable early studies were Tom Philbrook, *Fisherman, Logger, Merchant, Miner*, 1966; James C. Faris, *Cat Harbour*, 1972; Louis J. Chiaramonte, *Craftsman–Client Contracts*, 1966; Cato Wadel, *Now, Whose Fault Is That? The Struggle for Self-Esteem in the Face of Chronic Unemployment*, 1973. See also Ralph D. Matthews, *"There's No Better Place Than Here"*, 1976; and, for a useful collection, Maurice A. Sterns, ed., *Perspectives on Newfoundland Society and Culture*, 1974.

19   A welcome recent exception is the book edited by Linda Cullum and Marilyn Porter, *Creating This Place*, 2014. Other exceptions are Alison Kahn, *Listen While I Tell You*, 1987; and J.D. House, *The Challenge of Oil*, 1986, which are focused mainly on St. John's.

southeast side of the Bay. Born in 1841, George married Arianna Mary Ainsworth in 1867. She was the daughter of John and Sarah Ainsworth. John was a schoolmaster, and it may have been his influence that initiated the prevalence of the teaching profession in subsequent generations of Houses. George and Arianna had five children, one of whom they also called George. This George, Edgar's father, was born in 1876. He married Mary Ellen Day, who had been born into a fishing family in the nearby community of Champneys in 1872.[20]

As we shall see in Edgar's narrative, his father, George House, was an able and ambitious man who finished his Grade 11 (the senior year of high school at the time) and became a teacher, first in Champneys and then in Change Islands at the turn of the twentieth century. He then travelled to St. John's to further his education at Bishop Feild College, achieving the designation A.A. (Associate in Arts), which was the highest level of formal education attainable in Newfoundland at the time. Based on this academic success, he was offered and accepted a position as a Master (teacher) at Bishop Feild. By this time, George and Mary had one daughter, Edith, who had been born in Change Islands in 1903. In a pattern familiar to many Newfoundland families throughout the country's history, George moved his family from the outports to St. John's to take advantage of a new and challenging career opportunity. In 1911, Mary gave birth to their second child and only son, Edgar George. They broke a three-generation family custom by calling him Edgar rather than George as his main name; and Edgar was to break the tradition altogether by naming his only son John Douglas.

As the popular and academic literature cited above emphasizes, family and kinship have always been important institutions in Newfoundland and Labrador. For the first three centuries of its post-European existence, the British government treated Newfoundland primarily as a resource — "a great ship moored off the Grand Banks"

---

20 These dates should be viewed as best estimates. According to the family tree constructed by Barbara Moore, a descendant of the Day family, Mary Day was born in 1870.

— for curing fish to be exploited by the merchant houses of the west country of England — and as a "nursery for seamen" who could be called up to serve in the British navy in times of war.[21] Permanent settlement was discouraged and little attempt was made to establish formal legal and political institutions. This meant that those who did settle along the coast of the island and Labrador had to rely on themselves and their families and kin. This cultural pattern that places great importance on family and kinship persists to this day.

The House family was exceptional in one sense. At a time when Newfoundland families typically were very large,[22] with many children, Edgar's great-grandfather had four children, his grandfather had five, and his father and he had only two each. Nevertheless, family and kinship ties were very important to the Houses. As will be seen, Edgar's relationship to his father was one of the dominant themes in his life. Their relationship was clearly rather formal. Edgar's feeling towards his father was more one of respect than of a more expressive or sentimental type of love.[23] He clearly set great store by his father's opinion, notably in his career choices. It must have been a proud moment for George, a self-made man who became a Master at Bishop Feild College, when his son was chosen as Headmaster. In my own life growing up, whenever I accomplished anything, my father would often say to me: "George House would have been proud!"

Edgar's relationship with his mother Mary was more openly affectionate. He was somewhat ambivalent about the way she maintained her strong outport accent throughout her life; but he admired her strong work ethic and her ability to run their household effectively, a household that usually included, besides the immediate family, one or

---

21   The classic account is D.W. Prowse's *A History of Newfoundland from the English, Colonial, and Foreign Records*, 1895.

22   This was particularly so for Roman Catholic families, but Anglican families also typically were large until recent times.

23   Unfortunately, Edgar's father, "Gampy House" to my sister and me, died when we were too young to get to know him, so I am not able to draw on direct personal experience in this section.

more visiting relatives and, for a time, war hero Tommy Ricketts. Sadly, my only personal memory of Granny House, who died shortly after her husband in 1949 when I was only five years old, is the wonderful smell of the pot of homemade soup she always kept on the stove.

Edgar's upbringing and his relationships with his father and mother undoubtedly influenced his approach to his relationships with his children. My sister Janet and I enjoyed a happy childhood in a close family. But ours was not a family in which people were very demonstrative about their feelings. As a young man, when I first met my English fiancée's family I was quite struck that, unlike the stereotype of the restrained English, they were much more prone to hugs and kisses than was my family back in Newfoundland. In their later years, my parents did become more demonstrative in their relations with their grandchildren than they had been with their own children. The earlier situation may also have been influenced by the presence of our grandmother, my mother's mother, who came to live with our family for 13 years after her husband died. She was not a demonstrative woman.

In addition to its role in socialization and sociability, kinship was also important to the informal economic ties between outport and city in Newfoundland. Edgar recalls that George and Mary's house on Winter Place in St. John's was always full of visitors. It was a place where their relatives from Champneys and Trinity could stay when visiting St. John's, whether for educational, health, or recreational reasons, and enjoy free room and board. In what economic anthropologists call "balanced reciprocity,"[24] this was a two-way street. When Edgar and his father visited Trinity in the summers, they would stay with their relatives there. There was also a regular exchange of goods between town and country. Edgar and his family could look forward every year to receiving gifts of fish, game, and berries from their outport relatives. In return, they would provide items of clothing and manufactured goods to their cousins, aunts, and uncles in Champneys and Trinity. This kinship system provided economic value to

---

24   See, for example, Marcel Mauss, *The Gift*, 1967.

both the St. John's and outport relatives and improved their standard of living beyond what they enjoyed through the market system.

Friendship was also important, especially so to small families such as the Houses. Edgar's description of George's close friendship with I.J. Samson is a prime example. He became good friends with Mr. Samson's son, Art, his next-door neighbour. Later, while a student at Bishop Feild College, Edgar developed a coterie of lifelong friends including Bill Neal, Bliss Murphy, Stuart Godfrey, Val Earle, and Gordon Stirling. Edgar and Margie also cemented strong friendships through Margie's friends at Prince of Wales, notably Brenda Butler (née Marshall) and Florence Currie (née Hue). Some of these friendships were given special status in the idiom social anthropologists call "fictive kin."[25] In addition to "real" aunts and uncles — Auntie Edith, Uncle Wilf, Uncle Gel, and Auntie Dot — my sister Janet and I were equally close to our parents' friends — "Uncle Bill," "Auntie Marg," "Uncle Ches," "Auntie Bren," "Uncle Chancey," and "Aunt Florence." Their children became childhood friends of ours.

This special recognition through the idiom of fictive kinship also extended to our summer visits to Trinity. The wonderful fisherman/ carpenter/jack-of-all trades, Jacob House,[26] who became a good friend of our parents, we called "Uncle Jake." He was also known as "Uncle Jake" by most people in Trinity. This custom, according a well-respected older man in the community with the designation "Uncle," was common in Newfoundland outports, another indication of the importance of kinship as an idiom that permeated outport life. Interestingly, in the early years of our acquaintance, we called Uncle Jake's wife "Mrs. House," although later we referred to her as "Aunt Hattie."

---

25   Fictive kin: a term used to refer to individuals who are unrelated by either birth or marriage, who have an emotionally significant relationship with another individual that would take on the characteristics of a family relationship. For a good description of fictive kin in a very different setting, a black urban poor community within a Midwest city in the United States, see Carol B. Stack, *All Our Kin*, 1974, 57–61.

26   Although Uncle Jake's surname happened to be House, he was not a known relative of ours. He may have been a distant relative but this was never ascertained.

Their strong immediate family relations, as well as the great web of kinship and friendship that characterized their lives, provided a solid sense of security and of belonging for both Edgar's parents and for him and his wife. They helped them develop a strong sense of self-worth and contributed to their enjoyment of life.

City, Town, and Outport

During most of Newfoundland and Labrador's early post-European history, from the beginning of the sixteenth century to the middle of the nineteenth century, settlement and the establishment of strong modern social institutions were delayed by British policy, as noted above. Nevertheless, settlement did gradually take place, almost ex-clusively in small communities dotted along the coastline where peo-ple could exploit the inshore fishing grounds. These came to be called "outharbours" or "outports." Early on, St. John's, with its easternmost location and excellent harbour, emerged as the largest community and the seat of nascent political and social institutions. By the time Edgar was born in 1911, St. John's had become the capital city of the country of Newfoundland. Although small, it had an international flavour as a centre of shipping and trade involving people from many nations of the world.

By the latter half of the nineteenth century, after Newfoundland had been granted responsible government in 1855, efforts were made to diversify the economy from its almost total dependency on the fishing industry, which had reached its extensive limit in terms of how many people it could support (Alexander). By the early twentieth century, this effort met with some success with the establishment of two paper mills at Corner Brook and Grand Falls, and a number of mining towns at Tilt Cove, St. Lawrence, Bell Island, and Buchans. In the latter half of the twentieth century, three new towns were built in western Labrador: Labrador City and Wabush based on iron ore, and Churchill Falls based on the massive Churchill Falls hydroelectricity project. Initially, many of these were "company towns." They were built, managed, and regulated by the resource company that ran the mine or the mill.

Edgar House's career and life were affected by each of these community types.[27] He was born and bred in St. John's, received most of his education there, and pursued most of his teaching and all of his health administration career in the city. He lived "away" (off the island of Newfoundland) only for the two years he spent in Halifax in the early 1930s completing his B.Sc. degree, and he and Margie lived for three years in Buchans from 1941 to 1944.

Not only did he live in St. John's, but he lived virtually his whole life within the same neighbourhood. He grew up on Winter Place where his enterprising father and I.J. Samson built a fine duplex home, which is still occupied and in good condition today. The Houses and Samsons were something of an anomaly on Winter Place. Built on the Winter Estate,[28] the area was generally seen as a well-to-do neighbourhood, and most of the houses were large, single-family residences. Over the years, Winter Place has housed two lieutenant-governors, Fabian O'Dea and Gordon Winter, well-known media businessman Geoff Stirling, broadcaster/politician Don Jamieson, Judge Geoffrey Steele, politician/judge Bill Marshall, and several other well-known Newfoundlanders. It was a congenial neighbourhood in which to grow up, especially for an athletic boy like Edgar. He helped his father develop the Feildian Grounds, which are adjacent to Winter Place to the south; and, in what was then a mainly unsettled hinterland to the north (now midtown suburbs), he enjoyed skating and playing hockey in the winter and swimming and hiking in the summer.

During Edgar's boyhood and up until the 1950s, St. John's was a compact city centred on its fine sheltered harbour and its main thoroughfare, Water Street. The leading business people of the day, "the merchants of Water Street," as they were known, dominated not only trade in the country's fisheries but also wholesale and retail trade. Most of people's shopping was done downtown, mainly on Water

27   In recent years, a fourth type of community has emerged to prominence: towns that have become regional service centres, including Carbonear/Harbour Grace, Clarenville, Gander, and Happy Valley-Goose Bay.

28   See Chapter 2, note 18 (p. 99).

Street in locally owned stores. These were of two main types: large department stores, notably Bowring Brothers, Ayre and Sons, and London, New York and Paris; and specialty stores such as S.O. Steele (crockery ware), Neyle-Soper (hardware), and The Sports Shop (sporting goods). Many of the most prominent business families (with names such as Ayre, Bowring, Collingwood, Crosbie, and Hickman) formed a loose social alliance with some intermarrying and common social practices that distinguished them from the general population, such as sending their older children away to school and university and owning expensive summer homes outside St. John's. Although these mercantile families were generally referred to as the St. John's upper class or elite, there was a lot of turnover among them and upward and downward mobility as their business fortunes waxed and waned. Newfoundland and Labrador has never had an established landed aristocracy in the British sense.[29]

In 1938, the year before he married Margaret Butt, Edgar bought an unfinished house within easy walking distance of where he grew up, at the top of the hill just north of Winter Place. He and his father worked together to complete the inside of the house. Its address was originally 44 Robinson's Hill, and the city limits sign was directly across from it. Later, the name Robinson's Hill was discontinued and it was incorporated into Portugal Cove Road with his house becoming 20 Portugal Cove Road. It is situated on the north corner of Glenridge Crescent and is still in good shape today. More often than not,

---

29   The populist political leader, Joseph Smallwood, was to make much of what he called "the thieves of Water Street" in his campaign for Confederation in the late 1940s. While many St. John's business families were initially anti-confederate, most of them did quite well out of Confederation by becoming local agents of national corporations and benefiting from the construction and retail booms that came from the new flow of money into the province. Later, Water Street was superseded by suburban malls and, recently, big box stores dominated by national chains, and the old Water Street firms have gone into decline. However, Water and Duckworth streets have been reinvented as centres for boutique shopping, entertainment, and dining, with several restaurants receiving national recognition. Downtown continues to bustle as it once did, albeit in a different way.

my sister and I would go out through our back door and down a few steps to play with our friends on "the Crescent."

Glenridge Crescent was one of the first suburban housing developments in St. John's, but, unlike the Churchill Park area (Collier), it was an informal development.[30] In the late 1940s and early 1950s Glenridge Crescent became one of the most desirable housing areas in St. John's, and it continues to be so to this day. When we grew up it was a middle- to upper-middle class neighbourhood with an interesting mix of Anglican, United Church, Roman Catholic, and Jewish families. Many of Jan's and my best friends were Jewish, and it was only later that I learned that this socializing was not a common pattern among Christians in St. John's. Our favourite adult was Maurice Wilansky who ran the Model Shop on Water Street. We all called him "Uncle Maurice." He organized croquet games for the Crescent kids in his spacious back garden, showed popular movies of such Western heroes as Hopalong Cassidy and the Lone Ranger in his house on the weekends, and, on special occasions, would take us in his station wagon out to his country place on Topsail Pond for swimming, boating, and barbecued steaks. For several years, Maurice's wife Penny organized music programs for the children on the Crescent as well.

Although he was very much a townie, and an eastern St. John's townie at that,[31] Edgar was also profoundly influenced throughout his life by his ties to rural Newfoundland. His father came from Trinity, which at the time was an important fishing and merchant centre,[32] and his mother came from the nearby fishing village of Champneys. As a boy, he and his parents would travel to Champneys and Trinity most years by schooner, and Edgar enjoyed staying with his various

---

30   See Chapter 2, note 20 (p. 102).

31   As in many cities of longstanding, the citizens of St. John's differentiate themselves by various areas and neighbourhoods within the city. The broadest distinction is between west enders, who claim to have better weather and less fog, and east enders, who see themselves as the real heart of the city.

32   See Rev. Edmund Hunt, *Aspects of the History of Trinity*, 1981; Gordon Handcock, *The Story of Trinity*, 1997.

relatives there. He refers fondly to the many trouting expeditions he went on with his father. In those days, they could easily fill their baskets with mud trout, sea trout, and the occasional salmon; and they usually brought back a gallon or more of berries — bakeapples, blueberries, and/or partridgeberries — as well. During these visits, he also learned to appreciate the rigours and joys of outport living and fishing as a way of life.

In 1948, Edgar and his good friend, Dr. Bliss Murphy, visited Trinity and had the distinction of being the first guests to stay in the Trinity Cabins, which operate today. While there, Edgar spotted a small cabin nestled in the woods behind what was then the railway station at Trinity Junction. He decided to buy it and it became the House family's summer dwelling.[33] Going to Trinity, by which we meant going to the cabin that actually is located about a mile outside of the town of Trinity itself, has taken on almost mystical meaning for three generations of Houses, Squires, and their descendants. It's the place we go to relax and lift our spirits after the rigours of winter and work in St. John's or other urban centres.

When Edgar and Margie got married in July of 1939, his father loaned them his car for their honeymoon in Brigus. To them, at that time, visiting Brigus was as remote and exciting as honeymoons to Florida or Las Vegas are for newlyweds today. In the same vein, two years after their marriage they took advantage of a job offer Edgar received to move to Buchans. This adventure, all the way to a mining town in the interior of central Newfoundland, was the highlight of their early years of marriage, an adventure they often talked and reminisced about while viewing pictures in their photograph album throughout their 60 years together.

Edgar had been offered and was pleased to accept the position of Principal of Buchans Public School, a position he held from 1941 to 1944. This was an amalgamated school for boys and girls from each of

---

33 My sister, Janet, and her husband, George Squires, built a second cabin on the property in 1975. They continue to spend much of their summers there, keeping Edgar's old cabin, "Glen Avon," as their guest cabin.

the Protestant denominations. At the time, Buchans was a thriving company town. The school was well built and well equipped, and Edgar enjoyed having his salary supplemented by the company. This time was early days for Buchans, which have not been well documented. The few books available about the town were written much later by people who were not even born in the early 1940s.[34] Edgar is to be found but not named in a photograph with the caption "Buchans Public School Hockey Team, circa 1940s," in the book *Khaki Dodgers* (Red Indian Lake Development Association 117). He could also be said to have been included implicitly in the following comment about education in Buchans:

> Another positive feature of Buchans was education. A solid education was given to all of the children of the Buchans Miners. As a result, the cultural and economic life of the province has been greatly enriched by graduates of the two high schools, who went on to become professionals or tradespeople with a solid work ethic patterned after our parents. (Cranford viii)

Although they spent only three years there, these were formative years for Edgar and Margie. They came to appreciate what life was like in a company town, different in many ways from either St. John's or the outports.

Later, in his career as Director of Rehabilitation of the Newfoundland Tuberculosis Association, Edgar further broadened his understanding of and appreciation for most parts of the province. He spent many days visiting different towns, meeting with ex-patients of the sanatorium in St. John's, and trying to match them with various occupational opportunities in their hometowns and villages. He became a well-rounded Newfoundlander and this influenced his sense of his own identity and his attitudes on key issues of the day.

---

34 See Red Indian Lake Development Association, *Khaki Dodgers*, 1997; Derek Yetman, *Riches of the Earth*, 1986.

GENERAL INTRODUCTION   43

Religion and Denominational Education

Education was a dominant theme and passion throughout Edgar's
life. As a boy, from 1917 to 1929, he attended the Church of England
(Anglican) all-grade school, Bishop Feild College, where his father,
George House, was one of the masters (teachers). He completed the
first two years of his university education at Memorial University
College from 1929 to 1931, then went on to Nova Scotia for his B.Sc.
degree. He started as a teacher at Bishop Feild in 1933, taking a year
out to return to Memorial University College to complete his formal
teacher training in the academic year, 1935–36. After his years in
Buchans, in 1944 he returned to St. John's and served as Headmaster
at Bishop Feild from 1944 to 1952. He also served a term as the President of the Newfoundland Teachers' Association just after Confederation, 1950–51.[35] Edgar's sister Edith was also a teacher (at Bishop
Spencer College), and his wife worked as a teacher until they married.
Later, his daughter married a teacher and his son became a university
professor.

Edgar was respected and well liked as a teacher and headmaster.
Some of his philosophy of teaching comes through in the text of a talk
he was asked to give to the Teachers Training Department of Memorial University College in 1945 on the topic "So you're going to be a
teacher!" He stated that the purpose of his talk was "to show you that
teaching is a great profession and that, as teachers, we must be ready
to defend it against all scoffers." Some of the other points he made are
as follows:

- One of your greatest rewards in teaching will be the
  thrill of watching your pupils after they leave school

---

35 Teachers, including principals, were poorly paid in Newfoundland in the 1930s
and 1940s. It is ironic that, a year after teachers began to enjoy better pay and
working conditions, Edgar left the teaching profession for a career as a health administrator. In the long run, in terms of pay and pension when he retired, he would
probably have been better off if he had stayed in teaching. But he never expressed
any regrets about his career change.

and advance to fill responsible positions. I get a much greater thrill from hearing that some former pupil has been awarded a D.F.M.[36] or has started processing our cod fish in some more palatable fashion than I do in drawing my monthly cheque.

- Be proud that you are a teacher and start your work in September with enthusiasm. This point is most important. Let your enthusiasm be always apparent.
- Every teacher must try to become something of an actor. Learn to cultivate your dramatic possibilities for quite often a little touch of drama will be an aid in teaching.
- Cultivate your sense of humour and use it to good advantage. The sense of humour is based on values and helps us to see things in their true proportion. We must, however, be careful not to mistake sarcasm for humour; too many teachers use biting sarcasm as a weapon of punishment and there is nothing that can hurt a child more. Humour must be kindly. We must be prepared to laugh *with* our pupils, never *at* them.

Such a humanistic approach to teaching says a lot about Edgar and why his pupils liked him. These are timeless principles of sound pedagogy.

Despite his commitment to the teaching profession, Edgar was to make a dramatic career change seven years later. For reasons to be explained in his own words, Edgar changed career direction in 1952 when he took up the position of Director of Rehabilitation at the Newfoundland Tuberculosis Association. But this change was still about education. Edgar's job was to establish training programs for

---

36   Distinguished Flying Medal. "The award was made to non-commissioned officers and men for an act or acts of valour, courage or devotion to duty performed whilst flying in active operations against the enemy" ("Distinguished").

TB patients after they had been released from the sanatorium but were unable to return to their previous employment in physically demanding jobs, such as fishing and construction work. He held this position from 1952 to 1963, and then was promoted to the senior position of Executive Secretary, a position he held until his retirement in 1976. Edgar also served on both the Anglican School Board and the Board of Regents of Memorial University. After retirement, he contributed to the history of Newfoundland education by writing a book about Bishop Feild and Bishop Feild College.[37]

From 1843 until 1998 Newfoundland and Labrador had a denominational education system (Downer and Bull 2).[38] Although publicly funded and with a common core curriculum, most schools in the country/province were operated under the auspices of the three main Christian denominations: Church of England/Anglican, Methodist/United Church, and Roman Catholic. Later, the Salvation Army and Pentecostal Assembly also ran their own school systems.

Throughout the whole of Edgar's active working life, church and school were intimately related. Furthermore, both the Anglican and Roman Catholic school systems (but not the United Church) were divided into separate boys' schools and girls' schools. Until the establishment of larger city high schools in the 1960s, the denominational school system was also differentiated along class lines. The denominational colleges (Bishop Feild, Bishop Spencer, Prince of Wales, St. Bonaventure's, and Mercy Convent Academy) were more privileged than the other high schools, such as St. Michael's and St. George's (Anglican), Macpherson and Curtis (United Church), and St. Patrick's

---

37   Edgar House, *Edward Feild*, 1987.

38   For a good descriptive overview of the history of education in Newfoundland before Confederation, see Fred W. Rowe, *The History of Education in Newfoundland*, 1952. See also the two-volume history by Ralph L. Andrews, edited by Alice E. Wareham, *Integration and Other Developments in Newfoundland Education 1915–1949* and *Post-Confederation Developments in Newfoundland Education 1949–1975*, 1985.

and Holy Cross (Roman Catholic).[39] The colleges charged a small fee
and were purported to provide a higher standard of education than
the high schools.[40] The colleges and high schools were socially differentiated in many ways. For many years, there were separate sports
leagues for the colleges (the intercollegiate leagues) and the high
schools (the high school leagues).

There is a common misperception that the denominational colleges catered to the elite of St. John's.[41] While it is true that the merchant class did send their sons to Feild and the other colleges for the
lower grades, most of them sent their older children away to boarding
schools in England or mainland Canada. Most of the students at Bishop
Feild and the other St. John's colleges were solidly middle class, with
some from working-class backgrounds.[42] There is no doubt, however,
that many of those who attended Bishop Feild College believed that
they were lucky to be there and shared in a strong sense of "the
Feildian spirit." A colonial version of the English public school system
values of fair play and sportsmanship prevailed. Most of the Headmasters and many of the teachers at Bishop Feild were British. Edgar

39   For an informative discussion of the education of girls at Bishop Spencer, Prince of
Wales, and Mercy, see the article by Marilyn Porter, "She Knows Who She Is: Edu-
cating Girls to Their Place in Society," in Linda Cullum and Marilyn Porter, eds.,
Creating This Place, 146–78.

40   This may or may not have been the case. The same basic curriculum was taught in
the colleges as in the high schools.

41   In his biography of Joseph Smallwood, Richard Gwynn refers to Bishop Feild College as "where the headmaster was a B.A. (Contab.) and where the St. John's merchants sent their sons"; this view of the colleges as elitist is also present in author
Wayne Johnston's fictionalized account of Smallwood's life, *The Colony of Unre-
quited Dreams*, 1999 (I gave a copy of this book to my father as a birthday gift, but
he was upset by what he felt was an inaccurate and unfair portrayal of Bishop Feild
College). For a favourable description of life at Bishop Feild College in the late
1890s and early twentieth century, see Colton, *Newfoundland Rhapsody*, 23–54.

42   For example, Ches Parsons. When I was a boy at Bishop Feild I remember feeling
sorry for those of our buddies whose parents made them go away to school when
they reached the higher grades. We certainly didn't envy them.

was the first Headmaster to be both born in Newfoundland and educated in North America. He believed strongly in the same values as
his British predecessors and, as a teacher and headmaster, was adept
at inculcating them in the boys at Feild. He was respected and admired by most of his pupils and ex-pupils.[43]

Despite their representing different religious denominations,
common bonds united the Headmasters or Headmistresses and
teachers of the denominational colleges. The Headmasters of the
three boys' colleges enjoyed relationships of mutual respect and sup-
ported each other in promoting the intercollegiate system. They
shared a social class consciousness; the three colleges were united in
differentiating themselves from the less prestigious high schools. Edgar
married Margaret Butt, who was a teacher at Prince of Wales College,
and he was even approached about the possibility of becoming the
Principal of Prince of Wales (much to his father's consternation). As
one of his stories illustrates, he also helped the nuns at Mercy Convent
when they wanted to learn chemistry.

During all the years when Edgar was involved in schooling as a
student, teacher, and headmaster, education and religion were closely
linked in Newfoundland's denominational system.[44] Edgar and Margie
were Christian believers, but they were not fervently religious. My
mother had no difficulty in converting from Methodism/United
Church to Church of England/Anglican when she got married. She
thought the family members should be of the same religion. The
whole family attended church regularly for many years, but this was
as much a social as a religious ritual. I well remember my sister Janet
and I waiting impatiently after church while Dad chatted for ages (as
it seemed to us) with friends and acquaintances outside the church
after service. Initially, we attended the Anglican Cathedral, but after

---

43   This theme is illustrated in the Foreword and elaborated on in the Conclusion of
     this book.

44   With the exception of his three years in Buchans, when he was Principal of Buchans
     Public School, which included all the Protestant denominations in Buchans. There
     was a separate Roman Catholic school.

Dad had a falling out with the minister there we moved to St. Thomas' Church.[45] Our parents enrolled us in Sunday school when we were little, but later, when we protested, they gave in easily enough.

Religious values and practices were still prevalent in our household during our early childhood. Perhaps as a carryover from my mother's early Methodism, we were not allowed to play cards on Sunday. For many years, Edgar was the Chairman of the Grounds Committee of the Feildian Athletic Grounds Association, which looked after the Feildian Grounds located at the beginning of Portugal Cove Road just down from where we lived. As a boy, I remember going down to the Grounds with Dad on several Sundays when he would send away anyone playing games there on the Sabbath.

Later in life, after their children had grown up and the older generation died, my parents attended church less often. Nevertheless, in 1995 Edgar House was honoured with the Bishop's Award of Merit, Diocesan Level by Bishop D.F. Harvey. The old animosities between Catholics and Protestants (in the local idiom, the "micks" and the "blacks") gradually waned over the years. When my sister announced her engagement to a Roman Catholic my parents were not much fussed, and laughingly dismissed an edict from one of my mother's Methodist aunts who phoned her to say, "Margaret, you must stop it!"

Despite this gradual evolution away from religious rivalries and denominational education in Newfoundland that occurred during his lifetime, there is no doubt that his upbringing as a member of the Church of England and his time as a pupil, teacher, and headmaster at a Church of England school were formative influences on Edgar's character and self-identity. I will return to this theme after we have considered other key social institutions that shaped his personality.

Social Stratification and Edgar House's Social Class

All known complex societies exhibit evidence of social differentiation by which some members and groups are ranked higher than others

---

45   We never did find out what the falling out was about.

according to various criteria. Newfoundland and Labrador is no exception. To date, however, a systematic and definitive analysis of social stratification for our society has not been done.[46] Some social scientists have taken a Marxist approach,[47] but this would be of limited use for present purposes. Marx argued that within a capitalist society social class is primarily determined by one's relationship to the means of production, with the main division being between the bourgeoisie (capitalist class) and proletariat (working class). The former is dominant because it owns and controls the means of production.[48] This approach is limited for understanding class and status differences *within* Newfoundland and Labrador because ownership and control of most of the province's main industries — oil and gas, mining, and pulp and paper — rests with multinational corporations headquartered outside the province. The same reservation applies to C. Wright Mills's concept of the power elite (Mills). Many of the major political decisions that affect the province have been made in Britain historically, and in central Canada since Confederation in 1949.

For Canada as a whole, there have been some notable attempts at delineating the defining features of social stratification. The best-known example is John Porter's *The Vertical Mosaic: An Analysis of Social Class and Power in Canada* (1965). Porter's focus is mainly on immigration and how various ethnic groups have gradually found a niche within the Canadian social mosaic. While insightful for most regions of Canada, Porter's analysis is not so applicable to the mainly homogeneous white, English/Irish population of Newfoundland and Labrador. Another well-known approach to social stratification in Canada is Bernard Blishen's occupational class scale (Blishen 41–53). This would be helpful if applied systematically to Newfoundland and

---

46   For an earlier preliminary effort, see J.D. House, *Lectures on Newfoundland Society and Culture*, 1978, 175–86.

47   See, for example, Gerald M. Sider, *Culture and Class in Anthropology and History*, 1986; James Overton, *Making a World of Difference*, 1996.

48   See, for example, T.B. Bottomore and Maximilien Rubel, *Karl Marx*, 1956, 178–202.

Labrador, but would still be limited as it applies only to occupational status and not other aspects of social stratification.

A more promising approach for our purposes is Gerth and Mills's 1953 update of Max Weber's writings about social class and status honour, *Character and Social Structure*. Gerth and Mills distinguish four dimensions of stratification: *occupation*, which is "a set of activities pursued more or less regularly as a major source of income"; *class*, which "has to do with the amount and source (property or work) of income as these affect the chances of people to obtain other available values"; *status*, which "involves the successful realization of claims to prestige; it refers to the distribution of deference in a society"; and *power*, which "refers to the realization of one's will, even if this involves the resistance of others" (307). For current purposes, we would add that *educational level* plays an important role in determining any individual's life chances on each of these dimensions, especially occupation and status.

In popular discourse, the term "social class" is commonly used to refer to a kind of amalgam of each of the four dimensions of stratification identified by Gerth and Mills, which, for simplicity's sake, we will use here.[49] We also want to pay attention to *social mobility*, which refers to an individual's, family's, or social group's movement up or down the social stratification hierarchy, either during their own lifetime or from one generation to the next.

Keeping these criteria in mind, we can distinguish among four distinct social classes internally in Newfoundland and Labrador: the upper class (or elite); the middle class (which can be further divided into the upper-middle class and the lower-middle class); the working class; and the underclass (the poor and underprivileged). The elite are the most powerful and richest members of the society, with significant income from property investments. The middle class are generally well educated and enjoy salaried incomes, with the upper-middle class being more highly paid managers and professionals. The working

---

49   This approach is similar to that adopted by Cullum and Porter in their Introduction to *Creating This Place*, 7.

class work for wages and enjoy less job security than the middle class. The underclass is more or less left out of the labour market and is dependent on the state for support. This model is what Weber would refer to as an "ideal type," useful for analysis but not an exact depiction of social reality. There are no rigid boundaries between the social classes in Newfoundland and Labrador and both upward and downward mobility between classes is common.

Where do Edgar and the House family fit into this model? The family has exhibited both geographical and social mobility over the years. Edgar's grandfather was the captain of a small mail packet. His father achieved an Associate in Arts diploma, the highest level of formal education in the country at the time. He moved from teaching in a rural school to the city of St. John's where he became a master at Bishop Feild College, the country's most prestigious Church of England school. It is noteworthy that Edgar's mother, from a rural fishing family, took up bridge, the most popular card game for the urban middle and upper classes, when she moved to St. John's.[50] Outport Newfoundlanders and working-class townies prefer the traditional card game 120s or "Growl," which originated in Scotland and Ireland as "Maw" in the mid-fifteenth century.[51]

Edgar himself attained a university degree, and married a woman who also had a degree (and was herself upwardly mobile from a lower-middle class background); and he went on to become the Headmaster at Bishop Feild and, later, the Executive Director of an important voluntary organization.

As Headmaster at Feild, as the senior administrator of the TB

---

50   Grace Sparkes, who grew up in a well-to-do merchant family in Grand Bank in the 1910s and 1920s, is quoted as saying about entertainment in the home: "We could play cards: I could play bridge before I was sixteen." (Wright 28). Unlike most sports at the time, bridge and other card games were typically a mixed-gender form of recreation. For more on Grace Sparkes, see Chapter 2, note 13 (p. 96).

51   The *Dictionary of Newfoundland English* (hereafter *DNE*) defines "growl" as: Card game; Auction forty-five's; and one-twenty as: variety of the card-game, auction, in which the winning score is 120 points.

Association, and, later, as a member of the St. John's Rotary Club, Edgar rubbed shoulders and became personally acquainted with many members of the St. John's upper class. He was, in a sense, on the fringe of the establishment. He was well educated and held prestigious and respected positions, but he was never powerful or rich. He and Margie enjoyed a modest, middle-class lifestyle. They lived in a solid but unpretentious house in a desirable neighbourhood in which many of the houses were grander than theirs. Many of their friends were better off in material terms than they were, but this never seemed to bother them. Having grown up during the Depression, they were frugal and grateful that they never lacked the necessities of life. They enjoyed some luxuries, but not many. They could afford to spend a few vacations in distant locations: western Canada, Europe, the Caribbean, and Florida; but, most years, they were content with their annual holiday in Trinity.

Women and Gender Relations

It is appropriate to begin this section with some considerations about Edgar's wife Margie, the woman who had the most influence on his views about women and gender relations.

Margaret Butt was born and raised in St. John's. Her family lived at Masonic Terrace, off Gower Street, and she remembers having a great view of St. John's harbour out her bedroom window. At the time, that area of town was mainly a working-class/lower-middle class neighbourhood. The Butt family fit into the latter category. Her father Charles worked virtually his whole career as a clerk at T. & M. Winter Co., and her mother, Maggie Taylor, was a mother and housewife in the typical household division of labour of the time. Margie had two older brothers, Herbert and Gerald, neither of whom attended university. Their family being Methodist, Margie attended Holloway School and Prince of Wales College. She was bright and did so well at school that she was encouraged to continue with her studies after graduation. She went to Memorial University College, where in addition to her studies she played ice hockey, field hockey, and basketball. We have included photographs of the Memorial girls' basketball and hockey teams from 1930 on which Margie played. While at Memorial she became a favourite of its President, John Lewis Paton. She was prone to illness in those days, and President Paton would visit her (as he visited every student) and refer to her as "Lady Margaret." Edgar believed that it was probably Mr. Paton who suggested she go on to complete a university degree and arranged for her to get some financial assistance. Since Memorial University College did not offer degrees, this meant that she would have to go away to another country to complete the additional two years she would need to qualify for a degree. She chose to go to Mount Allison University in Sackville, New Brunswick, Canada, which was affiliated with the United Church of Canada at the time.[52]

Her illness, appendicitis, caused Margie to take an extra year to complete her degree. Although a year older than Edgar, she graduated from Mount Allison with a B.Sc. degree in 1934, a year after he graduated with his B.Sc. from Dalhousie. Margie was active in student affairs and sports, and was chosen to propose the toast to the *Alma Mater* at the junior/senior banquet on 12 May 1934.

On her return to St. John's, she accepted an interesting teaching position. In the mornings, she would teach kindergarten at Holloway School, and in the afternoons teach physiology to the Grade 11 students at Prince of Wales College. After a long courtship,[53] Margie and Edgar were married in the summer of 1939. As was the custom — unwritten law — in those days, Margie had to resign her teaching position once she got married.[54] As far as her children know, Margie expressed

---

52 See John G. Reid, *Mount Allison University*, 1984.

53 Times were hard during the 1930s and schoolteachers were poorly paid. Edgar and Margie saved as best they could so they could afford to buy a house when they got married. Edgar later expressed regret about waiting so long. But, if they had married sooner, it would have meant that Margie's teaching career would have been even shorter than it was.

54 In their study of four female Newfoundland teachers from the interwar years, Kay Whitehead and Judith Peppard note that "Although there was no official marriage bar in the education regulations, most women did resign when they married" (Whitehead and Peppard 2005). The marriage bar for female teachers is also noted in Cullum and Porter, *Creating This Place*, 274.

no real regrets about this change. It was simply taken for granted. She settled easily enough into her new role as housewife, and, five years later, mother. Earlier, she had given birth to a son who died of a congenital heart defect after only a few days.[55]

Two years after their marriage, Margie headed off with Edgar for their Buchans adventure. On their return, she settled into the role of supportive wife of a Headmaster, and was active in the Feildian Ladies Association that catered to various school events. She took up bowling, enjoyed attending community concerts and various sporting events, became a fine bridge player, and developed a wide and active circle of friends. After several years, when her own children reached university age, Margie did return to the paid workforce as a part-time assistant librarian at Memorial University. This was a job rather than a career, but she did enjoy the work and her interactions with students.

While it is tempting to elaborate about Margie, my main purpose here is to provide enough information about her for understanding the way Edgar's views about the role of women and gender relations evolved over the years. Although his own mother had little formal education and was strictly a wife and mother in a traditional household division of labour, Edgar was close to his mother, admired her for her work ethic and good spirits, and valued her advice on his life choices. He went on to marry a bright woman who had earned a university degree, which was rare in Newfoundland in the 1930s.

Edgar's views on women and gender relations were, in some ways, ahead of his time. As early as 1938, he gave a talk called "Sport Around the World" in which he reviewed the way in which different nations had developed their distinctive sport — soccer in England, baseball in the United States, ice hockey in Canada, etc. He concluded by arguing that Newfoundland should develop a national sport of its own that could be played by people of both sexes in small outports as

---

55   My parents never talked to me about this loss; they mentioned it briefly to my sister Jan. But Edgar did mention it one time to Jan's husband, George; and Margie talked about it to my wife, Jeannie. According to Jan the boy was christened Robert, after Margie's cousin Robert Butt, who died in World War II.

well as large towns: "What we need is a game which can be played by both sexes indoors or out of doors and one in which the equipment will cost so little that even the poorest can indulge in it." He went on to speak approvingly of "the crossing of sex lines in sport." "In these taboo-destroying days the sexes have crossed the traditional lines and are engaging in whatever games they wish. As women have entered into the political and economic life of most countries so they have entered the athletic."

When I was a teenager, most of my friends' parents lived in households where the division of labour was strict between men and women. Men did men's work and would not be expected to or, in many cases, not even be welcome to join in kitchen chores and other kinds of women's work. At the time, I was somewhat disconcerted by my father's being different: he regularly did the dishes, some of the cleaning, and even some of the cooking in our household. I didn't like it when my parents' female friends would say to me, as they often did: "You should just hope to grow up to be half the man your father is." Embarrassed at the time, I now feel proud to think that my father was ahead of his time in his attitudes towards women and the domestic division of labour.

Later in his life, well after he retired, two incidents come to mind that express his outlook. When the St. John's Rotary Club finally agreed to allow female members in 1992, Edgar, as one of the oldest long-term members of the club, was interviewed by a reporter for a local radio station. The female reporter asked him, "What do you think about women joining Rotary, Mr. House?" His answer: "It's about time!" Some years later, my daughter, Vanessa, screwed up her courage to tell "Pop" that she and her boyfriend, Cory (now her husband), had decided to live together in a flat in downtown St. John's. She was relieved when his response was the same as it had been to the reporter mentioned above: "It's about time!"

I don't want to overstate the point being made here. In many ways, Edgar was quite traditional in his attitudes towards and relations with women. He was quite content to be the breadwinner in the family and, to my knowledge, did not question the propriety of Margie's having to give up her teaching career to become his wife and the mother of his children, and her converting to become an Anglican. In some ways, he was quite old-fashioned. He would tip his hat to the ladies, hold the door open for them, and stand when they entered the room. While such actions would no doubt be frowned upon as sexist and demeaning by modern-day feminists, they were meant by Edgar and his male friends at the time to express their respect. On the whole, Edgar's attitudes and opinions about women and gender relations were progressive for his time, certainly more progressive than one might have predicted solely from his social background.

Voluntary Organizations and Good Citizenship

In the latter years of the twentieth century, several sociologists (e.g., Broom and Selznick 206–08) pointed out that modern Western democracies were characterized by numerous voluntary and community-based organizations.[56] These were of many types: recreational, religious, educational, promotional, self-improvement, and service provision of various kinds. Recently, this sector has been more systematically studied and is now more commonly referred to as the non-profit and voluntary sector. It has been defined as follows: "nonprofit and voluntary organizations are defined as organizations that have a structure, are non-governmental, do not distribute profits, are self-governing, and benefit from some degree of voluntary contribution of time or money"(Hall et al. vii).[57]

The non-profit and voluntary sector fulfills important functions within contemporary societies. In addition to their social contributions,

---

56   According to the 2003 *National Survey of Nonprofit and Voluntary Organizations,* there were 161,227 NVO organizations in Canada as of that date, of which 2,219 were in Newfoundland and Labrador (Penelope Rowe 6).

57   For more contemporary analyses of the financial and other challenges facing this sector in the early years of the twenty-first century, see Kathy L. Brock and Keith G. Banting, eds., *The Nonprofit Sector and Government in a New Century,* 2001, and Brock and Banting, eds., *The Nonprofit Sector in Interesting Times,* 2003.

such agencies also contribute significant economic benefits. They provide many jobs and satisfying careers, and several organizations in
this sector provide goods and services to individuals and families that
are not well served either by the market system or by state agencies.
Although this sector was neither clearly defined nor well researched
during Edgar House's working life, in retrospect he was intimately involved over many years both as a paid employee and as a volunteer in
the non-profit and voluntary sector.

As we have seen, for the final 24 years of his working career Edgar
was employed by one such voluntary organization, the Newfoundland Tuberculosis Association. The TB Association, as it was popularly
called, contributed significantly to the eradication of tuberculosis in
the province and to helping former TB patients find employment and
adjust to life after they had been released from the sanatorium.[58] His
work as Director of Rehabilitation and then Executive Secretary of
this organization provided Edgar with a satisfying career. Although
he had enjoyed his earlier career in teaching, his subsequent career
was less stressful and time-consuming than being a Headmaster who
also carried a heavy teaching load. He particularly enjoyed his 11
years as Director of Rehabilitation. In that work, he had the satisfaction of seeing the direct results of his efforts as former sanatorium
patients were able to start new jobs and reintegrate into their communities all over the province.

Less obviously and mainly behind the scenes, Edgar was heavily
involved throughout his life, both before and after his retirement, as a
volunteer worker for many voluntary organizations and associations.
He was President of the Newfoundland Teachers' Association after
Confederation and led the negotiations for teachers' improved con-
tract and working conditions in the new province. In 1950, he played
a lead role in establishing the St. John's Branch of the Victorian Order
of Nurses and served as its first President. During his 55 years as a member of the St. John's Rotary Club, Edgar exemplified that organization's

---

58   See Edgar House, *Light at Last*, 1981; and Harry Cuff, ed., *Take a Deep Breath*,
      2003.

stated aim of providing service to the community. In particular, he volunteered his time for many years working at the Waterford Hospital (the so-called "mental hospital") in St. John's, helping to run its canteen, its rehabilitation program for patients, and its annual Christmas celebrations.

Edgar was a member of Memorial University's Board of Regents the year the new campus was opened on Elizabeth Avenue in 1961.[59] He was particularly proud of his work on the Board's Medical School Feasibility Study Committee, which recommended that Memorial should proceed to establish its own medical school. In keeping with his lifelong interest in sport, recreation, and physical health, he also served as Newfoundland's representative on the National Physical Fitness Council. After retirement, he was the Financial Campaign Chairman for both the St. Luke's Home Chapel and the Waterford Hospital Chapel. His final volunteer position was as a member of Memorial University's Medical School Advisory Committee for Gerontology.

What motivated Edgar to put so much time and effort into unpaid community service? Edgar, like many others, had a strong sense of duty and responsibility towards his community. He identified with it and wanted to contribute to its improvement. Most of his volunteer work was done behind the scenes with little or no recognition, although he was liked, respected, and even admired in some circles. He was honoured with several life memberships and an honorary Doctor of Laws degree from Memorial University. But it would be stretching the point to suggest that he conducted his volunteer work in order to receive such recognition. He was, indeed, a good citizen of St. John's and Newfoundland; for him, that seemed to be reward enough in and of itself.

59   He is included in a picture of the Board of Regents at that time, which is currently on display on a picture board about Memorial's governance, located outside the current Arts and Administration building.

Self-Identity: An Anglo-Newfoundland Canadian

A person's self-identity is not mechanically determined by social and other forces. Rather, he or she constructs an identity based mainly on personal experiences in several different social milieux. For Edgar House, each of the social spheres examined above played a part in influencing his self-identity — his family, relatives, and friends; the urban and rural communities in which he lived and visited; his position as a white, Anglo-Saxon male in a mainly homogeneous white society; his upbringing within the Church of England/Anglican religion; his education at Bishop Feild College, Memorial University College, King's College, and Dalhousie University; his dual career experiences in education and then in health administration; his upwardly mobile middle-class standing and his many contacts with members of Newfoundland's upper class; his involvement in many voluntary associations — all of these (and other experiences as well) influenced the kind of person Edgar became, his sense of worth, and his self-identity.

In his 2012 study, *Beyond the Nation: Immigrants' Local Lives in Transnational Cultures*, Alexander Freund makes the point that immigrants to Canada often maintain two national identities, for example, German and Canadian (4–5). This kind of multi-faceted national identity is not necessarily confined to immigrants. Edgar House lived most of his life in a single neighbourhood in St. John's. Nevertheless, his self-identification involved a complex interplay among three different "nationalities": English, Newfoundlander, and Canadian. Edgar attended a Church of England school, Bishop Feild College, which was modelled to some degree on the English public school system. Its colours, light blue and dark blue, were the colours of Cambridge and Oxford universities. The Headmaster and many of the masters were English. At Memorial University College, he was heavily influenced by John Lewis Paton, an English educator who had been High Master of the respected Manchester Grammar School. He went to the Anglican church, and marched in the Church Lads' Brigade. He became a fan of the Manchester United football team and was instrumental in Memorial teams modelling their colours on that famous team. At home, we were taught to take for granted that English goods — bicycles, biscuits, chocolates, etc. — were superior. Edgar and Margie could not afford expensive holidays during the early years of their marriage but, later in life, they delighted in a few vacations to England.

Edgar's kind of quiet pro-English sentiment is more prevalent than is generally recognized. In recent years, a great deal has been made of Newfoundland's connections to Ireland. This is a positive development but it tends to obscure the fact that more Newfoundlanders trace their origins to the West Country of England than to Ireland.[60] Perhaps because England was the dominant country in determining Newfoundland's history, English Newfoundlanders have been less outgoing and vocal about their origins than their Irish counterparts. This connection to England no doubt helps explain the fierce loyalty that Newfoundland displayed towards Britain during two world wars,[61] and it also helps to explain why most Newfoundlanders were ready enough to temporarily suspend democracy in favour of rule by a British-dominated Commission of Government in 1934.

---

60   Religious identity roughly conforms to ethnic origins, with most Roman Catholics being of Irish descent, and Protestants of English descent (there is also a minority of Newfoundlanders of French, Scottish, and Aboriginal descent). In 1935, when Edgar was just starting his career as a teacher, 32.4 per cent of the population of Newfoundland and Labrador was Roman Catholic and 65.8 per cent was Protestant (32.0 per cent Anglican, 26.3 per cent United Church, 6.2 per cent Salvation Army, and 1.3 per cent Pentecostal). In St. John's, the percentage of Roman Catholics is significantly higher than for the province as a whole. In 1935, 47.5 per cent of the population of St. John's was Roman Catholic, 23.6 per cent Church of England, and 27.6 per cent other Protestant (United Church, Salvation Army, Pentecostal, Presbyterian, and Congregational) (Canada 1935, 4, 14). As of the latest census, in 2011, with less of the population identifying as Christian, 35.8 per cent of the population of Newfoundland and Labrador identified as Catholic, and 57.4 per cent as Protestant (25.1 per cent Anglican, 32.2 per cent other Protestant). In St. John's, those percentages were 45.6 per cent Catholic and 44.3 per cent Protestant (20.9 per cent Anglican, 23.4 per cent other Protestant) (Canada 2011, 5).

61   Newfoundlanders of Irish origin were equally committed to the cause, as likely to enlist, and as likely to be killed or wounded as those of English origin. By the twentieth century, they all shared a common identity as Newfoundlanders.

Despite his allegiance to Britain, Edgar was nevertheless a Newfoundlander first and foremost. He was a real "townie" in that he was born, raised, educated, and spent most of his life in St. John's. Nevertheless, both his parents came from the outports, he spent most of his summers throughout his life in his beloved Trinity, and his work for the Tuberculosis Association gave him the opportunity to visit many small communities in all parts of the province.[62] He spent three years in the mining town of Buchans in central Newfoundland and visited Grand Falls and Corner Brook on several occasions. Hence, he had a well-rounded sense of Newfoundland. During his work as a playground supervisor in Bannerman Park in St. John's and his many visits with his relatives in Champneys, he observed both urban and rural poverty first-hand during the Depression of the 1930s. His love for Newfoundland was expressed more in a social than political sense. He wanted things to be better for people, for poverty and diseases such as TB to be eradicated, for people to have better educations, opportunities, and life chances. These goals were more important to him than abstract political principles. From his point of view, when the fledgling nation of Newfoundland found itself in severe financial difficulties in the early 1930s, the temporary suspension of democracy under a British-led Commission of Government would have been seen as a price worth paying in order to get the country back on its feet.

As a fortuitous consequence of its strategic position during World War II, Newfoundland's economy and fiscal situation improved during the first half of the 1940s. Post-war Britain was preoccupied with its own reconstruction and was not much interested in the "problem" of what to do about Newfoundland. It established a National Convention, with representatives elected from each region of the province, to hold consultations and debate the country's future. In 1948, a referendum was held to determine which of three options the people preferred: a return to responsible government of an independent

---

62 Although Edgar visited some parts of Labrador, he was not very familiar with the mainland part of the province of Newfoundland and Labrador.

nation, a continuation of the Commission of Government, or Confederation with Canada as its tenth province.[63]

Edgar's views on Confederation have to be seen partly in light of
his concern about the well-being of the people of the province, and
also in terms of his impressions of Canada. During his two years at
King's College and Dalhousie University in Halifax, Edgar enjoyed his
time immensely and was favourably impressed by the Canadians he
met and came to know. His wife-to-be, Margaret Butt, was similarly
impressed by her experiences at Mount Allison University in New
Brunswick. Despite the Depression, Canada seemed to be a country
on the move and, as provinces of Canada, Nova Scotia and New
Brunswick would be part of that nation's future success.

The post-war period when the National Convention was formed
and carried out its debates, which were broadcast live to the people of
Newfoundland, happened to coincide with the time when Edgar returned from Buchans to St. John's to become Headmaster of Bishop
Feild College. In addition to his administrative responsibilities, Edgar
was required to teach several courses, a daunting and time-consuming
challenge. As attested to by many former pupils, Edgar was a successful Headmaster and inspiring teacher; but these responsibilities left
little time for other activities, including involvement in the affairs of
the National Convention.

Many of the people in Edgar and Margie's social circle were anti-
confederates, some of them fervently so. One of their best friends,
Chancey Currie, was the publisher of the *Daily News*, the city's morning newspaper at the time, which was strongly supportive of a return
to responsible government. Most of the merchant class men who sent
their sons to Bishop Feild were adamantly opposed to Confederation

---

63   Much has been written about the several contentious issues that characterized the
National Convention and the way in which Confederation was achieved that is
beyond the scope of my current focus on Edgar House's position on these matters.
See, for example, Raymond B. Blake, *Canadians at Last*, 1994; Bren Walsh, *More
Than a Poor Majority*, 1985; John Edward Fitzgerald, ed., *Newfoundland at the
Crossroads*, 2002; Greg Malone, *Don't Tell the Newfoundlanders*, 2012.

and to its strongest proponent, Joseph Smallwood. But Edgar had become quietly pro-Confederation. His earlier contact with Smallwood at Bishop Feild had impressed him favourably, as had Smallwood's compelling oratory when he gave a speech about the British Empire to the students and staff of Buchans Public School.[64] In a low-key act of defiance, Edgar invited Smallwood to be guest speaker at a Feildian "smoker" (a meeting for discussing issues of the day), and ignored a threat from a member of the elite that he would take his son out of Feild if he went ahead with it.

Edgar never regretted his support for Confederation, and felt vindicated when the benefits of being part of a wealthier country's social security system started to flow into the new province, thereby improving the standard of living of hundreds of low-income families. However, he maintained an ambivalent attitude towards Joe Smallwood, who reigned as Premier of the new province from 1949 to 1972.[65] He admired Smallwood for his energetic leadership in the confederate cause, and for his contributions to education and the growth of Memorial University. But he was upset by several of Smallwood's economic development schemes, his naivety in dealing with such wheeler-dealers as Alfred Valdmanis and John Doyle, and his autocratic ways. Like many Newfoundlanders, he wished that Smallwood had retired earlier rather than clinging on to power for as long as possible.

Edgar seamlessly became a proud Canadian. He went on to serve on the boards of several regional and national organizations, including the Royal Canadian Air Cadets, the Victorian Order of Nurses, the Maritime Conference on Social Work (President in 1963), and the National Fitness Council. He also served on the Canadian Lung Association and, in 1977, was recognized with an Honorary Life Membership in that organization. He and Margie enjoyed several visits to the

---

64 Edgar's own account of this event can be found below in his life story, "Chapter 12: Politics and Joe Smallwood."

65 Although he fashioned himself as "Joey" for his political persona, Smallwood was usually called "Joe" by those who knew him personally.

mainland,[66] including Nova Scotia, Montreal, Ottawa, and British Columbia. Like many Newfoundland couples, they saw some of their children, grandchildren, and great-grandchildren move away to other parts of Canada to attend university, work for several years, or even settle permanently.

As a consequence of Confederation, after 1949 Edgar assumed a third national self-identity as a Canadian. And like the immigrants described by Freund, Edgar maintained three national identities in comfortable juxtaposition. He was equally proud about being a British subject, a Canadian citizen, and a Newfoundlander.

Here, I have focused mainly on the broadest category of Edgar's overall self-identity — nationality — because this is key to understanding the position he took on the big issues that Newfoundland confronted during his lifetime. But his sense of identity, or, more accurately, self-identities, entailed many other dimensions as well: son, brother, husband, father, grandfather, friend, educator, Feildian, athlete, Church Lads' Brigade officer, health administrator, and Rotarian. I will not elaborate on these here because they are less controversial and more self-apparent in reading the text that follows in Edgar's own words.

A Note on Edgar's Spoken English[67]

Sandra Clarke, in her excellent book, *Newfoundland and Labrador English* (2010), delineates two main varieties of Newfoundland English (NLE): Newfoundland British English (NBE), spoken in most of the province including the Trinity area, where Edgar's parents were from, and Newfoundland Irish English (NIE), spoken on the southeast

---

66   Newfoundlanders typically refer to the rest of Canada as "the mainland."

67   This section was researched and written by Adrian House.

Avalon Peninsula, parts of Placentia Bay, and in St. John's.[68] Edgar, growing up in St. John's, would have spoken a different dialect of English from his parents, although even between them there were differences that were tied to socio-economic status. As he observes: "Mother . . . was almost as much a woman from Champneys when she died as she was when she arrived here. My father spoke very good English but the difference between Trinity and Champneys was very marked. Trinity was one of *the* towns at that time. It had a very good school, a very good teacher, and their speech was not the least like it would be down in English Harbour [near Champneys]."

Clarke (1986) demonstrates that the prominent NIE features in St. John's are more pronounced the further you go down the socio-economic scale, and also that stronger Irish features are stigmatized in terms of status (but not in terms of positive qualities such as honesty) (Clarke "Language" 27). Edgar, being middle class but highly educated and in a prominent social position as Headmaster, exhibits speech more in line with the upper strata. In terms of differences between his speech and that of a Catholic man in a similar position, Clarke concludes that such linguistic variation based on religious and ethnic background is minimal in St. John's (Clarke "Sociolinguistic" 74–75). Edgar's speech was firmly in the NIE tradition of someone born in 1911 in St. John's. Samples of Edgar's speech can be heard on the website for this book, www.edgarhouse.ca.

---

68 We are grateful to Sandra Clarke for reviewing this section. She offered the following interesting observation:

"I very much enjoyed reading what you've written about your grandfather's speech. I agree that since the traditional accent of St. John's had a primarily Irish-English source, someone born in the city a century ago would have been very likely to have some pronunciation features from that source, no matter what their religion and upbringing. I have to admit I was a bit surprised when I began studying St. John's speech three decades ago not to find more marked ethno-religious — essentially Irish-origin vs. non-Irish-origin — differences among city residents, given the strength of the denominational system."

Conclusion: "An Extraordinary Ordinary Man"

George Squires was born in St. John's and grew up on Gower Street in the downtown area of the city. Raised in a traditional Roman Catholic family, he went to school at St. Bonaventure's College and then earned a degree in education at Iona College in New York, as a novitiate in the Irish Christian Brothers. He then taught in Corner Brook at Regina High School. He later decided not to pursue a vocation in the Brothers and returned to St. John's to a teaching position at the Jesuit Gonzaga High School, while obtaining a Bachelor of Education degree from Memorial University. In 1968 he met Janet House, Edgar's daughter, and they married on 7 April 1969.[69] Theirs was what Newfoundlanders at the time called a "mixed marriage," that is, a marriage between a Catholic and a Protestant. Jordy, as George was called by his family, had married into the House family and came to have a strong affection for Edgar and Margie. Out of respect he always called them Mr. House and Mrs. House, or, fondly, after his children were born, Gampy and Nana. Jordy loved Trinity and he and Jan built their own cabin on Edgar and Margie's property in 1975. After Margie died in 2000 and Edgar retired from driving, Jordy helped by driving him when he needed to go to the bank, to get his hair cut, or simply wanted to go out for a drive; Jordy visited Edgar daily throughout his declining years.

When Jordy learned that Adrian and I were working on Edgar's life story, he commented that Mr. House was "an extraordinary ordinary man." What did he mean by that? Edgar was ordinary in that he was not rich, famous, or powerful. Like all human beings, he had his

---

69   Edgar's daughter, Janet Squires (née House), went on to have a successful career as a physiotherapist, Director of Physiotherapy at the Children's Rehabilitation Centre and, later, as Director of Adult Rehabilitation with the Health Care Corporation of St. John's up until 2011, and then was the Director of Professional Practice for Allied Health within Eastern Health. In 1970 she obtained a Certificate of Graduate Study — International Program, from Sargent College School of Allied Health Professionals, Boston University, and George was awarded a Master of Education degree from Boston College.

weaknesses as well as his strengths. He sometimes became impatient, spoke with a slight note of irritation in his voice, and occasionally showed his temper. As a teenager, I had a temper as well and this led to a few clashes between us. His language was always respectful, with his most common profanity being "Damn the devil and no man!"

Edgar was also reluctant to express strong views on the issues of the day. He tended to take the lead from others that he respected and to keep his opinions to himself. Ours was not a household in which we had lively discussions about politics and current affairs in the living room or around the dining room table. In his life story, Edgar expresses very few regrets; but the few that he does express — notably, going to Memorial College rather than to a Canadian university to do his teacher's training, come from his taking advice from authority figures rather than following his own instincts.

This was all ordinary enough; but what did Edgar's son-in-law and others, including former students, former TB patients, and many friends and acquaintances state or imply that was extraordinary about him? They were impressed by his integrity, his love of learning, his genuine humanity in dealing with his students and others who depended on him. They also appreciated his gentle sense of humour and his genuine enjoyment of the simple pleasures of life, an enjoyment that was shared and enhanced by his long, happy marriage with Margie, a woman who was equally content and appreciative of what life had to offer.

Edgar neither sought nor achieved much public recognition for the good work he did in his paid employment and his many volunteer activities. He worked mainly behind the scenes, but those in the know appreciated his many contributions to education, health care, and the social development of his city and country/province. They saw to it that he received various kinds of recognition, not so much with the general public but certainly within the specific sectors of the public in which he was known. He was clearly appreciated and respected by Bishop Feild College/Bishop Feild School; the Feildian Athletic Association; the Anglican Church; Memorial University; the Newfoundland

and Labrador Teachers' Association; both the Newfoundland and the Canadian Lung Association; the St. John's Rotary Club; and the Newfoundland and Labrador Soccer Hall of Fame.

More than this, the people who knew him, in particular the many students who were inspired by him during his prime as a teacher and headmaster, developed an appreciation for Edgar House the man and the humanist that supersedes his formal awards and recognition. We will return to this theme in the conclusion to the life story of this extraordinary ordinary Newfoundlander.

Introduction to the Text
Adrian House

When I tell people about my father's work in recording Edgar's stories and our work to edit them into this book, people often ask, "What did he do?" thinking that Edgar was famous in some way to warrant this treatment. My response is that he really lived his life, relished it, and had an incredible memory and a gift for telling a story. And so, whether you have a specific interest in Newfoundland or just enjoy a good story, we think that the following pages will be compelling. Turning these pages, you will be turning through a life that encompassed most of the turbulent twentieth century.

The stories and anecdotes are best appreciated if you put yourself into their times, if you identify with them. Yes, it was very different back then, one sees; but as well it was very similar. People built things, worked, fell in love, and coped with the joys and sorrows of life just like we do today. Some of it makes one appreciate what we have now, a time of relative peace and prosperity, while some of it awakens one to things that we have lost and could strive to re-establish, such as a closer sense of community and a keener sense of civic duty.

This life story contains stories of all different kinds: about childhood in St. John's, wartime, school, sports, teaching, holidays, city, and outport; those stories are sad, happy, funny, and serious, all told in Edgar's unique voice. Edgar, or "Pop," as my siblings and I called him, had an amazing memory, eye for detail, and skill at bringing the past to life. He had a different idea of Newfoundland from that of people growing up here today: he grew up in a different country. When he says, "Buchans has the best weather in the country," he means Newfoundland. His speech is that of old St. John's, and there are some good Newfoundland words in here, such as "sparable" and "quintal." With the help of the *Dictionary of Newfoundland English*, we have definitions for these in footnotes. We have also added notes expanding upon the various people, events, and places Edgar mentions in his narrative. Maps of Newfoundland and St. John's (see pages 15 and 16) have been labelled with the places Edgar identifies in his history.

Although he wasn't a rich, powerful person, Edgar knew many prominent Newfoundlanders personally. Tommy Ricketts, I.J. Samson, Sir Richard Squires, J.L. Paton, A.R. Scammell, Bliss Murphy, Joey Smallwood, John Crosbie, and Bob Cole all feature in his colourful stories. Reading them, one gets a virtual catalogue of the important figures of twentieth-century Newfoundland.

Some of the stories display a generosity that is heart-warming, such as the Boxing Day concert at the Waterford Hospital, or the building of Memorial Stadium with donations from people's salaries on Water Street. When people wanted something done that needed money, they often raised it themselves, not expecting the government or someone else to provide it for them. People felt a real sense of accomplishment and community in doing this and in working on these projects together.

Some of these stories our family heard again and again, but they were often told in a different way, for example, with a different inflection in the voices. "The Tie," about his and Margie's meeting, was a favourite. This would sometimes be a shorter tale, told in a bit more offhand way, while at other times he would get completely into it, and do a new, very convincing impression of my grandmother emphatically saying "I don't like that tie!" while he flicked the one he was wearing. This would send us all into laughter no matter how often we had heard the story before.

Edgar took pleasure and exulted, even, in the things he enjoyed: teaching, carpentry, sports, the Church Lads' Brigade (CLB), church, his wife and children whom he loved dearly, summer trips to Trinity, and Rotary. Sometimes there is sadness in the stories about things and people that have passed, but overall, Edgar was a happy, fulfilled man. He identified himself strongly with St. John's, and loved the city. While never one for radical social commentaries or criticisms, Edgar always was keenly involved in the community, and instead of idly complaining, he went out and did things when he felt things needed to be done, for example, improving teachers' salaries and pensions or cleaning Prescott Street with the Junior Chamber of Commerce. He was truly a great citizen of this city.

Edgar was a raconteur; he had a deliberate manner of reflecting on things and telling his stories. He would adjust himself in his chair, get comfortable, and his eyes would sparkle as he became transported in memory, remembering and creating. It was a play that he performed, often bringing dialogue, setting, and atmosphere to life. He held court in his living room, benignly proffering ginger ale and biscuits, and we listened, prompting him when appropriate. We'd like you to imagine him settling down in this way, the twinkle in his eye, as you let yourself be transported into the world that he is about to unfold for you.

THE LIFE STORY OF EDGAR HOUSE IN HIS OWN WORDS

1. Family

I was born in 1911 under difficult circumstances. Mother had an attack of gallstones, and I was no sooner born than she had to go back to hospital because of her gallstones. They had to get a nanny to look after me down on Torbay Road for several weeks until she was well enough to do the job. The nanny was lovely, apparently. She introduced me to tea. "You can't have just milk! Have a little drop of tea with it," she'd say. When I was only a month old I was drinking tea. I often wonder if that's why I've got good teeth — it's supposed to be good for your teeth. Anyhow, it worked.

Mother was one of a fairly large family, the Days, from Champneys East, or Salmon Cove, as it often was called in those days.[1] Champneys got its name from one of the governors of Newfoundland.[2] One of my father's first teaching positions was at Salmon Cove. That's where he met mother, and they went up to Port Rexton and got married. Her name was Mary; "plain Mary," she used to say.[3]

---

1   Mary Day was born in Salmon Cove in 1872. The community is located about five kilometres from Trinity, Trinity Bay, and has been a fishing community since 1675. Salmon Cove was changed to Champneys around 1911 due to the large number of "Salmon Coves" in Newfoundland (Smallwood vol. 1 "Champneys"; Canada 1901; Canada 1911).

2   Sir Ralph Champneys Williams was governor of Newfoundland from 1909 to 1913. A world traveller, he held colonial posts in Gibraltar, Barbados, and Botswana prior to his tenure in Newfoundland (Poole vol. 5 "Williams"). He wrote an autobiography entitled *How I Became a Governor* in 1913, in which he seems charmed by Newfoundland and to have taken an active role in the country as governor (Williams 404–17).

3   Edgar's wife also had only one Christian name and would refer to herself as "plain Margaret."

A few years after that, he got the school down at Change Islands, which was a bigger school, and a better school, I think. That's where Edith, my sister, was born, on Change Islands, in 1903. Eight years before I was. She was a young lady by the time they moved to St. John's, in 1909, and immediately went to Bishop Spencer College; she stayed with Spencer, as a pupil and then as a teacher, until she got married. If you add up her years at Spencer and my father's years and my years at Feild,[4] it comes to just over one hundred.

Mother's father was a fisherman. My grandfather, Dad's father, was a fisherman, but he was also a mail carrier. Grandfather was born in Trinity. I traced back to 1820, I think it was. The rector there at the time said, "In all probability there might be more records down at Bonavista." I never did get a chance to get down, to go any further. I should have!

But yes, the family all had to be fishermen down there, in Trinity Bight. That's all that there was. Her brothers became fishermen. Bill Day's father — you know Bill Day — was a fisherman and his older brother was a fisherman.[5] That was it for the most part.

One or two of them got out, managed to get away. My Uncle Jack, Dad's brother, started Goodyear and House in Corner Brook, a big firm.[6] He gradually sent to Trinity for employees, and he must have had six or seven employees in that area, out in Corner Brook — one of them was Bill Day's uncle in St. John's. Goodyear was one of the famous Grand Falls families. He was only in it as a silent partner. He put the money in.

Uncle Jack had been the manager of Ayre's retail store here in St. John's, which is where he got most of his experience. When Corner

---

4   Bishop Feild College.

5   Bill Day is the son of George Day, Edgar's mother's brother. George Day later moved to St. John's where his son Bill went on to a successful career as a banker.

6   Roland Goodyear, a native of Notre Dame Bay and a successful businessman, and A.J. House set up this retail store in 1924 (Smallwood vol. 2 "Goodyear").

Goodyear and House Limited, Corner Brook, c. late 1940s.

Brook started up,[7] he said, "Here's my chance," so he started up quite an ambitious business there. When he died, his sons, Ed and Hal, were both away during the war [World War II] and Ed, the older brother, got killed in the Air Force on a raid. So poor old Hal had to come home and look after the family business, shortly before the war ended. But he took it over and built up quite a business there. He sold it all out, eventually. Interestingly, he went bankrupt and then, later on, he bought all the buildings back again himself. The bank backed him. He was a smart businessman.

When they first came to St. John's, my parents rented a house up on one of those streets off LeMarchant Road, and then they had a house halfway down Prescott Street, just behind Spencer College. They lived there for a number of years, until they had the house

---

7   In 1923, the Newfoundland Power and Paper Company was formed, and a power plant at Deer Lake and newsprint mill in Corner Brook, plus 100 houses, were built at a cost of $51,800,000 (Smallwood vol. 1 "Corner Brook"). Corner Brook is now Newfoundland's second largest city, with a population of 27,202 in 2011 (Canada 2011).

completed on Winter Place. They must have been here for six or seven years living in rented homes.

"Don't you dare throw that out — I'll make a mat from that."

Mother adjusted very, very well to life in St. John's, but she did not adjust as far as her language was concerned. She was almost as much a woman from Champneys when she died as she was when she arrived here. My father spoke very good English but the difference between Trinity and Champneys was very marked. Trinity was one of *the* towns at that time. It had a very good school, a very good teacher, and their speech was not the least like it would be down in English Harbour.

Mother didn't get much formal schooling. She learned to read and write, and she wrote very well. She was a very intelligent woman; she learned to play bridge, and they spent sometimes as much as four nights a week playing bridge. Edith and I used to play with Wilf[8] and Mother sometimes.

She never worked outside the home, but certainly worked a lot inside and around the home. We had a hen house — Mother looked after the 14 to 15 hens we had. She was a very hard worker, never stopped. If she wasn't cooking and cleaning house, she was knitting. I can remember many times my father saying, "For God's sake, Mary, put away the knitting. Put away the knitting. You're driving me crazy!" You'd see a sweater growing in front of you. She did a lot of knitting for the Feildian Ladies' Association for their fall sales. She'd do socks and scarves and such, and things for the church sales.

She made a lot of homemade mats, too. She made a mat out of Tommy Ricketts's old uniform.[9] Tommy Ricketts was with us and shortly after he came, they supplied him with a new uniform. And so here was this old uniform. Tommy said, "I'll have to throw that out I guess, Mrs. House." "Don't you dare, don't you dare," she says. "I'll make

---

8   Edgar is referring here to a somewhat later time when he and his sister, Edith, would play bridge with their mother and Edith's husband, Wilfred Furneaux.

9   See Chapter 4 for more on Newfoundland war hero Tommy Ricketts.

a mat from that." She made a couple of very nice mats out of Tommy Ricketts's uniform. Too bad I didn't keep them afterwards. Mother was firm but she was a very loving type. We got on very well together.

She always baked her own bread. Made all her jam. In the fall of the year, we'd have a barrel, not a tub but a barrel of partridgeberries sent up from English Harbour or Champneys. A full barrel. We'd share them out with the Samsons next door. A half barrel of partridgeberries is a lot of partridgeberries. We just kept them in water all the winter. You'd have to go down and bring up some partridgeberries from the cellar, because they kept well in the cold water. So I'd bring up partridgeberries and she'd make up fresh partridgeberry jam. We had our bakeapples.[10] We had our potatoes and turnip and carrot and beet. All sent up from Trinity and Champneys. The Day family would pick the berries, and we'd pay for them. The schooners would bring it all up. There'd be no charge, just get a truck to go up to Ayre's wharf and pick it all up.

We made our own splits in those days because we had to light the fire every morning and it's most important to have nice dry wood,[11] so Mr. Samson used to get a couple of hundred, what he used to call "white ends." Flat Island in Bonavista Bay, where Mr. Samson was from, wasn't a farming community at all, but the men used to go off and cut a lot of wood and dry it out, peel it, and it used to come out when it was dried nice and white, great stuff for making splits. Everybody used splits in those days. We all used coal ranges so that was the job that Art [Arthur] Samson and I had every year, taking all these 15- to 20-foot lengths of white ends, and we'd saw

---

10 The bakeapple (a Newfoundland word) or cloudberry plant grows in boggy areas of Newfoundland and Labrador; the berries are sweet and amber-coloured, resemble raspberries in shape, and are much prized and considered a delicacy. Partridge-berries (Newfoundland word) or lingonberries are also much prized; they grow on a low creeping plant that produces small, tart red berries, related to cranberries. Both are made into jams and used in baked goods (DNE).

11 Split: "A thin piece of wood, about twelve to fourteen inches long, used chiefly as kindling" (DNE).

them up and chop them up for splits. Then I had to finish the job every night when I was old enough. I'd get up early in the morning before anybody else and come down and get the fire in, using the splits. So by the time Mother came down, I had the place reasonably warm. And that was a big house, nine-foot ceilings. It took a lot of heat to spread around.

Wintertime on Winter Place, c. 1920s.

When the fall came and the cattle were slaughtered in Trinity, we always had a big quarter of beef sent up, nearly always. Every time Dad went down to Trinity, he'd bring down a barrel of tinned goods, groceries, and so on of all kinds. To say a thank you, they used to send us up berries and fresh butter, as we used to call it because it was salted, it was no ordinary butter, and vegetables all the time.[12]

One of Mother's brothers became a captain of one of the coastal boats, passenger boats — Uncle Nehemiah Day, lived up on LeMarchant Road. He had a nice big double house up there, and we used to visit them, and they used to visit down on Winter Place when he was in town. Unfortunately, he got diabetes, and a month after he died,

---

12   This is a good example of the interdependence of the St. John's/outport or urban/ rural economy of the time.

they developed a cure for it. His daughter [Barbara Moore] came to see me, and she took that picture of me right there [points to a picture on his mantelpiece]. She was writing a history of the family. She came over here and quizzed me and took that picture.

"It's time now for you to take things seriously and learn how to drive a nail."

My father, George House, was born in Trinity in 1876 and raised there, and his father was a fisherman who had his own boat and crew, and also ran the mail packet across Trinity Bay to [New] Perlican. In those days the railway took the mail from St. John's down to Trinity, and it went from Trinity then across the bay, by boat, to Winterton and Perlican and so on. There was a letter in the paper, *The Telegram*, a few years ago by an old chap over in Perlican, describing how George House as a young boy used to come over with his father on the mail packet and sometimes they'd take a cricket team from Trinity and take time out and stay overnight.[13] Play a game of cricket against Heart's Content. The nearest cricket ground was at Perlican, so on one occasion my dad climbed up to the top of this hill and with his sharp knife, he carved his initials, G.H., into the rock, into a rock on top of the hill. This letter from an old chap in *The Telegram* describes how he went up there just a few years

---

13   In P.J. Myler's *Recollections of Cricket* (9), the author fondly recalls the heyday of St. John's cricket in the 1880s, when it was the most popular game in the city. There were enough clubs for two divisions, with the fiercest rivalry being between Shamrock and Mechanics. Matches were played at the Parade grounds and at Pleasantville. Games were informal, though competitive, and players often had nicknames, such as "Shinny," "Mummie," "Sticks," and "Stogger" (10). By the time of the writing of the book, however, the sport seems to have all but died out. Myler has several explanations for this, including that the youth now preferred football (soccer), as well as the distance of the grounds from town for spectators, versus the proximity of the football grounds, which were too small for cricket (37–39). The province has enjoyed a revival of cricket in recent years under the leadership of Cricket Newfoundland and Labrador, which was incorporated in 2010. See http://www.canadacricket.com/nlcricket/.

before and the names and G.H. are still quite visible on this rock. I've never gone up there. I've always been meaning to.[14]

My dad was in Change Islands in 1900, so I suppose he was 33 [actually 24]. He played cricket there, which had been introduced by an English clergyman. They had a three-cornered league down in Notre Dame Bay, where Fogo, Twillingate, and Change Islands all [each] had a team. George Earle's father Fred was a member, as was his grandfather Charlie, and of course there was the English clergyman. It's hard to believe that cricket was being played a hundred years ago in Notre Dame Bay.

A good story is told about George Earle.[15] After he had his first year at Memorial, he went back to Change Islands for the summer. Of course, when the coastal boat comes in, everybody goes down to the wharf. And so this old fella saw him and said, "Well, George me son, I suppose you knows it all now, shorthand and everything." George said, "Yes sir. I know quite a bit I suppose." He said, "George, say something to us in shorthand, will you b'y?" George remembered a verse of Cicero that he had committed to memory and he rattled it off as fast as he could, in Latin. This old fella said, "Oh . . . I don't see what makes that shorthand." George said, "If I wrote that out for you, it would take me about three days to write it all."

Dad taught during the year, and in the summer he used to mark examination papers. The Council of Higher Education would farm out the grades, and intermediate grade geometry would go to George

---

14   Doug, Adrian, and Jeannie House (Doug's wife/Adrian's mother) visited this site in the summer of 2014. It provides a beautiful view over Trinity Bay and must have been an ideal spot for viewing the mail packet en route from Trinity to New Perlican. There were many footprints and initials carved in the rock, but we could not clearly distinguish the "G.H." mentioned by the old chap to whom Edgar refers.

15   Canon George Earle was born in Change Islands in 1914. Ordained as an Anglican deacon in 1938, he later became Principal of Queen's College (an Anglican theological school in St. John's, now part of Memorial University), and in 1971 Canon of the Cathedral of St. John the Baptist, St. John's. He was also a well-known Newfoundland humorist, and was awarded an honorary degree of Doctor of Divinity by Memorial University in 1979 (Smallwood vol. 1 "Earle").

Change Islands cricket team, late 1890s. Standing (left to right): Arch Scammell, Dorman Elliott, Rev. E. Clench, Arthur Seeley, Fred C. Earle, George House. On ground (left to right): Fred R. Earle, Edmund Hyde, Charlie Scammell, William H. Earle, Elam Elliott.

House. So all the books from all over the island for Grade 11 would be sent to him. He had to mark each paper individually and get paid so much per book. I did the same.

I was just looking at my toolbox down in Trinity — it's used now for my splits. I was only five years old, and my dad decided that I should have some tools. So he made this tool box about two and a half feet long, I suppose, eight-and-a-half inches wide and five to seven inches deep. It had a cover on it, hinges on it, and it was stained and varnished, with handles on the end. It was a lovely looking thing. He bought a small saw and a hammer and a few screwdrivers to put in it. He gave it to me when I was five or six I guess. "Here," he said, "here is your birthday present. It's time now for you to take things seriously and learn how to drive a nail." Anyhow, I hung on to the old tool box and never did part with it. It was quite useful.

In the spring of the year, there was a church service at the Cathedral — I suppose it was around Lent — to which Spencer and Feild turned up. Before it began, my father said to me, "Come find me after the service is over; I want to take you down to Water Street." So after the service, we went to Ayre & Sons and looked in the window, and here was the first Hercules bicycle to be imported into Newfoundland, the very first one.

I said, "Oh boy, that's a beauty, isn't it?"

He said, "Yes! How would you like to have that?" My eyes nearly popped out. Anyhow, to make a long story short, he bought the bicycle for me, the first Hercules bike, and that was the best make there was at the time. We took it down off the rack and put it out on Water Street. I could already ride; I had already practised on other fellows' bikes. So I drove home on my bicycle. Had to walk up Prescott Street [a very steep street going downtown], but the rest of it was easy, and my dad took the streetcar at Adelaide Street and came up to Rawlins Cross, and walked home from Rawlins Cross. That was really a highlight. I was about 15, I guess.

Edgar, age 14 or 15.

"I came to with my head resting on the Victoria Cross."

It seems we always had an extra person in the house when I was growing up. We had a spare bedroom and we had a lot of outport uncles and aunts and cousins, and somebody was always coming into St. John's for something, even for operations. The General Hospital was always filled to the brim. Nobody could get into the General Hospital except a serviceman, so operations often had to take place in the home.

Our kitchen table became an operating table for Dr. Murphy, Bliss's father,[16] and Dr. Macpherson,[17] who gave the anaesthetic. Dr. Murphy used to always wear a khaki-coloured dust coat for driving and goggles. He was an EENT, eye, ear, nose, and throat doctor.

We had several operations done on our kitchen table, and I was one of them, for adenoids and tonsils. In those days, there were no antibiotics so when you had septic tonsils and adenoids, it was a common thing to have them whipped out. So I had mine removed, and I was coming to just as Tommy Ricketts came in the door. He'd been on a special parade somewhere, and he had his complete uniform on, plus all his medals. He had the French Croix de Guerre on as well as the Victoria Cross and a couple of other war medals, all strung across his breast. He came in the door as I was coming to, and he said, "Oh Mrs. House, I'll take Edgar upstairs and put him on his bed now." I came to with my head resting on the Victoria Cross and the Croix de Guerre and at least two other war medals and ribbons! That really made an impression on me at the time.[18]

---

16 Dr. Bliss Murphy was one of Edgar's lifelong friends. A graduate of Dalhousie Medical School, he was the director of radiotherapy at the General Hospital in St. John's, and until the late 1950s the only radiotherapist in the province. Dr. Murphy trained the first radiation technologists in Newfoundland and was instrumental in establishing cancer care in the province. Bliss Murphy died in 1992 at 78, and a year later the new Dr. H. Bliss Murphy Cancer Centre in the St. John's General Hospital was named in his honour ("Tireless Physician").

17 Born in St. John's in 1879, Dr. Cluny Macpherson earned his degree in medicine from McGill University. He is best known as the inventor of the gas mask, while serving with the Newfoundland Regiment during World War I. He spent several years in Labrador as part of the Grenfell Mission, and was president of the International Grenfell Association. Macpherson received many honours, including being made a Companion of the Order of St. Michael and St. George (1918). He died in St. John's in 1966 (Smallwood vol. 3 "Macpherson").

18 Edgar loved making puns, so much so that his family affectionately referred to them as "Edgarisms."

Major (Dr.) Cluny Macpherson, 1917. (Courtesy
The Rooms Provincial Archives, from *Newfoundland Quarterly*)

Dr. Macpherson and Dr. Murphy did a lot of that. They did this one on the kitchen table and shortly after that, Art Scammell[19] — our family knew the Scammells because Dad taught down in Change Islands — Art Scammell had to have his tonsils out. After a few of these, Dad eventually said, "We've got to get another bulb for the kitchen." Dr. Murphy complained that "that 60-Watt bulb . . . (two thirties really!) . . . is not powerful enough. Not enough light, even with the kitchen window." So we finished up with a couple of big bulbs there for the benefit of the people who came after me. I think I was the first one.

"Fine, you can get out now."

Mother had a distant relative, a girl, came up from Champneys. She nearly always had somebody there to help her, because she needed it, and they'd stay in the spare bedroom. We had a cousin from Champ-neys came up and did her teacher training, and stayed with us.

I can remember Warwick Wells, who was a student at Queen's College [the Anglican theological college in St. John's]. At Lent time,

---

19   Born in Change Islands in 1913, Arthur Reginald Scammell was well known as a Newfoundland educator and writer. He was the author of one of Newfoundland's best-known songs, "The Squid-Jiggin' Grounds," which he wrote while fishing with his father at age 14. Scammell taught in Newfoundland until 1940, when he moved to Montreal and taught there until his retirement in 1970. He received many honours, and in 1987 became a member of the Order of Canada. He died in 1995, aged 82 (Pitt vol. 5 "Scammell").

when Lent had come and gone, all the students at Queen's, a dozen or so divinity students, decided to do what the monks of old did, and shave their heads. Which they did! When Mr. Facey, the Principal, saw them, he said, "Fine, you can get out now. Find a place somewhere and come back when your hair is grown out." He kicked them out. Warwick Wells came to Mother, and begged her on bended knee to take him in until his hair grew out. So we had him for a while.

George and Mary House, late 1930s.

2. Margie

Margie's mother was a Taylor from Carbonear, around the Bay [i.e., Conception Bay]. She married Charlie Butt, who was also from around the Bay, somewhere around Job's Cove.[1] But he started out as a boy with T. & M. Winter in St. John's and he and Tom Furlong's[2] father worked side by side at T. & M. Winter for over 50 years, bookkeeping, making out orders, and taking orders for all the things that they carried in their warehouse. T. & M. Winter was a fairly big outfit at that time.[3] They had some of the best goods, like well-known baking powder and tea and all that stuff.

The Butts lived first on Mullock Street, off Monkstown Road. But all the time I knew them, they were in a house down on the Masonic Terrace. It's still there. So he didn't have very far to go to work at T. & M. Winter, except coming back it was all uphill. It was very convenient

---

1   Job's Cove (which used to be called Devil's Cove) is one of a number of small outports located on the west side of Conception Bay between Carbonear and Bay de Verde (Smallwood vol. 3 "Job's").

2   Tom Furlong was born in St. John's in 1911. A key figure in the Boy Scouts movement in the province, his involvement with scouting began when he was 25 and continued throughout his life; in 1987 he won the Silver Acorn Award for exceptional service. For many years he wrote a weekly scouting column in the *Evening Telegram*, as well as a history column for the *Newfoundland Herald*. The author of several books, Furlong died in 2005, age 94 (Stacey "Scout Master").

3   T. & M. Winter, commercial agents and importers, was formed by Marmaduke and Thomas Winter towards the end of the nineteenth century (*Dictionary of Newfoundland and Labrador Biography* [*henceforth DNLB*], 1990: 366).

for Margie going to Holloway School, on Long's Hill.[4]

Mr. Butt was a very keen baseball fan, locally and for the national games, too. So he'd always take his holidays in the late fall when the playoffs [World Series] were on. On the radio, that was. He used to rent a house in Manuels, not far from the old CLB [Church Lads' Brigade][5] campgrounds. So the family would go in as soon as school closed and stay until the

Maggie (Taylor) and Charlie Butt, c. 1930s.

end of August, the whole summer, and he would come back and forth every day by train and walk down from the station.[6] Margie said she

4   Holloway School was opened in 1926 after the Methodist College burned down. It became an elementary school after Prince of Wales College was built in 1928. Declining enrolment led to its closure in 1979, and the building was controversially demolished in 1984 (Smallwood vol. 2 "Holloway School").

5   The Church Lads' Brigade, the motto of which is "Fight the Good Fight," is an Anglican paramilitary program geared mainly towards youth, with components such as drill, camp, sports, marching band, badge work similar to Scouts, and leadership skills. It started in England in 1891, in Newfoundland in 1892, and is still active today. According to the CLB website, "A Company #119 C.L.B. has the honour of being first C.L.B. Company in the Colonies (1892)." "C Company" was the branch of the CLB at Bishop Feild College. As Newfoundland had no military when it went to war for Britain in 1914, the CLB was one of the sources for many of its soldiers and officers (Smallwood vol. 1 "Church Lads"; "Early History").

6   Construction on the Newfoundland Railway began in 1881, and the line across the province was completed in 1898 by Robert G. Reid's company. Several branch lines were added in the beginning of the twentieth century. After Confederation and the completion of the Trans-Canada Highway in 1965, Newfoundlanders opted to drive more instead of taking the train. In 1969, passenger train service was abandoned, despite a huge public outcry. Freight service continued but gradually slowed until the railway was closed permanently in 1988 and dismantled (Pieroway Rails Across the Rock xii–xiv).

often used to go up to the train to meet him because he'd always have some oranges or apples or some treat.

"He was a bit of a lad."

She had two brothers: Herb, who worked at T. & M. Winter's for a while, and Gel [short for Gerald], who worked in the bank for a while. Herb went off out west to Sault Ste. Marie, and Gel went out west in Newfoundland. First, he was bookkeeper for one of the big fish firms out there, in Bonne Bay, and then he moved from that to the Glynmill Inn in Corner Brook. They didn't go to university. As far as I can understand, Gel had all his textbooks sold before the end of the year in Grade 10. He was a bit of a lad. Herb went out to Sault Ste. Marie and did quite well out there. He married a girl from there, Mona.

Gel's wife, Dot, was a Jardine from St. John's. Rather interestingly, her mother was quite musical and in the early days of the silent movies, she used to do the piano accompaniment at the Nickel Theatre. She was very good at it, too, you know. I mean if it was a love scene, she'd have very soft music in the background. If it was a troop of horsemen, she'd gallop over the keys.

Margie attended the old Methodist College, the name of which I think was changed to Prince of Wales at just about the time she moved to Memorial.[7] Then after she had a couple of years there [at Memorial College], she went on to Mount Allison in New Brunswick.

---

7   Methodist College had its beginnings in 1859 as Wesleyan Academy. It became Methodist College in 1886 with the construction of new buildings, only to be completely destroyed in the Great Fire of 1892. A new brick structure was rebuilt, but was destroyed again by fire in 1925. The next year Holloway School was built and then Prince of Wales College in 1928. (Smallwood vol. 3 "Methodist"; Rowe 20; "The Story of the Wesleyan").

"I don't like that tie!"

I'd known her before we were at Memorial. I knew who she was from the Feildian dances — everybody went to the Feild dances — but I hadn't really met her until we chanced into the library on the first day we were at Memorial. I had a beautiful expensive white-coloured silk tie on, and was passing her in the library, and she said, "I don't like that tie!" and she flicked the tie. Foolishly, when I got home I took it off and put it away, never wore it afterwards. So I packed it up with old clothes going down to Champneys to our relatives down there. And so the next place I saw my tie was my cousin wearing it at a church service in Champneys. It looked just as good as ever.

"She was Smooch to everybody I think."

She acquired from her brothers the name "Smooch."[8] There were eight or 10 of us that got together at Memorial, a clique I suppose, and she was Smooch to everybody I think. Oh, she was good fun, very good fun. She played ice hockey, she played field hockey, she played basketball. She tried tennis but she wasn't a natural, though she persisted.

She loved dancing, and the old Feildians had this Saturday night dance going to earn money for the Grounds and so on, and so a bunch of us went to all the Feild dances. They were very popular. They were about the only ones at the time that had regular dances, because the floor was so good. We nearly always had two or three fellows for the orchestra. One of them was a chap Cowan, who had a dairy farm out on Topsail Road. Cowan and Bob MacLeod were the duo. There were only two dances in those days, the fox trot and the waltz. We had a lot of fun. The Feildian Ladies used to cater for our dances. There'd be a dance until about half past ten and then everybody would stop for half an hour and have supper, coffee and sandwiches and soft drinks, and then back to it again.

---

8   The term "smooch" is not defined in the *DNE*, but is defined in the *Oxford Dictionary of Canadian English* as an informal verb meaning: 1 kiss. 2. cuddle or caress.

Memorial girls' basketball team, 1930. Margie, fourth from left.

Memorial girls' hockey team, 1930. Margie, second from left, second row.

In the fall of '29, Margie and I were at Memorial together, and she had a boyfriend from her days at Prince of Wales. Nobody liked this fellow — nobody! And I used to cut him a bit, I guess. She ditched him and replaced him with me in 1929, and we didn't get married for another 10 years. We were both working on degrees. She lost a year at Mount A [due to illness], so it wasn't until 1934 that we really got together again. It took five years to

Margie and Doug, c. early 1980s.

scurry up enough courage and money to buy this little place, and in 1939 we were married. Nobody had much money then.[9]

I remember when I was an officer at the CLB camp in Topsail. They were short of officers so I went out there full time. At the same time, Margie's Girl Guide company had a camp out at Beachy Cove.

Church Lads' Brigade Camp, Topsail, 1937. (Courtesy CLB Archives)

---

9   Edgar and Margie had a long, 10-year courtship and engagement. At the time, it
     was a common middle-class practice to save enough money to buy a house and
     furnishings before getting married. This was difficult to do during the Depression
     of the 1930s.

So for a couple of nights, if I got off, I would take the car with some-body else who was off duty and drive out to Beachy Cove and go up to the Girl Guides' camp. The girls would be having a campfire there and a sing-song, and I went up to get Margie, who was in uniform, as I was, and the girls would all sing out as we were leaving, "Let Me Call You Sweetheart." I remember that so plainly; Margie was so embarrassed.

Margie (second from left) and Girl Guides.

"She was the head girl at the residence."

She studied chemistry [at Mount Allison University]. She always said how stupid she was to do it, instead of taking home economics or something like that, something that would have been useful for her. Because she did advanced mathematics, including calculus, and she never used it. She didn't use her physics and chemistry that she knew, either, except to help in her physiology. She was the head girl at the residence, and had to sit at the head table with all the girls. They brought all their worries to her. I suppose she got that because she went in as a scholarship winner. I have no doubt that Mr. Paton[10] gave her a glowing letter of introduction.

She played basketball up there, and made a place on the team, but developed appendicitis and had to come home. She immediately went into hospital here. I remember that well, because she had four aunts here at the time. After she had her appendix out, after school one afternoon, I went up to visit her, carrying my little box of Moirs chocolates. When I got there, no less than four of her aunts were all around the bed, visiting Margie. Then, of course, they had to eye her boyfriend. So they stayed for a while. She almost owned a bed in the Grace Hospital. We counted that, in one year, she made 13 visits to the Grace Hospital for one thing or another. It put her behind a year at Mount A. Every time she was there, the appendix flared up. Eventually, though, she was chosen to propose the toast to the *Alma Mater* at the junior/senior banquet.

"Edgar, what's physiology?"

She returned to St. John's in the spring of '34. She was hardly back in town when she had a call from Ray Gushue,[11] the Chairman of the Board at Prince of Wales.[12] He said, "You've got a degree in science and no doubt you know your physiology. Would you be prepared to take a new class, girls that have never done physiology, a completely new class?" She said to Gushue, "Oh, yes, of course." When she got off

---

10 John Lewis Paton. See Chapter 9, "Education."

11 Raymond Gushue was born in Whitbourne in 1900. He earned a law degree from Dalhousie University in 1925 and practised law for 10 years in St. John's. He eventually became President of Memorial University from 1952 to 1966 and in 1967 he became the first Newfoundlander to be appointed to the Order of Canada (*DNLB* 137).

12 Prince of Wales College, a United Church school for junior and high school students, was opened in 1928 on LeMarchant Road due to lack of space at Holloway School. Later, increased enrolment required a separate high school, Prince of Wales Collegiate, which was built on Paton Street in 1960. The LeMarchant Rd. location closed in 1982, and the building was developed into condominiums. See also this chapter, note 7 (p. 90), on the Methodist College (Poole vol. 4 "Prince").

the phone, she came into the room where her father and mother and I were and she said, "Edgar, what's physiology? I told Mr. Gushue that I could teach physiology."

I said, "Well, it just so happens that was my best subject the past year." So then I spent the summer, July and August, going through my textbook in physiology and teaching her all I knew about physiology. She taught for five years, five physiology classes in Grade 11, and didn't have a failure.

There were very few women with degrees.[13] They were personal friends of Margie's, I guess, most of them. I think Mr. Paton was partly responsible for her getting a degree. He encouraged her and found a Mount A scholarship for her, which was enough to cover her tuition there, I think. I think he was the one that encouraged her. He encouraged all of us.

She taught kindergarten in the morning, at Holloway, and then she'd trot up to LeMarchant Road for the afternoon classes in physiology at Prince of Wales. I think she enjoyed her teaching years, but in those days there was no thought of carrying on. Once you were married, that was it! No married teachers. If you were a woman and you married you had to quit — it was the law.[14] So her teaching days were finished, then. She just accepted it because everybody else did.

---

13   One of the first was Grace Margaret Sparkes (née Patten), who also went to Mount Allison University. She was born in Grand Bank, Newfoundland, in 1908. She started at Mount Allison in 1924 and graduated in 1928 with a Bachelor of Arts degree, major in biology. She went on to a long, distinguished career in education, politics, journalism, and community service, and was also a devoted patron of the arts. Sparkes campaigned with Peter Cashin for responsible government during the 1940s, ran for the Progressive Conservative Party both federally and provincially, and wrote for the *Daily News* from 1951 to 1957. She taught at Prince of Wales Collegiate until 1973. She died in 2003 at age 95 (Riggs "A Newfoundlander"; Cuff "Sparkes"; Benson, A12). For more on Grace Sparkes, a contemporary of Edgar and Margie House, see Marie-Beth Wright, *Grace Sparkes: Blazing a Trail to Independence*, 2014.

14   See General Introduction, notes 53 and 54 (p. 53).

"We had a lovely honeymoon over in Brigus."

We always felt we would like some place of our own. We could have rented I guess, but we didn't. We should have. She saved some and she bought the bedroom set that we still have. That was her big contribution. There was a little bit of a fire down at Royal Stores, so they had a fire sale. There wasn't a mark on this bedroom set. She bought it ahead of time. Actually, I had it in here and stowed upstairs before the house was finished.

We had a lovely wedding at the Cochrane Street Church at which Brenda Butler, Margie's best friend, was supposed to be the bridesmaid, but she was highly pregnant at the time. So Edith [Edgar's sister] became the bridesmaid, and Florence Currie and Brenda watched from the rear of the church.

Edith House at 7 Winter Place, early 1930s.

My best man was a very prominent old Feildian, a good friend, Stuart Godfrey, and Gordon Stirling headed up the ushers. Stuart and I had been good friends at Feild since his father arrived from India. His father was an Englishman, and he'd been out in India for a number of years and Stuart was actually educated, for several years, in India. He came into Feild when he was 11 or 12 years of age, not knowing anybody, and I guess I befriended him then.

Cochrane Street Church was your mother's church; that's where she and her mother went. I don't think her father or Gel or Herb were regulars, but Margie and her mother went there often. So we naturally went there to be married. There's a picture of it somewhere. She took the confirmation classes in the Cathedral afterwards and decided to

Wedding, 1939.

become an Anglican.[15] She said, "You know, the children don't want to grow up with two religions."

We had a very lovely reception out at Topsail at Paul Johnson's place, going down the hill, and then we hopped in my father's car which he was good enough to give us for 10 days. We went to Brigus, where we had the use of a nice little summer place owned by Harry Roberts's father, who was a good friend of Margie's father. So we had a lovely honeymoon over in Brigus, which is a good place for a honeymoon because it's such a central spot that you can take little trips around the place in a car. We had a big Chev overland touring car.

---

15   Margie grew up a Methodist, and became United Church when it was formed in 1925 with the union of the Methodist, Congregational, and some of the Presbyterian churches. In 1921 there were 17,746 Roman Catholics in St. John's, 8,374 Anglicans, 7,623 Methodists, 980 Salvation Army, 1,047 Presbyterians, 348 Congregationalists, and 326 "others" (Poole vol. 4 "United"; Canada 1921).

The back seat could come forward, and you could make it into a bed if you wanted to. I think we spent a couple of nights while we were there in the car, camping out.

"When I bought it, it was just a shack, really."

I bought the house [at what was then 44 Robinson's Hill, now 20 Portugal Cove Road] in the fall of 1938, the year before we got married.[16] The fall and winter and spring of that year, my father and I finished it enough for it to be habitable. When I bought it, it was just a shack, really. The man that was building it ran out of funds. He had it well finished outside, but hardly a thing done inside, and so we had to start from scratch. My father and I laid the floors here and upstairs. We put in the windows, the French doors there. I was lucky enough at the time to be able to get all those cobblestones from Water Street to put up my garden wall.[17] When I think of it, I did a lot of work on this house.

Margie and Edgar, 1930s.

Dad and Mr. Samson paid rent to the Winter Estate for their land, and I paid rent to the Winter Estate for this house here.[18] You paid for

---

16 Edgar was to live in that house until a few weeks before he died in 2006.

17 Water Street was paved with cobbles in 1899 with the introduction of electric streetcars; they were replaced with asphalt on 29 Aug. 1949, after Confederation. Mayor Andy Carnell cut the ribbon to officially open the street, and the Lion's Club organized a street dance on the same day (O'Brien).

18 The estate of the wealthy Winter family. The land, about 20 acres to start with, was granted to James Winter by Governor Molineux Shuldham in 1774. It passed to his son George in the "56th year of George III," 1814, to be leased and done with as he pleased. This leasing continued until at least the 1970s (Shuldham).

Margie, 20 Portugal Cove Road, after a storm, late 1970s.

30 years or so, at which point you could buy it at a very reasonable price, which I did.[19] I don't know what's happened to the Winter Estate now but I suppose it's still on the go. I guess some of the Winters get some of it. When we came back from our honeymoon in Brigus, we moved into this house immediately. I had it ready enough to be able to live in it — sitting room and dining room, kitchen and one bedroom and a bathroom. This was late in the summer of 1939. We had a little bit of money at the time I suppose, saved up, and one of the first things I did was go down to Ayre & Sons and buy a little radio. I brought it home and turned it on, and the first thing we got was the Declaration of War. The very first thing that came on.

It was particularly upsetting for me, I think, because I was not as young as most of the fellows. A lot of my friends did go. A lot of them

---

19   Edgar paid $1,000 to purchase his land in 1973.

didn't come back. My eyes were not good. My doctor, Dr. O'Reilly, told me I wouldn't get to the war. "Now," he said, "soon as they hear you're a teacher, that's what you'll be doing." So I did, but it was hard, those years throughout the war, there were so many Feildian casualties. Every one of them was a boy that I knew. Some of them I knew well. There'd be an announcement at prayers in the morning that Corporal So-and-So or Squadron Leader So-and-So had been killed in action. It was tough going.

Chancey Currie, the publisher of the *Daily News*, and his wife, Florence Hue before she was married, were good friends of ours; Florence was a great friend of Margie's. He was married before, and had to go to South Africa. It

Land grant to James Winter from Governor Molineux Shuldham, 1774. (Courtesy St. John's City Archives)

was much easier to get a divorce if you went down there and worked for awhile, which he did. He worked for six months with an English firm, a pottery firm, as a salesman down there so that he could qualify to get his divorce. And it worked.

The four of us got together quite often for bridge and bowling and movies, but on the night that they were engaged, they dropped in to announce their engagement. I didn't have a thing to drink in the house except apricot brandy, and we didn't have a fire in the grate — we'd been out I think. And so the four of us sat around out in the hallway there around this big cabinet heater we had. It was nice and cozy, and we drank apricot brandy to the announcement of their engagement. We polished off a bottle of apricot brandy.

Glenridge Crescent

Charlie Hutchings was the designer of the first housing development in St. John's, I guess, Glenridge Crescent [directly behind Edgar's house].[20] That was quite a big thing, to have a housing development like that in those days [early 1940s]. I guess the Parsons were our first neighbours, Dick and Phil Parsons's father, next door here. Then the Alderdices, Knowlings, Bairds . . . it didn't take long for Glenridge Crescent to develop once it started.

Your and Jan's [Doug's younger sister Janet] playpen was out the back door, onto the Crescent. You had a 14-foot playpen, a bit larger than the ordinary one, which I did for the summertime, and a sandbox too. You had a great time.[21] Margie used to have a hand bell she'd ring when it was time to come in. We had those down in Trinity, too. Yeah, we used it down there to call you up from the beach. I think it's still down there.

Doug and Janet House, c. 1950.

20   It appears to have been an informal, privately initiated development. Charles Hutchings was administrator of the Winter Estate, and sold the land to the city of St. John's for $1.00 in 1942. The first planned development was Churchill Park (the first of its kind in Canada), which began in 1944 (Conveyance; Sharpe 83).

21   Unless otherwise specified, when Edgar uses the word "you" it refers to his son, Doug House, to whom he was talking in the conversations that were taped for this life story.

3. Jerry and Georgie

"They built those two houses even to the point of making their own bricks."

My father and Mr. Samson both came in to Feild in St. John's to do what they called the A.A., Associate in Arts, in about 1900 [perhaps 1904 or 1905, after Edgar's sister, Edith, was born in Change Islands]. The A.A. was about the equivalent of Grade 12 but it involved some teacher training. And as soon as they finished their teacher training at Bishop Feild, perhaps they would get a job, they thought. Examinations were set and marked in England. There was a Council of Higher Education, CHE as they called it, and if you had your A.A. that was about as far as any of our local teachers went.[1] We usually had an Englishman or two with a degree to teach Latin, French, and so on, sciences. The local teachers, I wouldn't say any of them in my day had a degree.

So they both came in to do this and completed it, and they were both appointed. It was a big promotion. They both had good records

---

1   Examinations for selected Newfoundland pupils began to be set up and marked by the University of London (England) in 1890. The CHE was formed in 1893 to organize these exams. From 1918 to 1920 the exams were sent to Dalhousie due to "transportation difficulties," but then continued to be sent to England until 1931, with the establishment of the Common Examining Board of the Maritime Provinces and Newfoundland (for which Edgar later worked). They were then sent to Windsor, Nova Scotia (Fizzard; Newfoundland "Report of the Public Schools").

Bishop Feild staff of 1913. Standing: I.J. Samson, H.W. Stirling, R. Rowsell, H.W.F. Blackall, G. House, A. Raley. Sitting: Miss Wills, A.E. Bernard, R.R. Wood, C.F. Jeffery, Miss Steed.

in the outport schools, so Dr. Blackall[2] appointed both of them to the staff at Feild. Mr. Samson's initials were I.J.,[3] which stood for Israel Joseph. One of the boys one day asked him what "J" stood for and he said "Jerry." From then on, he became Jerry Samson. My father was always Georgie House. So the two of them were great friends and walked back and forth to school together, worked together, and everybody knew them as Jerry and Georgie.

---

2   William Walker Blackall (1864–1943), a native of Middlesborough, England, was Headmaster of Church of England Academy and College, later Bishop Feild College, 1891–1908. On his recommendation, the name was changed in 1894, and he instituted the college song, uniform, and crest, as well as Sports Day, manual training, intercollegiate sports, and much more. By all accounts he was responsible for developing Bishop Feild's academic and athletic reputations. His other contributions include a large role in the forming of Memorial College in 1925 (House 119; Cuff "Blackall").

3   I.J. Samson Junior High School in St. John's (closed 2011) was named after Mr. Samson.

Mr. Samson and my dad, both on the staff of Feild and both good outport men that could do anything with their hands, decided when they got together at Feild that they'd build a house together. They acquired land down on the north side of what was then called the old Tannery Field, because there used to be a tannery, quite a prosperous one, where Riverdale Tennis Club is now. The area down on the south side of Winter Place became their garden, where they planted their potatoes and their carrots and their beets, and so on. The gardens were rented out from the Winters. Five dollars a season for quite a big piece of land — where Gordon Winter and all those homes are now. They had quite a nice garden there. We also had a back garden in which Mother had her lettuce and beets and a few black currant bushes and stuff like that.

On the north side, they built their house. Everything that went into the house was built by them. Everything, even the bricks for the chimney! They built those two houses even to the point of making their own bricks. The brickworks were up on Flavin Street, and the manager was George Daly, a member of the Cathedral congregation. My dad had the nerve to ask him if, on Saturdays, when the brick factory wasn't working, they could go up and make their own bricks. So he gave them permission, and they did. And so those bricks in the two chimneys down in Winter Place are handmade by George House and Jerry Samson, around 1910–11. They've never given any trouble since as far as I know.

They bought all the lumber here from Horwoods, which was still going way back then, or in a few cases had lumber sent up from Bonavista Bay or Trinity Bay by schooner. They even built their own oak mantelpieces. Mr. Samson was teaching woodwork at the time, and was a very good carpenter. They were both excellent at the work, and they imported their six grates for the fireplaces from England and all the tiles to go with them. They installed them themselves, put the tiling on themselves. Oh yes, they were really jacks-of-all-trades! They did have to get the plumbing done. The plastering was done by the father of a Conway out here. They built the two houses together, a duplex, with an adjoining, opening door under the stairway so that we didn't have to go out. If I wanted to go and play with the Samson youngsters, I had to just open the door and go through. They built a very fine house there.

Looking across Rennies River and Feildian Grounds to Winter Place, late 1920s. The House/ Samson house is the second from the right on the far side.

"Luckily, he had on a very strong scarf."

I remember one terribly stormy day, very stormy, so bad that Mr. Wood, the Principal, decided that the boys had better get home as fast as they could — this is about nine o'clock in the morning. He packed them all off home. My dad and Mr. Samson always walked home together from Feild because they lived next door to each other, and so on this very windy, snowy day, they started home. When they got down to the Rennies River Bridge, which at the time was a wooden bridge, I think, but with a metal railing on the side of it, the snow was so heavy that it filled up the bridge so that you could just barely see the railing. Mr. Samson and my dad, Jerry and Georgie, walking home together, got down to Rennie's River Bridge and they started to cross, but it was hard to see where the bridge was because the snow had drifted right over it. Anyhow, Mr. Samson stepped off the bridge and disappeared down towards the river!

Luckily, he had on a very strong, heavy, knitted scarf that his wife had knitted him and my dad had an almost identical one that Mary House had knitted for him. Anyhow, my dad was able to get his scarf down to Mr. Samson, who was up to his neck in snow, and would have gone farther, right into the river. They managed to tie the two scarves together and with the help of the scarves and my dad leaning over and tugging, they managed to get Mr. Samson back on the rail and onto the bridge. If he had been by himself, that would have been the end. They came home, and they were shaking when they got to the house.

"They didn't know what to make of it."

I never went mummering,[4] but my father and Mr. Samson did. It was rather interesting because here on Winter Place you had these richer houses, and then there was our house and the Samsons'. Next to that was Goodland of Gray and Goodland, the booksellers and printers, a great fellow; next to that was J.A. Winter; next to that was a man Rennie, who was employed by the government; and next to that was the Emersons.[5] So here you have Winter Place with these two upstarts, outport men from Trinity Bay and Bonavista Bay, building this big double house next to the well-to-do townies and next to the lane near where the Emersons and so on were.

Anyhow, these two outport men decided that it was Christmas time and that they'd go mummering. Nobody down there had ever heard of it, I suppose. Well, they might have heard of it but never experienced it at all. So the two of them got some big white sheets and one thing or another and dressed themselves up, I can just remember, and off they went to all these aristocrats on Winter Place. They didn't

---

4   "Mummering" is described in the *DNE* as "The practice of visiting houses disguised as a mummer at Christmas." A "mummer" is "an elaborately costumed and disguised person who participates in various group activities at Christmas." When Doug was a boy, the term "mummering" was used to refer to children dressing up and going trick or treating on Hallowe'en.

5   See General Introduction, note 17 (p. 31).

know what to make of it. They were gracious enough and polite enough but they didn't know what it was all about.[6] I mean, they were carrying on, singing. Yeah, they gave them quite a surprise.

"He could walk the legs off me."

They did very well one summer fishing down in Quidi Vidi. They went down and found an old fellow who wasn't going fishing any-more and had a big motorboat. And so they rented it for the summer and walked every morning from Winter Place, before daylight, down to Quidi Vidi Village [about 3.5 km]. They took the boat and went out and did their fishing in Freshwater Bay and Blackhead Bay. Took their fish into Job's and sold it green [unsalted], then took the boat back to Quidi Vidi and walked home from there. You can imagine the physical condition that they were in by the end of it. They quit the middle of August because my dad said he had to have his couple of weeks down in Trinity. They had a good summer. He was as hard as nails. I used to go trouting with him down there and he could walk the legs off me.

I went out squid jigging with them once, Mr. Samson, my dad, and myself[7] — the three of us. I had to get up before daybreak and go down with them to Quidi Vidi. Get into this big hard fisherman's boat that they had down there. We went out to Blackhead Bay and the squid were there. So we had a great time. I was filthy when I came back. Oh!

---

6   Mummering did actually take place in St. John's, including as part of a Mummers Parade. The parade and the practice waned after the colony-wide ban on mum-mering in 1861, which Chris Brookes presents as a suppression of the working class by the elite following a period of civil unrest and a murder (Brookes *A Public* 29). Horwood, however, vividly describes visits from mummers in his childhood in St. John's in the 1920s (Horwood 54). Mummering was all but gone when Brookes and his theatre group, The Mummers Troupe, revived the practice in St. John's in 1972 (Brookes *A Public* 43), and in 2009 the Mummers Parade was re-vived by the newly formed Mummers Festival. The parade has developed into an annual event with upwards of 500 participants (Halpert 51; Davis 43; Maclean).

7   The squid were used as bait for catching codfish.

I don't know what they did with their squid. I think they had an arrangement with an old fellow down in Quidi Vidi that had some ice. He kept the squid for them so that they didn't deteriorate too much, and then they used to take what they wanted when they went out. It made a big difference. If they had the bait, they got the fish. Like everything else, squid seemed to be more plentiful in those days than they are now. Yes they were. That was back in about 1924.

They went to New York once. They went down to a summer school at Columbia University, a big teaching summer school. They showed a lot of initiative at that age. That's where the set of bridge chairs came from — I've passed them on to Jan. Yes, they're 75 years old. He bought them up in New York, and that was his present to Mother when he came back. A very useful and very much used present it was, too. They played a lot of bridge.

They went by boat straight from here to New York, which was *the* way to go. There was no other way to go except cross-country from Halifax, and that was a long, long journey. They took special courses for teachers given there in the summer. My dad stayed with a cousin, so his board didn't cost him anything. And I think Mr. Samson stayed there too. Facey, one of the Faceys who was a caretaker for the big cathedral of St. John the Divine in New York, was a distant cousin. He had come from English Harbour originally. They went up for six weeks. It was, you know, an unusual thing to do for teachers at that stage, 1925. Some of his fellow teachers went. I thought it was very brave of them.

"He did things that I'd hardly expect of him."

My dad had a strong character, a great deal of determination. He did things that, you know, I'd hardly expect of him. When the war broke out, World War I, four of the teachers on Bishop Feild staff immediately joined up. They had a remarkable war effort, but my dad and Mr. Samson were a little too old for it so they didn't join up. It meant that the CLB and C Company lost their officers; they had all joined up, four of them, one of whom was killed in action. So my dad, who had no CLB experience at all, was granted a commission by the Bishop and became a second lieutenant in the CLB. He took a crash course up at the Armoury, and he headed up the C Company until the fellows came back from overseas. And he did a good job, too.

Church Lads' Brigade, "C" and "K" companies, 1932. Front row, left to right, officers Capt. (Rev.) H.L. Pike, Major George House, Lieut. L.C. Colley. These officers "carried the load" during World War I, when several fellow members of the College teaching staff, who were officers of "C" Company, joined the armed forces. (Courtesy CLB Archives)

Mr. Samson wasn't the type to be an officer, but he consented to be the quartermaster. He looked after the uniforms and the money, the bit of money there was. But my dad, he got textbooks on physical training and all the rest of it. I remember particularly having these exercises in the CLB, in the old gymnasium, where he would have us march in a circle around the outside of the gym and do exercises as we were marching. Arms raised, this sort of thing. I see some of them when I'm watching the TV now.

Dad built a rifle range in the old gym. He put up a backboard, a big sheet of lead he got from the plumber, thinking it would stop every shot that went out from the rifle range, which was facing Colonial Street. And it did stop nine hundred and ninety nine out of a thousand, I guess, but one of the Cannings, Bill Canning on this occasion, wavered to the point where he missed the backboard and it went on across the street into a plate glass window of the shop that was there, the Tuck Shop. That's where we used to go for a drink and a chocolate bar recess time. The old lady that looked after the thing was in the place at the time and it went past her and into a can of tomatoes that was on the shelf. Oh, that was an amazing thing! So, after that they enlarged the backboard. One of the people that came out to teach us on the rifle range was Reg Knight; Reg and Tommy Winter were the ones involved in the earlier days of the Feildian tennis courts, the original courts.

Dad was a very keen supporter of the Feildian teams. He never missed a hockey game or a soccer game when the Feildians were playing; he was always there.

The Society of United Fishermen (SUF)[8]

My father and Jack Cheeseman, the Honourable John Cheeseman, became the two top mucky-mucks in the SUF (Society of United

---

8   The Society of United Fishermen was founded in 1862 by Rev. George Gardner as a form of social assistance for fishermen in Heart's Content and neighbouring communities. The organization quickly grew to encompass all of Trinity Bay and, after its collapse due to diminished funds, was reformed in 1873 as a secret society. The SUF had a lodge, "grand masters," and "degrees" that members could pass through. The lodge expanded throughout Newfoundland and even into Canada in the 1920s, with up to 90 lodges operating at one time, its focus remaining one of assistance towards fishing families. Welfare brought by Confederation and the disruption of resettlement both contributed to the decline of the Society, however. The Society remains active today, albeit diminished from its former stature, and in 2008 there were 18 active lodges in the province. George House was grand master, 1924–28, and John Cheeseman, 1933–40 (Hodder; Pike).

Fishermen), the Grand Masters.[9] They did a lot of travelling together, going to various branches around the country. It wasn't a fishermen's union, although there were a lot of fishermen members; 'twas more of a fraternal society, and it was quite strong at one point. Nearly every Sunday afternoon, he used to go down to the General Hospital and visit the SUF members there from the outports. There were always a few of them around. Like the Orangemen, they used to have their parades occasionally. They had quite handsome regalia that they used. It was a bit like the Masonic Order; sometimes they existed side by side. At one time there was a Masonic Order down at Trinity as well as the SUF.

No. 1 Heart's Content Lodge

No. 2 Winterton Lodge

Society of United Fishermen lodges. Top: Heart's Content; bottom, Winterton. (Courtesy Centre for Newfoundland Studies)

"They might as well have come in naked."

Before 1920, quite a few of the men wore big, wide moustaches, as did my father and Mr. Samson. And then, on the way home one day, they both decided they were fed up with them. They were going to shave off their moustaches and not say a word to anybody. And so they both came down to breakfast in the morning with no moustache. They might as well have come in naked.

---

9   John T. Cheeseman (1892–1968) was a businessman and politician from Port aux Bras, Burin Peninsula. He started out with his father's fishing business, and represented Burin as an MHA, 1919–1923. In 1934 he became Chief Fisheries Officer of Newfoundland. He returned to politics as a Liberal MHA in 1956. John T. Cheeseman Provincial Park was named in his honour (Smallwood vol. 1 "Cheeseman").

It was weird for us after so many years of seeing them with the big moustaches. I think Mother was rather pleased. She said, "It makes you about 10 or 20 years younger."

In the mid-thirties, Dad and Mr. Samson decided they'd learn to drive a motor car. Dad mastered the driving, but Mr. Samson didn't. Mr. Samson ran the car into Windsor Lake! So he left it there. His daughter Mildred[10] went in and got it out. He never drove afterwards, but my dad persisted, and I'm very glad he did. Dad's first car was a good second-hand car which belonged to a canon at the Anglican Cathedral. He took it down on the Feildian Grounds, and he took it down on the north side of Quidi Vidi, and in no time, he was driving. To get your licence, you had to go up and drive around Fort Townsend, that's where you got your licence. He got it all right, and Edith got hers, but poor old Mr. Samson just couldn't master it, although he did help Dad build a lovely two-car garage.

You don't remember being ditched out in the bushes. My mother said to you, and I think you were about six, "Would you like to go for a little drive with Gampy?" "Oh yes, that would be lovely," you said. So you got in and the two of you drove across Winter Place, and up that little lane that goes up to Winter Avenue. He negotiated the lane all right and was nearly out on Winter Avenue, when the door next to you opened suddenly and you disappeared! As the Lord would have it, there were three or four big bushes right there, raspberry canes actually. When you went out the door, you went smack out into the raspberry bushes. And Dad retrieved you with not a scratch or a mark on you. I would say you were about five or six.

---

10   I.J. Samson's daughter Mildred later became godmother to Edgar and Margie's daughter Janet.

4. War and a War Hero[1]

One of my earliest memories of the war [World War I] is a sad one. The Goodlands' son, from two doors over, was in the Forces, the only one in our neighbourhood, and they were right up at the front. He was the only veteran that we had down there so everybody knew him and everybody was praying for him, hoping that he'd come through. About two weeks before the Armistice, he was killed by a sniper's bullet. Of course that threw the whole neighbourhood there, Winter Place and Winter Avenue, into grief.

That was a bad one. And by a rather weird coincidence, in World War II my very next-door neighbour, who was a wing commander in the Air Force, Arthur Samson, who I think was the highest ranking officer that we had among the Newfoundland group, when the war was over, even though he had a wife and two children in England, decided to stay in uniform long enough to get some prisoners of war out of Burma. And taking one load of prisoners of war out from Burma, he had plane trouble, and the plane crashed into the sea and that was that. We never heard a sign or sight of him afterwards.[2] So that was two neighbours lost in two different world wars.

---

1   The story of Tommy Ricketts illustrates how we build up heroes in our society. Whether they like it or not, we create them, heap honours upon them, and have demanding expectations about how they should behave on returning to civilian life. Tommy Ricketts clearly felt uncomfortable and ambivalent about this role for the rest of his days.

2   Wing Commander Arthur James Samson of the Royal Air Force was lost on 8 Sept. 1945. His name is inscribed on the Singapore Memorial at the Kranji War Cemetery, Singapore, along with those of over 24,000 other soldiers of the British Empire and Commonwealth who served in Southeast Asia and whose bodies were not recovered. He received the Distinguished Flying Cross "For gallantry and devotion to duty in the execution of air operations" ("In Memory Of").

"The war is over, the war is over!"

I vividly remember the end of the First World War. On Rawlins Cross, just south of the corner, there was a little post office and telegraph office. I had been sent out there to buy stamps, I think, and while I was in the post office, the word came through on the telegraph line that the war was over. In five minutes, there were four or five hundred people dancing with joy on Rawlins Cross. The word spread from house to house. Everybody out dancing around and singing on Rawlins Cross. Oh, it was really something![3]

I had only one idea, and that was to get home and tell them that the war was over. "They don't know at home so I'd better get home and tell them," I said. And so, at eight or nine years old, I ran the whole distance and when I got home I was too breathless to tell them what it was all about. But when I caught my breath a little, I managed to get out, "The war is over, the war is over!" And so the news spread up Winter Place, and soon everybody was out celebrating the good news.

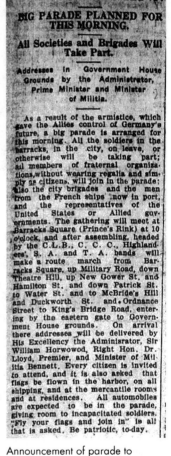

Announcement of parade to celebrate armistice, from the *Daily News*, 18 November 1918.

---

3   The Armistice was declared on 11 Nov. 1918. The next day a large parade was arranged in St. John's, where "Every citizen [was] invited to attend" ("Join in the Celebration"). Celebrations of note also took place in Twilingate, where "At night the dwelling houses were beautifully illuminated, joy guns firing, bells ringing and bonfires blazing, until the whole town was a delightful scene" ("Magistrate").

Tommy Ricketts and the Victoria Cross[4]

Tommy Ricketts.

They [the Royal Newfoundland Regiment] were attempting to get a German gun which was beating the hell out of them, and Tommy and one of his buddies volunteered to cross the couple of hundred yards and try to shoot these snipers or capture the gun. They did just that — an NCO went with him, I think, but it was Tommy who went back when they ran short of ammunition; it was Tommy that ran back over a hundred yards of completely open ground and got another round of ammunition and crawled back to his buddy, and they managed to capture this gun and take four or five prisoners.

I think his buddy was a corporal or something, so he was the one that saw it all and recommended Tommy to his commanding officer for the Victoria Cross. He saved a lot of lives and he captured a number of guns and a number of prisoners. Apparently he had done a lot of shooting of bears and that sort of thing as a boy, in his home in White Bay, which paid off when he went to war.

---

4   Edgar's version of the story of how Ricketts won the V.C. aligns with printed sources. The action took place in Ledeghem, West Flanders, Belgium, on 14 Oct. 1918, near the end of the war. The only book that discusses Ricketts in any depth seems to be Joy B. Cave's engaging 1984 account, *Two Newfoundland V.C.s* (in which she thanks Edgar); otherwise, the main sources are articles from newspapers and journals such as the *Newfoundland Quarterly*. Most sources describe Ricketts as a very shy, withdrawn, and modest man, who shunned any attention relating to his medal and resulting fame. One article illustrates his generosity and kindness (see this chapter, note 11 (p. 122)).

They had a terrific parade when he came home,[5] and he was presented with all kinds of gifts, hundreds of dollars of gifts from Water Street merchants, and other citizens. Yes, he came home with a backload of one thing or another. The thing that interested me the most were the fishing rods. He had three or four of those. I thought eventually I might get one, but I never did.

We all gathered down by Dr. Murphy's (that's Bliss's father), right down by where the War Memorial is now to watch the parade. Calvert's had a big fruit store right next to Murphy's, and that's where we gathered, in front of that, and we saw Tommy Ricketts walking by. Funny

Peace Celebration Parade, St. John's, 5 August 1919. (Courtesy The Rooms Provincial Archives, E 23-39)

---

5   The citizens of St. John's gave him a hero's welcome, pulling him through the snow on a sleigh with ropes attached: "Never in the annals of our history were there such scenes of enthusiasm and spontaneous welcome. More than half the populace of the city were along the streets, and thousands followed the procession throughout its march." ("Reception to Ricketts, V.C." 9). As Cave notes, "for the painfully shy young Ricketts it must have been an overwhelming experience" (77).

things just stick out in your mind. Mrs. Samson was with us. I don't know where Mr. was but Mrs. Samson was with us. She became faint. She fainted off right at Dr. Murphy's doorway, I remember that quite well. I believe Mr. Lawlor, a cab man, drove her home afterwards.

Tommy won the Victoria Cross in action in 1918, only 16 years of age. King George V was a remarkable man, and when he heard at the time that this young man had won the Victoria Cross, the King and Queen were on their way to one of their castles for a little rest and change, and to get over the death of their own son who had been killed just at that time. And when they heard that Tommy was on his way home, they gave up their visit to the castle to see to it that Tommy got his Victoria Cross presented to him before he left to come back to Newfoundland. There was only one other person present for that, and he was the oldest Victoria Cross winner in England from the Boer War. And Tommy Ricketts was the youngest ever.[6]

Postcard showing the Royal Newfoundland Regiment in training at Fort William in St. John's. (Courtesy The Rooms Provincial Archives, VA 37-15.4)

---

6   Edgar has made a slight error in Ricketts's age: he was 15 when he joined the army, and 17 when he won the V.C. However, as confirmed in other sources, the other facts about the presentation ceremony are correct (Cave 45, 47, 75).

He falsified his age when he joined up — he was 14, and pretended he was 16 in order to be able to join. When he won the Victoria Cross, they discovered his age, and so they discharged him home. His brother was a little older. There were no birth records where they were from, so there was no way to prove their age, because there were only a couple of families. The only time people got a birth record was when a clergyman came around and did a christening. They came from Seal Cove in White Bay. By a strange coincidence there was another Tommy Ricketts down there in White Bay, on the other side of the bay, and he was killed in action just about the time that Tommy got his Victoria Cross.

"Mother ended up looking after him for three years."

Towards the end of the war, when Tommy Ricketts came home, they wanted him to get some education. He was completely illiterate when he arrived back. There was no school in White Bay. He didn't learn to read or write until he went to Bishop Feild at the age of 16. Dr. Black-all entered him into Bishop Feild, and persuaded my father to take Tommy Ricketts in to live with us for a year so that he could help him with his homework, help him get on his feet. He lived with us. Mother ended up looking after him for three years. That included not only bed and breakfast and all his meals, but washing his clothes and mending his socks, and all the rest of it. His parents were dead — they died young. He'd never go back to White Bay.

He was a natural to be made an NCO in the C Company in the CLB, but it was a mistake because he was only a private when he was discharged, and there were boys in C Company who had gone from recruits right up to becoming sergeants and sergeants major. They were much better fitted to lead the Company than Tommy Ricketts was.

He was very withdrawn, very quiet, and Dr. Macpherson said he was suffering from what we called shell-shock in those days. He showed the effects of a couple of years' war in the trenches. It was all too much for him. He just withdrew into himself completely.[7] He would never, ever speak of his war experiences. He was wounded once, actually. He got a leg wound and was invalided back to England early in the war, early after he joined up, and then went back to the front again.

Memorial Day parade, 1 July 1924, members of the Royal Newfoundland Regiment marching down Water Street. (Courtesy The Rooms Provincial Archives, B 5-75)

He didn't do anything around the house; not a thing. But my dad decided that he was going to build a workshop for himself out in the back garden. Tommy asked if he could help him with it, and he did. He was a considerable help. It showed that up until the time he was a boy, 14 or 15 at White Bay, he had learned how to use a hammer and a saw.

He was still a young outport boy who had lost his boyhood. It was

---

7   Other accounts confirm that Ricketts was shy and shunned the spotlight. One of his former employees recalls his being curt with a magazine reporter who wanted to interview him (Roberts A1).

very natural, therefore, in the spring of the year when the ice broke up on the pond, that the first thing that he wanted to do was get a trouting pole and go fishing — which he did, using one of the highly expensive rods that were given him when he arrived back in Newfoundland. So he did the natural thing when the spring came, and asked my father where he could go to look for some trout.

"He passed an exam in pharmacy."

He went as far as he could go at Bishop Feild, really. He went up to the equivalent of Grade Six and then, very foolishly, I think, they pushed him on until they felt that he had the equivalent of Grade 11.[8] He had no real background in English, history, and literature, with the result that the same day he went to Memorial, he was advised to quit, he just didn't have the background. So he was taken down to McMurdo's Pharmacy, and the people at McMurdo's helped him to the point where he passed an exam in pharmacy.[9]

So, eventually, Tommy got to the point where, with the money he had been given and he had made, he had enough to open up his own

---

8   Whether he was "pushed" or not, Ricketts did reasonably well in school: "In 1921 he was third in order of merit in his form. The next year, in the lower Sixth, he was placed exactly in the middle of the examination lists; and the same applied in his Upper Sixth year" (Cave). (Lower and Upper Sixth are from the English system, and equivalent to today's Grades 11 and 12.) This was verified by examining the Feildian magazine for those years. It seems that Ricketts's Upper Sixth year was 1924, so it must have taken him a few years to get to that point. His tenure at Memorial, however, does seem to have been brief before he took up pharmacy.

9   Thomas J. McMurdo, a native of Scotland, came to Newfoundland in 1830. Thomas McMurdo Co., Chemists was opened on the north side of Water Street in 1846, after the original buildings were destroyed by fire. A pamphlet by the Newfoundland Pharmaceutical Association relates that "Nearly all the pharmacists of the period 1830 to 1930 served their apprenticeship with the McMurdo firm." Among those who trained there was Alexander M. Bell, father of Alexander Graham Bell. The store continued in operation at this location until its closure in 1973 ("Pharmacy"; Smallwood vol. 3 "McMurdo"; Poole vol. 4 "Pharmacy"; O'Mara 29).

drugstore, up opposite the railway station, on Water Street West.[10] He was there for a number of years, and all that's there now is a little memorial to him. There's a place fenced off, grass about 14 or 15 feet square and a little monument to the effect that this was the site of Tommy Ricketts's drugstore. It's right opposite the old station.

A lot of people used to drop in there. If you were going out on the train, it was a good place to buy your magazines and chocolate bars and one thing or another like that.[11] The trains were busy in those days. He did very well for a short while there. I had a number of chats with him. I used to go out on the train occasionally, and I used to drop in occasionally there and talk to him. He got married, his wife is still here.[12] His son was given the same name, Thomas; he went through Feild and then pre-med, and finished up as a doctor. He's a doctor now in Toronto.

Tommy Ricketts died young. He wasn't that old.[13]

---

10   There seems to be little information about Thomas Ricketts's drugstore, which he operated until he died. He is listed as "Thomas Ricketts, Prescription Druggist" in the 1948 St. John's Business Directory (Baggs 10).

11   A touching instance of Ricketts's kindness is related by Fred Carter, who was severely sunburned as a boy of eight or nine. Ricketts treated him with bandages and ointment for several days until he got better. Tommy supposed that the boy had little money, which was true, and so didn't charge him, treating him "gently and humanely." (Carter A11).

12   Edna May Ricketts (née Edwards) was born in 1913 in St. John's and attended the Methodist College. Athletic and musical, she eventually trained as a stenographer. She and Tommy met when he boarded at her family's home, and they were married in 1933, eventually moving above the drugstore on Water Street. The shy Ricketts wrote her daily love letters during a spell in Long Harbour, Placentia Bay. After Tommy's death Edna retrained and began work at MCP, the provincial Medical Care Plan. She died in 2010, aged 97 (Sullivan 20)

13   Tommy Ricketts died on 10 February 1967, two months before his sixty-sixth birthday.

5. Old St. John's

"You live in a very exclusive neighbourhood."

There were very few people [in the Winter Place/Winter Avenue neighbourhood] when I was young. It was out in the country, a bit [now midtown]. The only other house nearby was the Bailey family's up on the hill; there were almost as many in that house as there were in the whole of Winter Place. It was a two-storey house, and there were three Bailey boys and three girls. Mr. Bailey was the Secretary of Agriculture, and as such, he had quite an experimental farm going all up around the area which is now Glenridge Crescent. He had a big barn which was right next to a little pond there, our skating pond, and he had all kinds of experimental crops and ducks and geese and hens. We had a whale of a time with this big barn as youngsters, cows and horses and stuff. The barn was always there where we could change our boots to go skating out there, too. It was nice and warm before we went out on the pond. You could always go and sit in the hay and have a snack when you were taking a break.

When there was a good sheet of ice on the pond, Doug Bailey, who was a CLB bugler, got up on the roof of his house and blew a certain tune, north, south, east, and west, and within 15 minutes, you'd have two hockey teams on the pond there. Two or three of the Bailey boys were very good hockey players, and one was particularly good. The oldest, tall, lanky fellow, he played in goal for the school team. He was quite famous to the bunch of kids that were around.

So we had an interesting childhood. The Baileys were our companions. They were a little older than we were, some of them. When I say "we," I mean Art Samson, who was my buddy from next door, and myself. And there were two Goodland sons, and a few more.

Edgar, Bliss Murphy, Art Samson, Eric Calver, c. 1925, on what is probably the pond that used to be where Glenridge Crescent now is.

The pond itself filled up a space from across here [Edgar's house backed onto Glenridge Crescent], the Ewings' and Knowlings' places, right over to what used to be the Wilanskys', just where Glenridge Crescent is. Of course to build there, the Chief of Police, Hutchings — he was the one that started Glenridge Crescent — had the pond drained to the river behind, and had the city dump there for a long time to fill the pond up. So actually, the house that used to be the Knowlings' there was right in the middle of a little pond.

Of the other houses there in the 1910s, immediately to the east [of George House's house on Winter Place], there was another set of double houses, very much like the one that my father built. One of them

belonged to Goodland of Grey and Goodland, well-known booksellers, and the other belonged to Alec Winter, a well-known lawyer. He
later sold his house to Grant Patterson and built a lovely house on
Winter Place that was later bought by Don Jamieson.[1] So, as the
teachers at Bishop Feild used to say to my dad, "You live in a very ex-
clusive neighbourhood." There were just a few other houses there, including a big stone house down at the foot of the hill which was built
by two McNamara brothers, one of whom was a well-known jeweller
with a family jewellery store on Water Street.[2]

The Emersons also built a big house down on Winter Avenue.[3]
They were Nova Scotians. He came here as a young lawyer and built
that big home down here. There's a picture of me taken at the back
gate of that home, on a wooden rocking horse that my father made for
me. There were almost no houses on Winter Avenue then.

Further out, there was a huge big summer house that belonged to

---

1   Donald Campbell Jamieson, 1921–86, was born in St. John's. He was opposed to
     Confederation with Canada in 1949, favouring economic union with the U.S.
     instead, but went on to become "one of the most influential Newfoundland and
     Labrador representatives ever in federal politics." He and Geoffrey W. Stirling built
     a network of broadcasting stations across Newfoundland, eventually starting the
     Newfoundland Broadcasting Co. and television station CJON in 1955. Jamieson
     entered federal politics in 1966 and went on to become a federal cabinet minister
     in Pierre Trudeau's government from 1969 to 1979. He ended as Canada's High
     Commissioner to Great Britain (Cuff "Jamieson").

2   An obituary for Alfred McNamara, who resided in the stone house on Robinson's
     Hill opposite the entrance to Winter Place, appeared in the *Daily News* on Monday,
     18 Jan. 1926, which describes him as "one of the best known of the business men
     of Water Street, where for the past thirty years he had conducted a jewellery busi-
     ness, which is well known throughout the country." We are grateful to Heather
     Wareham, Maritime History Archives of Memorial University, who currently lives
     in the stone house, for providing this reference.

3   The house, now 130 years old, was recently demolished after a controversial deci-
     sion by City Council. Heritage status was recommended for the property, but re-
     jected to allow development (MacEachern A1).

McNamara house, Robinson's Hill. (Rennie/McNamara Collection, The Rooms Provincial Archives)

Carla Emerson's grandfather, a beautiful big home.[4] I think it was used as a sanatorium during the war when a lot of the fellows came back with tuberculosis. When it was empty after that, my mother used to say, "Now, you boys, if you're going swimming in Kent's Pond, don't you go near that house." Eventually it was bought by a German who was a purser on the boat going from here to New York. He bought it and was going to develop a farm there, and then just before he was setting out to sea the war broke out. The poor fellow was incarcerated. I don't know what happened to him afterwards, but the house just lay idle in there for years.

---

4   Carla Emerson was a harpist with the Newfoundland Symphony Orchestra. Born in St. John's, she attended Juilliard Conservatory in New York City after World War II, and worked in England for five years before returning to Newfoundland to play in the orchestra and teach privately (Marion White).

"Dad, where's the car?"

Bliss Murphy's absent-mindedness was exceeded only by his father, who was the most absent-minded man I've ever known. His country house was in there beyond the Colony Club,[5] and there was quite a big field there. We'd be playing ball there, and Bliss would look up and suddenly see his father coming in on foot. "Dad, where's the car?"

"Damnit, I left it down by the office. Don't let your mother know!" The office was down on Duckworth Street opposite the War Memorial. He'd cross the street then to Lawlor's farm and get the old man to hitch up his carriage and drive him back out to Water Street to pick up his car.

"A sleepy little city."

Until the Americans came, St. John's was a sleepy little city.[6] It really was. It woke up every now and then when all the schooners came in

---

5   The Old Colony Club was a popular dance club on Portugal Cove Road frequented by military servicemen in the 1940s. It was built in 1941, and then rebuilt in 1943 after a fire that killed four people. As with the 1943 Knights of Columbus fire that killed 99, the fire was suspected of being caused by enemy spies (Darrin McGrath A1). The newly built building was representative of "moderne" architecture (Harris 377). It was the main nightclub in St. John's after the war, and it continued its operations until it was closed and demolished in 1999. Currently the provincial Research and Development Corporation sits on the site (Harris; Darrin McGrath; "Old Colony").

6   Edgar's description of old St. John's contrasts a bit with Harold Horwood's in *A Walk in the Dreamtime*. Horwood describes it as a busy "hive of small industry, with five or six thousand people working in factories" (3). He also mentions the Labrador fishery, specifically the seal hunt, as a pinnacle of activity. Edgar may mean, however, that it was sleepy in comparison with the busy, car-filled St. John's of today, which developed during and after World War II. Indeed, in Steven High's *Occupied St. John's*, interviewee Ann Abraham remembers how "The town was so small before the war," during which cars and jeeps replaced the sounds of horses and carts (117).

from the outports to get their supplies to go down to Labrador.[7] It was a great sight when the schooners were coming in. Then we went to sleep again. We didn't have that many tourists, although there was a Tourist Bureau way back.[8] We didn't come awake again until the fall, when the schooners came back with all their fish. Water Street again became a thriving spot. People like my cousin, Mark Wells, would come in from English Harbour to supply his little store down there. He'd come in every fall and stay at the same boarding house. He'd go to the wholesale places like Neal's, him and his father, stock up on all kinds of stuff.[9]

I would say that St. John's in the 1910s, and I'm only guessing, probably had about 40,000 people.[10] It really was a small, sleepy town with cobblestones on Water Street and no paving at all on Duckworth Street, so that it became a sea of mud in the springtime. They had to have these crossing boys so that if a man wanted to go down Prescott Street and cross over to the other side of the street, where Royal Stores had a

---

7   The migratory cod fishery from Newfoundland to Labrador consisted of schooners, mainly from Conception Bay South, fishing the Labrador coast from June to September, though some departed from St. John's, too. St. John's was better known as the centre of the seal fishery. A huge flock of ships (steam, by the 1920s) would gather in the capital in the winter, sail to the front for several months, and return in the spring loaded down with pelts (Smallwood vol. 3 "Labrador"; Poole vol. 5 "Sealing"; Ryan).

8   The Newfoundland Tourist and Publicity Bureau existed as early as 1900, the date of a detailed pamphlet published by the Bureau about St. John's. The *Encyclopedia of Newfoundland and Labrador* says that the Newfoundland Tourist and Publicity Commission was formed in 1925 to promote tourism in Newfoundland, which had been steadily growing since the building of the railway in the 1880s. Eventually, the Commission became a government department (Poole vol. 5 "Tourism"; *St. John's*).

9   George Neal Ltd. was a wholesaler's started in 1894 by George Eric Neal, a native of St. John's. The business continued until the early 1990s, when it was dissolved by a grandson of the founder (Poole vol. 4 "Neal").

10   His guess is good — the actual population of St. John's in 1921 was 36,444 people. Newfoundland had 263,033 people. As of the last census, conducted in 2011, St. John's had 106,172 people in the city itself, and a total of 196,966 in the greater St. John's area. Newfoundland had 514,536 (Canada 1921; Canada 2011).

furniture store, he had to be swept over by a crossing boy. This was a boy with a birch broom who, for a penny, or more for those who happened to be generous, swept the man across the street. He'd go in front and swish the mud, right and left, right and left so that the man could go across without going over his rubbers; otherwise, he didn't have a chance.

I saw the same condition exactly after World War II when I was visiting Stephenville, where there were soldiers stationed at the American base. The mud on the main street was three or four inches deep, to the point where I had to take a taxi from a jewellery or watch repair shop on one side of the street, to go to a dry cleaners on the other side in order to avoid getting my shoes full of mud. The American soldiers would come in from the base and they'd take off their shoes and roll their pants up to their knees and they'd slosh through all that to do a bit of shopping.

"The racers would sit in sleds behind the horse."

They used to have horse races on Quidi Vidi Lake. Horseracing was a regular feature at Quidi Vidi around February or March. The racers would sit in sleds behind the horses. It was exciting! There were a number of very good horses, one of which was owned by my old friend Mr. Lawlor, the cabman. Very popular. He used to win quite a few races.

Mr. Lawlor was one of two cabmen that had a stand on Water Street, just opposite where Royal Stores used to be, so he was known by half the people in St. John's.[11] He lived on a farm just opposite the present Colony Club. Every time he was driving home in the evening, if I happened to be on the road, he'd stop and give me a lift from Rawlins Cross or somewhere into Winter Place. Very generous. He had a sleigh in the wintertime. Even if he had a passenger he'd always stop and you could stand on the runners behind and hold on and get a lift.

---

11   Little could be found about Mr. Lawlor, cabman; apparently the Lawlors were a family of cabmen, so the one Edgar remembers could be Walter or his father Thomas. John Lawlor, Walter's brother, died in 1910 ("City Council").

Quidi Vidi horse race, 1925. (Courtesy Centre for Newfoundland Studies)

He always insisted on having the very best of horses. He always wanted them with white forelegs, if he could possibly get them, so that during the July 1st parade down to the War Memorial, it was always Mr. Lawlor's horse that was used by the head of the regiment, Colonel Nangle.[12] Mr. Lawlor broke his hip one time, and they said he'd never walk again. He drank a bottle of rum every day until his hip healed. And it did. He walked and drove. He preserved himself in alcohol. He drank a lot but the old horse always got him home. All they had to do was point him up Prescott Street and he was as good as home.

Yes, the cabmen were very popular, made a good living. There was no other way to get to what we used to call the "higher levels"; the streetcar only went as far as Queen's Road. So they were kept busy.

Right here near my house, I can remember several winters when

---

12 Thomas F. Nangle was born in St. John's in 1889. He was ordained as a Roman Catholic priest in 1913 and in 1915 became the chaplain of the Newfoundland Regiment in France, eventually being promoted to lieutenant colonel. Nangle was known for his non-sectarian ministry to the troops, and admired as an entertaining and engaging speaker. Key in the establishment of the war memorials both in St. John's and France, Nangle left the priesthood in 1929, married, and moved to Rhodesia (now Zimbabwe). He died there in 1972 (Browne; Poole vol. 4 "Nangle").

the snow was so bad and the road covered over so badly, the horses used to have to go into the field up here, and they'd break over the fence going to the fields and then cut back to the roads further on. There were no snowploughs. Cars were all put away for the winter.

Old St. John's businesses

On Colonial Street, just down below Bond Street and on the east side there was Caul's Grocery, which was very convenient.[13] My dad would drop in with an order, or Mother would phone out an order. They used a horse to deliver, and we ate well. It was a good grocery store, N.F. Caul's. They were Roman Catholics but his son went to Bishop Feild and was a very good soccer player. Made his place on the old Feildian team, too. I often went in to W.J. Murphy's, a very old business.[14] Mother would give me a little note and say, "On your way home go into Murphy's and pick up such and such."

There was Royal Stores[15] in the east end of Water Street, the south side of course, and then you went up a little bit and you came to Garland's Bookstore,[16] which was between Royal Stores and London,

---

13 Caul's Grocery is listed in the 1924 and 1932 city directories as located at 22 Colonial Street.

14 W.J. Murphy's Grocery was a fixture at Rawlins Cross for 91 years. It was sold in 2000 ("W.J. Murphy's").

15 Royal Stores was founded in 1895 by Campbell and Archibald Macpherson (father of Dr. Cluny Macpherson) and William Carson Job. The firm ran a clothing factory in St. John's for 50 years at the corner of Duckworth and Prescott streets, a furniture department, and a department store on Water Street. Between 1910 and 1953 Royal Stores expanded to Grand Falls, Buchans, and Mackinsons. The business continued to thrive through the 1960s but declined in the 1970s until it was eventually placed in receivership on 6 Jan. 1977 ("The Royal Stores"; "Royal Stores").

16 Garland's Bookstore was opened by Samuel E. Garland, a native of Catalina, Trinity Bay, and was for many years the largest in St. John's. Garland opened the store in 1888, and it was destroyed by fire twice, in 1892 and 1908. Garland's, also a publisher, produced several books and also Newfoundland postcards. In the 1920s Garland closed his retail shop and ran the business from his home (Smallwood vol. 2 "Garland").

Water Street, 1920s, looking east, with Jewish-owned businesses on right: Sheffman's, Rosenberg's, Levitz's. Also Murphy's. (Courtesy The Rooms Provincial Archives, VA 14-30)

Water Street, 1920s, looking west, with Ayre & Sons on left. (Courtesy The Rooms Provincial Archives, A 3-39)

New York and Paris,[17] and then you went west and you came to Trapnell's Jewellers.[18] Trapnell's has been there for a long time. Then to Ayre & Sons,[19] which wasn't too far from Bowring's,[20] and then Sears. Ayre & Sons had a very good music department, cheap music, records, record players. Most of the outport men that came in on schooners went to Ayre & Sons or Bowring's, but particularly Ayre & Sons, to buy things. On the north side of the street there was a

---

17   London, New York and Paris Association of Fashion Ltd. was a St. John's clothing store opened by Harris Goldstone in 1917, and managed by Joseph Goldstone. The firm thrived for the next 50 years and was sold to Maxwell Janes in 1973. After expansion in the 1970s, the company went out of business in 1982. It continued for a time as a retail store as the London Ltd (Smallwood vol. 3 "London").

18   Trapnell's Jewellery was founded in 1898 and operated for 108 years. Robert H. Trapnell, the founder, sold the business to Lorne Hiscock in the early 1930s and Hiscock operated the business as a combined jeweller's and optometrist's. With his death in 1973 his son Geoff took over the business, and ran it together with his wife Carla and eventually their son David until its closure in 2006 ("The Jeweller").

19   Charles Robert Ayre opened a store on Water Street in 1859, and the firm of Ayre & Sons, importers, wholesalers, and distributors, was formed in 1884. The premises were destroyed in the fire of 1892 but soon afterwards a large new department store was opened on Water Street. In the next 30 years the company opened a five-storey building to expand their line and even started a radio station, VOAS. The company continued expanding after Confederation, opening supermarkets and purchasing a shipping company. After further expansion in the 1980s and following the recession of the early 1990s the firm was forced to declare bankruptcy and close its 60 retail outlets in March 1992 (Smallwood vol. 1 "Ayre"; Gorham 30).

20   Bowring's began as a business in 1811, and in 1815 Benjamin Bowring, a watchmaker from Exeter, opened a shop on Water Street. The business rapidly expanded and the firm entered the cod and seal oil trade, acquiring several schooners. Bowring's flourished throughout the nineteenth century, providing retail service and outfitting cod and sealing vessels, and in 1911, as part of the Centenary celebrations, opened a 50-acre park to the west of St. John's (Bowring Park). After changes in the fisheries Bowring's began to focus more on retailing, opening stores throughout the province. Bowring's sold its retail outlets in the 1980s, and the company was then sold. In 2004, however, the name returned to St. John's as a new Bowring store was opened on Stavanger Drive. This store and another 63 stores across the country are now owned by the Everett family in Winnipeg (Smallwood vol. 1 "Bowring"; Baird D1).

well-known hardware store, Neyle-Soper's.[21] That was there for a
long time. I think the Sports Shop opened in the late twenties or
early thirties, because my sister Edith had a few dates with Neil
Murray, who was the proprietor and owner.[22]

McMurdo's was *the* drugstore on Water Street.[23] It was the place
every morning where half a dozen of the Water Street young merchants would go for coffee. It was the coffee shop for Water Street.
That's where business was discussed — Bowring's, Ayre's, Baird's — it
was almost like a London club.

There weren't many factories. You could tick them off with the
fingers of your hand. The tobacco company was quite prominent.
There were a few others. One making soft drinks, and the Carnells
had a carriage factory down on Cochrane Street.[24] They moved it later.
That was a fairly big business in those days because there were lots of
horses and carriages and carts around.

---

21   Neyle-Soper Hardware was opened in 1849 by Richard Neyle (1828–1917), a native
     of Devonshire. Albert Soper was listed as vice-president of the business in the 1927
     Who's Who in and from Newfoundland (292). The business continued until 1989
     (Poole vol. 4 "Neyle").

22   The Sports Shop was actually opened on Water Street in 1947 by Arthur Murray
     and Frank Dyke, Sr. It was the first fully equipped sporting goods store in the prov-
     ince, and held a popular Victoria Day weekend trouting contest for many years.
     The business was going strong until April 2004, when the building was destroyed
     by fire; after the temporary location was robbed two months later The Sports Shop
     did not reopen (Power 12; Bennett A4).

23   See Chapter 4, note 9 (p. 121).

24   Carnell's Carriage Factory was begun in the early 1800s by Gilbert Carnell. His son
     John continued the business, building carriages and sleighs, and also performing
     undertaking services. Under the management of Andrew Carnell (1877–1951, later
     mayor of St. John's) the company expanded to include many types of vehicles, and
     included motor vehicle repair among its services. Carriages stopped being built in
     1940, and the company narrowed to specialize in motor vehicle repairs and funerals,
     opening Carnell's Funeral Home on Freshwater Road in 1966. Both the funeral
     business and the auto repair business, Carnell's Spring Service (now Hiscock's
     Spring Service), continue to operate today, making the business over 200 years old
     (Smallwood vol. 1 "Carriage"; Carnell's).

"Everywhere he went, he trotted."

We had a few characters around St. John's.[25] We used to say, "He's a character, you know." They were just different. We had one old fellow that never walked, he ran. Everywhere he went, he trotted. He got the nickname "Trotters" McCarthy. He was very well known, old Trotters McCarthy.[26]

---

25 Edgar makes other remarks about St. John's characters in a text for an undated/untitled speech the editors found:

"Peggy Stack was a little woman from Logy Bay who had a quick wit. There was a story that one day she sold a salmon to the Bishop, and when the cook was preparing it for His Lordship, she discovered that it was loaded with sand. The Bishop reproached her for defrauding him, and she replied, quick as a wink: "Sure, me Lord, the day that salmon was caught it was pretty rough weather, and that accounts for the ballast he had on board." After that she got the nickname "Ballast the Salmon."

Then there was Noftall, who's remembered as the man who was "forty on the pork and lost it." [Refers to the game of 45's, when you're one trick short of winning.] Apparently "Nofty" had the trump card but forgot to play it, and so lost the prize, which was a side of pork ("Wayfarer"). He was a fish-vendor who would peddle his wares on a small cart which he wheeled around the town, and he'd sing:

"Salt herring fresh from Fortune Bay,
Come this week by the schooner May;
If they're too late for your dinner
You can have them for your tay."

Another was Tom Murdock, who worked for Lindberg's Brewery, which made one of the favourite beers in the early days, Bavarian Beer. The government, for tax collection purposes, ruled that this was an alcoholic beverage, and so the company tried to prove that it wasn't intoxicating. Tom made a statement that he had many times drunk several quarts of the delicious beverage at a time without becoming in the least intoxicated. The company lost its case but there was a rhyme made up about Murdock:

"When Tom Murdock is dead and in his grave,
For Bavarian Beer he will not crave,
But on his tombstone will be wrote,
'Many's the gallon went down his throat.'"

26 Trotters McCarthy had a physical deformity that made it easier for him to run than walk; he was once featured in Ripley's *Believe It or Not* as "The Man Who Never Walked" (O'Neil 792).

Mayor Andy Carnell was really a character. He was a most generous soul. He'd start off from the house on Cochrane Street to walk to City Hall with a pocket full of small coins. By the time he got to City Hall, he wouldn't have a cent in his pocket. Every youngster that passed, he gave them a bit of money. And those were the days of poverty, especially on New Gower Street, and the youngsters got to know about him, they'd tag along.

"I've got to have a leak."

I was going down to Water Street one day and came to the corner there at Prescott. I was about 12 or 13. The young fellow that was selling the papers there said, "Can you do me a favour?"

I said, "I'll see what I can do."

He said, "I've got to have a leak." That's just the way he put it. "I've got to have a leak and that's all there is to it." He said, "You take my papers and sell them while I'm gone." He was longer than I expected, I think. He found it difficult to find a suitable place, I guess. When he came back, I had sold a number of papers, so he paid me for it. He paid me two pennies, I think it was, two of these big pennies, four cents, and then I had to cross from the corner of Prescott Street north to the south side through the mud. I earned enough to go to Garland's Bookstore, which was a well-known bookstore at that time, run by Sammy Garland. They stocked everything. It was located almost opposite the post office, on the south side of the street, just about where London, New York and Paris was. I can remember so clearly because I had earned that little bit of extra money, and I was able to buy the English *Boy's Own Paper*, which we very much liked. A good magazine. That was my bonus.

"The boys just wouldn't let you stop."

I really became aware of poverty in the summertime when I went down to Trinity and Champneys and English Harbour, but not so much here in St. John's until I went to work with the Playgrounds

Association in late '29, '30, '31, '32. Some of the boys that came to the playground every day were the poorest of the poor. They reminded me of the youngster in *Angela's Ashes*.[27] Of course, there was a lot of poverty in that area, around New Gower Street. The Rotary Club did a survey up there, a health survey of the whole area. It was so well done that, when the Commission of Government came here,[28] they adopted the Rotary report as the basis for some of the things that they did and suggested to the British government. One thing that came out of it was that tuberculosis was rampant in the centre of the town.

Because of all the poverty downtown, Neddie Outerbridge, one of the Outerbridge family, started a playground movement. He collected funds and bought equipment, and Bannerman Park and Victoria Park became a haven for all these poor youngsters that had no place to go. And so the East Enders went to Bannerman Park and the West Enders went to Victoria Park. I worked out in Bannerman Park July and August, all day every day except when it was raining. Margie did too, for one year. I had four years at it. We used to have softball games, basketball games, and soccer games between the two parks. And then we'd get together once a year and have a combined picnic in Bowring Park, with probably five or six hundred youngsters. Most of them would take the streetcar to the end of Water Street, and walk from there. Although the Rotarians provided some transportation too, I

27 The best-selling book about poverty in Ireland by Frank McCourt: *Angela's Ashes: A Memoir of a Childhood*. For a more contemporary (1960s) account of growing up in central downtown, see Robert Hunt's *Corner Boys*.

28 Democratic government was voluntarily suspended in Newfoundland from 16 Feb. 1934 to 31 Mar. 1949, and the British Parliament appointed a Commission of Government made up of six commissioners (three from Britain and three from Newfoundland) and a governor to run the affairs of the country (Smallwood vol. 2 "Government"). The conventional reason given for this is economic depression; however, in his book *Suspended State*, Gene Long explores the more subtle political factors behind this drastic change in Newfoundland's governing structure, including the central involvement of union leader William Coaker. Chris Brookes produced an award-winning radio documentary about the events in 2005 called *Not Fit for It: How Newfoundland Gave Up Elective Democracy in 1933* (Brookes, *Not Fit*).

know, especially for handicapped youngsters. They were very, very interested in the playground.

My job was to organize soccer and softball, and swimming classes up in the Rennie's River pool. I'd take them on hikes, picnics. It was an interesting, healthy two months. I got the noble sum of $50 a month, plus a bonus at the end of the year. I worked for four summers on the playground, and when I say I worked, I really mean I worked because there was nothing out there. The boys just wouldn't let you stop at all when you were supervisor of the playgrounds at Bannerman Park. It was nothing to have three or four soccer games and three or four softball games just in one day. Five o'clock in the afternoon I was beat, and yet that didn't stop me from going out to Bowring Park to play tennis at five o'clock.

Jack Squires was a big boy on the playground when I went there. I was 18, I think. Claude Howse and I were the only two at Memorial in 1930 that got a job for the summer, which was amazing, there wasn't a job to be had anywhere.[29] The outport fellows were lucky, very lucky, because they could go home and go fishing with their fathers. As I was saying, there was this big fellow Squires who was a member of our softball team, a very good athlete. This day I came in and he was there with a big jackknife, tearing the bark off a tree. So anyhow I went after him, he was bigger than I was. Up the tree he went, one of the big trees down the far end of the park, and I chased after him. When he got out so far on the branch, the branch broke and down he went. Luckily, I jumped and landed on top of him, and knocked the wind out of him completely, and I pummelled him. The poor fellow. I didn't realize that he was breathless but after that I didn't have to raise a finger to anybody in the park for the summer. They said, "Don't go up against Mr. House, he'll kill you!"

29   Claude Howse (1907–96) was born in Burin, educated at Memorial and Dalhousie, and became a government geologist in 1941. He later became Deputy Minister of Mines under Joey Smallwood. Moving on to work for the Iron Ore Company of Canada, he was a central force in developing the large iron ore mines in Labrador. He retired in 1974 and was awarded an honorary D.Sc. by Memorial (Smallwood vol. 2 "Howse").

As a matter of fact, Jack Squires became a professional boxer. Arthur Johnson was arranging some bouts at that time down at the old stadium, the old Prince's Rink, and unfortunately he offered this boy money to take part in a bout. And he did, and by taking the money, it made him a professional boxer. So he could never box in amateur sport again after that.

"It was the cleanest street in St. John's, before or since."

I was a member of the Junior Chamber of Commerce. It was in the spring of the year and the town was filthy, as it always was in the spring, in the old days. So we decided we'd set an example of one street to lead the way for St. John's to clean up. This was about the mid-thirties, I would think. We decided to have one clean street, Prescott Street. We got together with the fire department, got one of the heavy hoses which they had and hooked it up to the hydrant at Rawlins Cross there and got several firms to donate washing powder. So we arranged these packages of powder, about 30 of them, right across the top of Prescott Street, dumped them out, pile after pile, and then got the big hose, swished all that washing powder down over Prescott Street and into the harbour. There was one great white foam right to the top of the street. We used the really powerful hose, and swished it all out into Job's Cove as it was then. You could have eaten your dinner off Prescott Street when we were done! It was the cleanest street in St. John's, before or since. Boy, I remember that so plainly. There were hundreds and hundreds of people who turned out to watch it all.

"Sir, can I use your phone to phone for a cab?"

Screech wasn't called that in those days.[30] The Board of Liquor Control, dark rum, it was called. No, it wasn't called Screech until the Americans came here, during World War II. They got right into it, to

---

30   Screech: "Popular name for a variety of cheap, dark Demerara rum bottled in New-foundland; trade-name of a type of rum marketed with the label 'Screech'" (*DNE*).

the point where at some of their parties, they'd get out of hand completely to the point where I guess they were screeching. They put the nickname on it. Screech!

Right opposite here [44 Robinson's Hill, now 20 Portugal Cove Road] was the city limits sign, and so I was half in and half out. I paid suburban taxes, which were considerably less than the city taxes. During the blackout period in World War II, at night you just drove with your parking lights on. One of these American fellows stationed here came to the door one night and said, "Sir, can I use your phone to phone for a cab?" I said, "Look, you go and sit on the side of the road over there, right under that city limits sign. I know the cab man down at King's Bridge and I'll phone for a cab for you." He was a Texan, had a Texan drawl. You could recognize it, and he was half slopped. So I said, "You sit on the bank over there, under the sign, and when the taxi comes up the hill, he can't miss you because you've got the city limits sign with you." So fine, off he went. When I looked out a few minutes later, he was sitting in the middle of the road with the city limits sign in his hand, facing down the road so the taxi would have to run him over to miss him. So the taxi stopped and he took the sign under his arm and off he went! We never saw it afterwards. They moved the city limits about a mile out, then, and my taxes went up by a multiple of four. He wasn't very popular with me, I'll tell you.

I had a crash one time. I was going to the bowling alleys up on New Gower Street with three of the Feild College teachers to go bowling one afternoon. I was driving down by what used to be the theatre at the foot of Queen's Road, and this big American truck from Pepperrell[31] came around the corner and forgot that he was driving on the

---

31   The United States government acquired the rights to build military bases in Newfoundland under a Leased Bases Agreement with the United Kingdom in 1940. It built a base in St. John's in an area called Pleasantville on the north shore of Quidi Vidi Lake in 1941, which it named Fort Pepperrell (Higgins "Fort"). For more about the American and Canadian "Invasions," see Steven High's wonderful book, *Occupied St. John's*.

left and he crashed into my little car.[32] It was an English car, a small car. Buckled in the door. And at that time, there was no way he could compensate me. So he just said, "You bring that car down tomorrow and I'll have the door rolled out." He said he'd fix it.

I said, "No way!" I said, "I want a new door." So he fought it.

I had to get Gordon Stirling to represent me and altogether — this is amazing — I signed 21 different papers in connection with that. They had to pass a special act of Congress in the United States to set aside funds for civilian damages overseas. So I was responsible for the United States passing a special act of Congress! Anyhow, having attended 21 sessions, and having Gordon Stirling represent me, I went on out to Buchans that year and a month or so after I was out there, I got the cheque from the United States government. I think it was for $140. It was unusual, completely.

32 Newfoundland was the last region of Canada (independent at the time) to switch to driving on the right side of the road; it did so in 1947 (Dyer).

6. Sports and Recreation

"The Prince's Rink was 'the' rink."

Dad skated very well — he taught me to skate. I was about four or five years old when I started off on what they used to call double runners, with two blades. Soon got rid of those. It was so convenient having the pond right here, and the marsh in by The Colony Club which used to freeze over. Kenny's and Kent's Pond weren't very far away, Long Pond, too.

There used to be a rink up near the CLB Armoury, but it was very small; and then of course there was the Prince's Rink down behind Queen's College, by the hotel. The Prince's Rink was "the" rink, and for a number of years Arthur Johnson, Paul's father who was in the insurance business, was the manager.[1] He did a great job.

Ice-making was quite a job at that time, quite an art. Open the windows, let the cold in, and close the windows to keep the warm out. When you got it all frozen, you close the windows as fast as you could to keep the cold in. We had nothing like you have now, you know, pipes going under, artificial. It was just done simply on the frost that seeped into the building.

A couple of afternoons a week and in the night after a hockey game, there'd be a general skate. You'd go to the game and take your skates and have a skate after. Very popular. We had a three-piece band, saxophone and French horn and trombone, I think it was, Bennett's Band, which provided the music, and so you got out and skated to the

---

1   The Prince's Rink was opened in 1899 by R.G. Reid of the Newfoundland Railway Company, and destroyed by fire in 1941. Memorial Stadium was built to replace it, but it took 10 years to raise the money for its construction. For more, see *Souvenir Booklet*.

music with your partner. Margie and I went skating there. She wasn't a good skater but she was a brave skater. She made out. I wouldn't have much life left in my arm after we stopped skating.

On one occasion, Bully, the band master, used his presence of mind to great advantage. During the hockey game, a fight broke out on the ice between the two teams that were playing. Things were getting nasty because some of the spectators were starting to get into it. And suddenly he started to play "God Save the King." Everybody listened. Everybody stood at attention and by the time he stopped playing, everything had calmed down. It was the most amazing thing I ever saw!

In the late spring, when it got mild, you could rent the ice for half price — 20 cents each we used to put in, and a dozen of us would have the rink for an hour with a half inch of water on the ice. We had a lot of fun. We'd go home drenched. Absolutely drenched.

"Once St. Bon's got the rink we didn't stand a chance."

There's been club hockey since about 1900.[2] The big three were St. Bon's, the Methodist College/Prince of Wales, and Feild. Then, the Methodist senior team became the Guards, the Methodist Guards (at

---

2 Again, Edgar's memory is accurate. Hockey was introduced to Newfoundland by Canadian tradesmen in the late nineteenth century, and the first recorded game was on Quidi Vidi Lake in February 1896. The sport quickly took off and in 1899 the Newfoundland Hockey Association was formed, with club hockey beginning the next year. There were seven teams to start with: Victorias, the Bankers, Feildians, St. Bon's, St. Andrews, the Star of the Sea Society, and the City Team. By 1921 it had become "our winter game" (Thomas 2), with competitive teams throughout the province. The Herder Memorial Trophy competition for senior hockey began in 1935 and continues today. St. John's currently hosts an AHL franchise, the St. John's Ice Caps, and from 1991 to 2005 hosted the St. John's Maple Leafs. Over the years several Newfoundlanders have played in the NHL, including Stanley Cup winners Daniel Cleary (2008), a native of Harbour Grace, and Michael Ryder (2011), a native of Bonavista. Competition remains healthy at all levels of amateur and professional hockey, with both men and women involved (G. White; Thomas; Abbott; Poole vol. 5 "Sports").

one time there was a Methodist Guards, which was like the CLB). Some years, they won the championship. Feild and St. Bon's used to have their share. Of course, once St. Bon's got the rink, in the twenties, we didn't stand a chance. We were always handicapped because we didn't have the numbers — if we had 30 in Grade 11, St. Bon's had 60 or more; they always had two to one to pick from. The same with the Methodist College — they had far greater numbers than we did.

I played hockey at Memorial College. There were a number of commercial teams we played against: Bowring's and Harvey's and Royal Stores, Ayre & Sons. These teams were always looking for a team to play against, and also we went over to Harbour Grace, Carbonear, and Bell Island. The businesses had pretty good teams. They acted as a feeder for the club league. Some of the fellows, the better ones on Bowring's and so on, would make a place on the other regular league teams.

There were a number of good players. When I was a youngster going down to watch hockey, the outstanding Feildian player was Bert Tait.[3] He later became a Rhodes Scholar and captain of the Oxford team. He was a very fine, all-around athlete. He made a big name for himself during the war. Joined up as soon as the war started and came back and played hockey again after the war for a while. He and two of the teachers became very well known in the Newfoundland Regiment, outstanding officers.

There were some interesting players. Duke Winter, one of the

---

3   There is a glowing description of Bert Tait in a tiny book called *Newfoundland Hockey Guide (for the vest pocket)* by A.H. Thomas: "Height 5 ft. 5.5 in. [average player height was about 5'8"]; weight 160 lbs. His is a most brilliant record and one which will live for years. As a hockey player, born, bred and reared in this country, he has few, if any, equals. Being elected Rhodes Scholar in 1910, he left for Oxford" (19–21). There, as Edgar remembers, he played for the Oxford team and was captain in 1913, winning several European championships. After his stint in the Regiment, he returned to play with the Feildians, and was still doing so when the booklet was published in 1921.

Winters. Marmaduke, grandson I guess of Sir Marmaduke.[4] He was quite a player, a defenceman, and Randell, a good defenceman. Yes, there were several.

I played hockey with the school team, and then I started with the Old Feildians. I had to quit with the Old Feildians because by then I was wearing glasses. There was no way in those days that you could wear glasses and play hockey, so I had to give it up. The soccer ball I guess is so big that I could see it; it didn't affect me, really. I played without glasses.

When I was 14 or 15, at a practice down at the old rink, I was tripped and landed on my right ear, right on my head. I was out cold for a couple of minutes. When I came to, there was a bit of bleeding from the right ear and I was a bit stupid, but I wasn't too stupid to walk home myself. I wouldn't let the fellows come with me. I walked home on my own. The next morning, in the middle of the morning, I blacked out at school. I had to get in a dark room for two weeks following this concussion. I had a lovely cauliflower ear on my right side, and three or four days later, I developed mumps. They came out on the left side. The fellows would come in to visit me and they couldn't see me at first but when they got used to the semi-light and could see the shape I was in, they had a great time . . . laughing at me.

---

4   Sir Marmaduke Winter was a St. John's businessman and politician. Born in 1857, he started T. & M. Winter Co. (employer of Margie's father) in 1878, provision wholesalers for the seal and cod fisheries. He built Winterholme, one of the biggest mansions in the city (currently a bed and breakfast) in 1905, and in 1910 he was appointed to the Legislative Council. He started a hospital for veterans during World War I, and was knighted in 1923 (Poole vol. 5 "Winter").

Football [Soccer][5]

There was a football field down there at the old CLB camp in Topsail, which was immediately next to the beach. So every now and then, somebody would get hit or trip or something and finish up out on the beach. I was unfortunate — I got hit by a big fellow. Oh, he must have been 190 or 200 pounds I guess! He gave me the shoulder and I was only a youngster then. He let me have it anyhow, and I landed out on the beach. Of all places I landed right on my right elbow. Knocked a bone chip right off.

An officer in the CLB who lived in Manuels took me in the car and drove me down to the General Hospital to get my arm set. And all the way out — I was in terrific pain — he had a bag of walnuts in the shell and he'd take one of these walnuts and crack it and take the meat out and pass me the nuts. Then he'd take the shell and put it up on my shoulder here. He said, "Now, you're a second lieutenant." Another one he'd put up and he'd say, "Now, you're a first lieutenant." Finally, he had three on my shoulder. I was a captain then! It certainly distracted me somewhat from the arm.

---

5   In Newfoundland at the time, the term "football" was used to refer to what most North Americans now call "soccer." It only began to change after Confederation with Canada in 1949. Soccer and rugby, after its recent revival, are still the only organized forms of football played in Newfoundland and Labrador. Soccer arrived in Newfoundland in the mid-nineteenth century via English sailors, and, according to oral sources, the first league of six teams was formed in St. John's in 1898 (Carberry 2–3). The game became more formalized with the formation of the Newfoundland Soccer Association in 1950. The main hotbeds of soccer were, and still are, St. John's and the Burin Peninsula on the south coast. The French island of St. Pierre (just off the Burin Peninsula) also had a large influence on Newfoundland soccer, as teams travelled to and from the island for games and tournaments beginning in the 1880s. Results include Memorial University winning the national Intercollegiate title in 1970–71 and Holy Cross winning the 1988 Challenge Cup. Women began competing formally in 1976, with competition focused on the Corner Brook and St. John's leagues. Eventually women's competition spread province-wide and nationally, Newfoundland and Labrador fielding competitive teams in each Canada Games, and several women being selected for the national team (*Newfoundland Soccer* 1–8; "The Ten Best" 19).

We had two bone specialists here at the time — well, not specialists really, but they did work and they worked on it and couldn't do anything with it. One of the doctors later came down from Halifax and they got him to look at it. "Too late," he said, "the bone is grafted there now. I wouldn't dare break it and try to reset it." So I've been left with a crooked arm ever since. That's as far as I can straighten it [illustrates by trying to straighten his arm]. It didn't stop me from playing tennis or hockey or anything, though.

"The second half was quite lively."

There was no field for football in Trinity. The present field was a swamp, with all these humps. The only place to play was up on the side of Gun Hill.[6] You'd have to take a ball way up Gun Hill, and there was one flat spot up there. That's where you had to go to have your soccer practice. I remember it well because the night before a garden party at Trinity, we were up there and had a practice and the ball used to roll down over the hill and it would be a 10-minute rest until you got it.

There was a game we played against Catalina where I got badly kicked in the shin by a fisherman's boot. I was 14 I think at the time, but I could probably play soccer as well as anybody down there so they had me on the team. I was the youngster on the team. Oh, what a brutal kick I got! None of the fellows had football boots but they had heavy walking boots and that's what I got, oh, such a kick! The poor old doctor there felt tenderly all around it and he said, "I'm going to have to send you for an X-ray I think. I'm afraid that might be broken." Anyhow, he kept it up and finally he said, "No, I don't think it's broken. Just badly bruised." There was a big lump there. So it was a week I suppose before it went down. Very tender.

---

6   From a letter in the *Atlantic Guardian* by Richard Bugden, 1951: "The guns were part of the English defences of Trinity during the English–French wars, and rolled into the sea when the French captured the port at one time." They lay in the sea until he and some other young boys pulled them out and set them up again on Gun Hill, or Rider's Hill as it was also called (Bugden 9).

Trinity soccer team, c. 1925. Rear: Harvey Green (left) and Edgar and Peter Outerbridge (right); front: Bill Gent (second from right); others unidentified.

The next game was over at King's Cove. In King's Cove, Father Fitzgerald put up a tent so that we had a tent to change in. A very nice tent, too, but I was the youngster on the team; all the rest were men. Anyhow at halftime, Father Fitzgerald produced a bottle of Newfoundland rum and passed it in to the boys and they went around from mouth to mouth, you know. I didn't have any, for two reasons: I didn't want it, and my father was there at the time, watching. So the second half was quite lively. We had a series of four games, I think it was, two in Trinity and two in King's Cove. Good fun. Everybody in the place turned out.

When I was at school, they had under-15 football and rugby. The junior clubs at Feild were divided up into houses. It reflected the Boer War because the names of the houses were Boer War names, the Harts and the Butterflies and the Springboks. [Currently, in honour of Edgar, one of the houses at Bishop Feild School is called House House.]

With the Feildian club, I played left half at first, I guess, but then I found I could kick with both feet, and so I moved into centre half. I enjoyed playing centre half, the same as you did.[7] I remember all my teammates, I guess. The biggest was one of the Goldstones, the people that owned the London, New York and Paris store.[8] He played full-back. He went out to Vancouver eventually. I think I'm the only one of the team that's alive now. Jack Harnum became the Lieutenant-Governor.[9] He played in goal, a good goalie, too.

I played against Margie's brother, Gel Butt. He was a centre forward on the Guards for several years, and I was centre half on the Feildians. It was my job mainly to mark him and he was slippery. He was very good.

"I'll take it to the Minister, then."

The year 1929 was the first time that Memorial had their own jerseys. I was secretary of the Athletic Union, and so it was my job to order the jerseys, and being a Manchester United fan, I said, "That's the style we'll have." We'd have them with the colours of the Newfoundland Regiment, because we were Memorial College and their colours were maroon and white which are, you know, fairly nice colours for a jersey, similar to Manchester United, and so that's what I ordered. When they finally came in, it was my job to go down to the customs and try to get them through. They were going to charge the regular custom fees on them for clothing, and I said, "These are educational material. You can't do that."

---

7 When the Feildians won the St. John's senior soccer championship in 1961, the *Daily News* featured an article about the last Feildian team to win, in 1930, which pointed out that: "Edgar House played centre-half with the club that year and filling the same position with the 1961 champs was his son Doug." (B. Bennett "Like Father").

8 See Chapter 5, note 17 (p. 133).

9 Ewart John Arlington Harnum, lieutenant-governor of Newfoundland, 1969–1974, was born in Sound Island, Placentia Bay, in 1910. He attended Bishop Feild College and had a successful career in the insurance business, from which he retired in 1974. He was active in the community, including chairing the Canada Games for the Disabled and the Grand Lodge of Scotland. He died in 1996 (B. Bennett "Former Lieutenant").

"Nonsense, it's not educational material."

"I'll take it to the Minister, then," I said, which I did. Peter Cashin was Minister of Finance, so customs came under his care, and I spent nearly two hours with him trying to persuade him that this was educational material and therefore we shouldn't have to pay any customs duty on them.

We argued back and forth and he swore, oh, and he finally said, "Damn it, House, you're a tough customer!" He said, "Take your uniforms. I won't charge any customs duty on them. We'll regard them as necessary for the education of the students." His language was really something.

I said, "Will you give me a note to take to the customs people?"

He said, "Oh, yes!" He scribbled something, cleared it all.

We had spent every cent we had buying the uniforms. They would have had to stay there if we hadn't got them in.

I don't know how I got to be a Manchester United fan! I used to read some of the English papers and so on. I followed them closely, and old Foster the butcher, he knew the name of every player on every

Memorial soccer team, 1930; Edgar, back row (second from left)

team, I think. Yes, he was really very keen, and because he was a football referee here at St. George's Field in the local league, he got to know me. I was one of his meat customers. He'd keep me down there in the shop sometimes for an hour bringing me up to date on all the latest in English football. He had Scottish papers, English papers coming to him all the time. He was right down by the War Memorial on Duckworth Street.

I never played down on the Burin Peninsula myself,[10] but I remember going down there when I was working with the Lung Association and passing the field at St. Lawrence, which is on the way to the hospital. There were two teams playing there, young fellows 12 to 16 I suppose they were. They were playing really good football. No wrangling over offs or anything at all, no referee. I had to stop and watch them for a quarter of an hour, I suppose. I said to myself then, "St. Lawrence is going to have a championship team one of these days."

My first memories [of the Feildian Grounds] are of the "Tannery Field" and the Old Feildians coming in to play soccer in the evenings, and the CLB going down there on parade. Feildian Grounds was not ready for actual play until I was in Grade 11. Before that it was a swamp for the most part down at the east end. They had just enough dry ground up at the west end to have one field running east and west. It was called the "Tannery Field" because there was a prosperous tannery out by where the tennis club is now. It burned to the ground, and so that's the way the ground was when they managed to buy it, in the

---

10   The Burin Peninsula region of Newfoundland produced several fine teams and players over the years from small communities including Burin, Grand Bank, Marystown, and St. Lawrence. Edgar's son, Doug, played for the Feildian team that won the Challenge Cup (the provincial championship) in Grand Bank in 1964. Between 1967 and 1991, teams from this region won the Cup 14 times (Poole vol. 5 "Sports"; personal knowledge).

early twenties. There we played soccer and rugger for years. It was a very rough, crude ground but I grew up on the Tannery Field.

The Old Feildians, the Feildian Athletic Association, formed the Feildian Athletic Grounds Association, and working together they got enough money to buy the grounds. I think it was $4,000. In those days everybody who had a big business or a hospital was burning coal, so they got the bright idea of filling up the Feildian Grounds, the swamp there, with the ashes, dumped there by city trucks, from 1922 to 1924 or '25. I remember it very vividly. I would say that the field at the east end was raised by as much as four feet with ashes. When they felt they had it high enough, after adding some special French drains down in the east end, they topsoiled enough to make a double football field and have a cinder track going around it.

They felt there should be a fence around the grounds along Robinson's Hill [now Portugal Cove Road], and at that time schooners used to come up from Bonavista Bay with these pickets like they used in Bowring Park. My dad said the cheapest way we could put a fence along the grounds was to buy a boatload of these pickets, which he did. And so he and I and a bunch of the senior boys and a few of the teachers, the Old Feildians, built the first fence that went right from the corner of Bill Watson's house [at the corner of what is now Portugal Cove Road and Winter Place] right out to the bridge, to the tennis courts. That was there for years. Gradually, it rotted out, and so then we replaced it with a chain link.

"How many government grants did you have to help you do it all?"

Grants? We had no grants. We raised the money through donations, partly, and through the dances at the school. One thing and another. Eventually, we got the bowling alley going at the school, and it was the bowling alley that made the money to pay off the mortgage on the Grounds.

How short-minded it was of the directors at the time not to raise the money somehow to buy the other beautiful piece of property where Sir

Leonard Outerbridge built his house, all up Pringle Place there. Beautiful piece of property, along the river. They could have had the new school there instead of building a new school on Bond Street, right opposite a bakery and garage and so on. They could have had a beautiful school there with a boarding school. Dad could see the way things were going. He said, "Oh that crowd [the Bowrings and the Outerbridges who were responsible at the time for the board], if they only had any vision at all, they would have bought that other piece of property for the school."

"How about trying out for the Old Feildian soccer team?"

When the Feildian Grounds officially opened, the Old Feildians played the school team. It was 1929, my last year at Feild as a student. I recall the little dressing room we called after R.R. Wood, the old Principal who was very keen on soccer, very keen. He was a good soccer player and coached a lot of the teams. He had three boys and they all turned out to be good players, as well. They had a summer home over at Salmon Cove, and when they went over at the end of June, they didn't come back until the first of September. They spent their summer in their bare feet on the sand in Salmon Cove, and played soccer and all the rest of it in their bare feet. So when they came back, their feet were well toughened up.

We played the Old Feildians in the very first game. I was in my second year, Grade 11 again that year because my father said I was too young to go to Memorial. It was stupid — I wasted a year. So I went back for a second year in Grade 11 and when we played the Old Feildians in the opening game, I must have played fairly well because I was grabbed afterwards and they said, "You're finishing school now, how about trying out for the Old Feildian soccer team?" Which I did. I had a place on the team in the very first year, that very summer actually, in 1929. I guess I ended up playing with them for about 10 years.[11]

---

11   Edgar House was subsequently inducted into both the St. John's Soccer Hall of Fame and the Newfoundland and Labrador Soccer Hall of Fame, in 1999. Unfortunately, he had retired from the game before his children had the opportunity to see him play.

A big fuss about Sunday playing came up. We had to go to the Bishop, because of course we all wanted to play on Sundays. The Bishop was open-minded about it. He said, "Don't have them open during church time." Eleven o'clock to one o'clock. He said, "Before and after, go to it." That was old Bishop White. So that was exactly what happened.

I graduated from Dalhousie in 1933, and my father was already chair of the Grounds Committee for the Feildian Grounds. So as soon as I got home, he said, "Good, now you can take over." As far as I know I was on the Grounds Committee until the early eighties.

"It didn't matter how big they came; he had the knack, and he'd grab them around the knees."

Prince of Wales/Methodist College was the only other school besides Feild that played rugby. St. Bon's never did. St. Bon's Brothers for the most part came either from Ireland or New York. If they came from Ireland, they knew a bit of rugby, and soccer, but if they came from New York, they knew basketball. So when basketball started, St. Bon's had a great advantage. Rugby died out in the early thirties, sadly.[12] The Methodist College had an unfortunate accident in '30 or '31 in which a boy, an outport boy, received a head injury and never did recover properly. And so the directors of the College decided to cut out rugby. It's a pity because it was all because of a high tackle; and after

---

12   According to the Newfoundland Rugby Union's (NRU) website, formal rugby was reintroduced to Newfoundland in the early 1970s by Noel Browne. A *Telegram* article also attributes the resurgence to Mike Luke; together and with a small group they formed the NRU, and rugby began a steady growth in Newfoundland. By 1996 the Canadian men's national team had three Newfoundland players, and was coached by a Newfoundlander, Pat Parfrey. Parfrey is credited with being the driving force behind Newfoundland rugby. The Rock, Newfoundland's men's provincial team, won the national championship in 2005, 2006, 2008, and 2010 (Brown 10; "Newfoundland Flavour" 23; "History: Rugby"). The women's game has struggled in the province, though there have been some good results such as the under 20 team winning bronze at the 2010 Eastern Championship (Browne "Plenty" B4; "Under 20").

their team died out, Bishop Feild had nobody to play except the Old Feildians and a nondescript team made of Lewis Brookes and a bunch of fellows that had been to England to school. So eventually it died out at Bishop Feild, too. I always felt sorry about it because it was a good game. I enjoyed it very much. It's good to see it coming back.

Clyde Elworthy was one of the most prominent athletes that we ever had at Bishop Feild. I don't know where he came from, up north somewhere I think, but he turned into a wonderful soccer player and a marvellous rugby player. He was outstanding. You could always count on him for two or three tries in every game. On one occasion, though, he slipped. Down on the Feildian Grounds around 1929, he slipped close to the racetrack — went out, skidded, and somehow struck his head. When he got up he was concussed and didn't know which way he was playing. He didn't know if he was up or down. He managed to score a touchdown, but it was on his own team. There was nobody that could stop him! He went to work in New York, eventually.

Feild rugby team, 1929; Edgar, front row (right).

Albert Perlin was the editor of the *Evening Telegram* (currently called *The Telegram*) for quite a while. His brother Ted played fullback on the rugby team. Not a very heavy-set lad, but he was a deadly tackler. It didn't matter how big they came; he had the knack, and he'd grab them around the knees.

"It's a shame for that boy not to get a real chance."

Intercollegiate basketball started around 1928, I think. We were at a great disadvantage because St. Bon's had Christian Brothers who had been in New York, and they knew basketball. But we had an advantage that they didn't know anything about in that we had a boy, a very interesting case, who came from St. Anthony. His father was a mail carrier, taking mail from St. Anthony across the peninsula by dog team, and then coach. One of the nurses at St. Anthony hospital took a shine to this boy when he was about 12 or 13, and said, "It's a shame for that boy not to get a real chance." She asked the father if she could send him up to New York and get his education up there. She was one of the "WWOPs," they were called, Workers Without Pay, from the States, with Dr. Grenfell. So she sent him off to the mainland. He went to New York for a couple of years and then she felt that he should finish his education in Newfoundland. And so he finished up at Feild College, starting at Feild Hall,[13] and by this time he was a very accomplished basketball player.

He was tall. His hands were so big that he could hold the ball with one hand. When they started intercollegiate basketball in 1927, '28, he would notch up 40 or 50 points a game. The other schools couldn't get near him at all. Len Coates was his name.

He joined the Mounties when he left Feild, and when he retired from the Mounties in Baffin Bay, Baffin Island, he retired to the west coast of Newfoundland to do some farming over around Codroy Valley.

---

13   Feild Hall was the residence hall, located on Military Road, mainly for outport boys (with some exceptions, including Joe Smallwood), which operated from 1918 to 1933.

Unfortunately, towards the end of his life, the poor fellow became completely blind. Very sad. I went to see him once. He and Hal House[14] were good friends because they were both staying at Feild Hall together at one point. He was a real husky fellow.

"That was a big thrill for me."

My cousin, Claude Hall, played baseball with the B.I.S. [Benevolent Irish Society][15] when I was a boy, and I got interested in that as well, right after the war. The B.I.S. had a very good baseball team. They played up on what we called the Shamrock Field, opposite St. George's Court. If Claude was pitching, I was always taken to a baseball game to see cousin Claude play. In fact, his team, the Cubs, won the championship, I remember, the year after the war, in 1919. That was a big thrill for me, seven or eight years old, going up to see my cousin as pitcher of the Cubs baseball team. He was short, but he had long arms and he really could throw. He could throw the ball very well. He lived down on Mullock Street.

He was a character. His mother was my dad's sister, very, very different, and Claude was one of the best-known fellows around St. John's for three reasons: he sold insurance and did very well, he played baseball, and he played cards at the City Club and he was a real card shark! I'm sure he made a lot more money playing cards than he did with insurance sales.

Another cousin, Ed, from Corner Brook, became very good at baseball as well, but unfortunately was killed overseas in the Second World War. He lost his life in the air force over the North Sea. And his brother Hal was just studying, taking his papers to become an officer

---

14   Edgar's cousin.

15   Established in St. John's in 1806, the Benevolent Irish Society is Newfoundland's oldest charitable and social organization. Officially non-sectarian, the society was formed by Irish citizens who wished to alleviate the poverty they saw in the colony. The B.I.S. eventually started a school and an orphanage in the hopes of combating poverty with education. Social events such as dances and theatrical performances were also organized (Smallwood vol. 1 "Benevolent").

in the [Royal Newfoundland] Regiment, when their father died in Corner Brook. It was a big business so Hal had to have compassionate leave to come home and look after the business. He never forgave fate for it. All his buddies, some of them were Feild boys, became officers in the Regiment and he would have, too, but he didn't get the chance.

When the Americans were here during World War II, baseball made a big comeback, I must say. There was baseball way back in 1918 after World War I, but it didn't make a real comeback until the Americans came here at Pepperrell. Yes, it made a good comeback then on the old St. Pat's Field and then it died out again.

The first tennis courts were down at the east end of the grounds, and the famous Tommy Winter, who was a great loyalist, was determined he was going to have a red, white, and blue court. He got a lot of the old bricks torn down from the old school and had them pulverized, and made one court with the red brick. Next he got some almost white clay and made the second court, and then somehow or other he got hold of some blue clay. So he had the red, white, and blue courts! Bliss Murphy, Doug Pinsent, Herb Feder, and four or five others of us half-killed ourselves watering and rolling those courts trying to get

Riverdale Tennis Club, c. 1930s. Edgar, top row, far right.

them to settle down. The red one never did bind — the brick just didn't bind at all. The white one didn't bind either, so we finished up by having them all from that blue clay. Then, of course, we still had to water and roll, water and roll, water and roll. And that was the early Riverdale Tennis Club.

"I asked for $120,000 and we got it."[16]

I had a bit of a bug at one time about physical fitness, and I did a couple of radio broadcasts, and so Paul Johnson's father, Arthur Johnson, asked me if I'd be the Newfoundland representative on the new national Physical Fitness Council. I was delighted because it took me up to Ottawa two or three times a year and I got close to what was going on.

One thing I was able to do and improve upon was a recreation centre on Torbay Road. Art Johnson said, "Look, that Canadian Forces drill hall on Torbay Road — it's no longer used by them. It's being turned over to the government to do what we want with it." He said, "We're going to need a lot of money to repair the floor. You come in with me and have a look." So we went in. The building hadn't been heated for a couple of years, and the beautiful hardwood floor that covered the whole thing was buckled right up in the centre. The centre had swollen up, oh, it must have been three or four feet high with the dampness. He took one look and he said, "There's money available in Ottawa. You're going on up with the Physical Fitness Council, I want you to make a bid for $80,000 so that we can repair that and get it in working order."

I said, "Art, I'm going to do more than that."

He said, "What do you mean?"

I said, "I'm going to ask for $120,000. They can only cut me down to $80,000."

---

16   The Provincial Recreation Centre in Torbay was opened in 1967, acquired, as Edgar states, from the Canadian armed forces. For many years it operated as the training centre for top provincial athletes, and was also used by various sports groups such as the Newfoundland Table Tennis Association. It closed permanently in 2002 amid controversy due to lack of maintenance (Short C3; Miller).

He said, "You should be in the government!"

Anyhow, I asked for $120,000 and we got it. When we repaired the heating in there, got the furnace going, the floor went right down beautifully. It went right down in place. All we had to do was sand it and do the coating over it. And so the rest was money in the pocket that could be used for other things. They did a good job of getting that drill hall ready for use. It's been well used I think. Adrian Miller was the manager there for a long time.[17]

"If you want fun, that's a game where you get a lot of it."

If you want a lot of fun at a party of about 10 or 12 people and you have a large dining room table, the only equipment needed is a couple of little goals, and you can make those quite easily, and a bunch of straws and a ping pong ball. You all kneel down around the table, the two teams, centre the ball in the middle of the table and then everybody blows through the straw with the idea of getting control enough of the ball to be able to throw it down to the opponents' goal. I'll tell you, if you want fun, that's a game where you get a lot of it. Especially when you have a few drinks in of potent blueberry wine!

---

17   Adrian Miller was a star athlete originally from Bell Island. Moving to St. John's after high school in the 1950s, he became a standout competitor in track and field and hockey. He went on to a career in coaching and sports administration, and became the manager of recreation facilities for the provincial government, based out of the Provincial Recreation Centre. He retired in 1994, and lives in Logy Bay (B. Bennett "Flashback"; Miller).

7. Trinity: The Early Years

"Oh, there was lots to do!"

My first memory is not of Trinity, it's of Champneys, where my mother had a brother, Bill Day's grandfather, who had a big family. He kept, in addition to fishing, a little general store there, attached onto the house. Above the store were a couple of extra bedrooms, and so there was always lots of room for us. We always wanted to go down there.

We'd have three or four nights at Champneys West and we'd roam the place. We'd go out to Fox Isle picking blackberries, and we'd go cod jigging out in the Arm there. Oh, there was lots to do! I could get out in the boat and just paddle around the harbour and have a great time, and watch the men come in and gut their fish and put them out on the flakes to dry. The women would help do that part of it. It was quite a sight.

I admired these women because when the men were fishing, they had to build the kitchen gardens and tend them. They grew a lot of potatoes and turnips, carrots and beets — the usual things. Sometimes they'd have to make the hay. Cut the hay and make the hay. They had to do all that. They worked hard, these women.

They kept cattle — horses and cows. My mother's sister over in Champneys West always had a cow. When I think of the chances we took when the cows were being milked, going over with our little enamel mugs and holding them under the cows and getting our drink of milk, and a lot of tuberculosis going around at the time.[1] My mother's brother, in Champneys East, and her sister in Champneys

---

1   Bovine tuberculosis could be transferred to humans and cause human tuberculosis. This, however, was deemed to be a rare occurrence, as Edgar describes in his book on tuberculosis in Newfoundland (House *Light at Last* 152–54).

West were just about self-sufficient. They fished, so they had lots of fish for the winter. They grew vegetables, they had hens. I think all of our relatives, except for in Trinity, kept hens. They had cows and sheep and goats. I remember the goats down in English Harbour and drinking the goat's milk, which I hated. I was told it was good for me.

"There were lots of cousins."

I had cousins there, a little older than I was but not much — George Day, and John Day, who went out to Corner Brook later — Uncle Jack got a job for him with the papermaking. Oh, yes, there were lots of cousins, lots of people to play with and lots of room to play. We used to enjoy making hay. I used to die with hay fever, though. Didn't realize then what it was.

George Day is here now [in St. John's]. He's a first cousin, a little bit older. He came up to St. John's as a young man and got a job as an odd-job man down at Ayre & Sons, doing repairs and any carpentry work they wanted. It paid fairly well for those times. He was such a good carpenter that he built his own home down there off Higgins' Line, even though he wasn't married. Eventually he married a girl from Trinity Bay. He did very well and of course his son, Bill, whom you knew, did very well. He's Manager of Canada Trust in Ottawa. George goes to church, he goes to St. Thomas'. I never see him but anytime I do go, he's there.

There were quite a few sheep, all the way from Bonaventure down to English Harbour. I suppose every five or six homes had a loom and they made their own wool. They knitted sweaters and socks and so on. There weren't many horses, but there were dog teams. Down in English Harbour, people used to keep dogs under the stages there, where they were drying the fish. And they'd feed them the insides of the fish when they cleaned them.

Mother had her siblings in Champneys, and two first cousins down at English Harbour, Mark Wells and his sister. So we were welcome anytime we went to any one of the places. We were given a royal welcome. Mark was mother's first cousin, and Mid was his wife.

Mark had been in the American Navy during the war, the First World War. He happened to be up there working in New York at the time the war broke out, looking for work like half of English Harbour, on the Great Lakes. If they took all the English Harbour people off the Great Lakes, they'd have closed down the shipping industry there. I had a cousin, Mary Freeman from Champneys West, who was married to a captain of a boat on the Great Lakes. All of his crew, every man he had on his crew was from English Harbour. Anyhow, Mark decided to join the American Navy, and when he came back, he built a nice home for himself in English Harbour. He was a little bit ahead of his time — he got one of these wind generators and generated his own electricity. He was the first person down there with electric lights. He started a little store down on the beach and did very well really. I think he did all right, Uncle Mark. They didn't have any children, which was sad. Mid was a wonderful woman.

Later, we would visit them with you and Jan; we were always welcome there. She had a cellar under the kitchen and she used to take up this cover and go down a ladder and come up with raisin buns, already baked and just needed heating. They were cold, almost frozen.

"They tied my mother and myself into the bunks."

My first memory of Trinity itself is of going down there from St. John's the end of June, with my mother, on a schooner captained by my mother's brother, Uncle Ben Day. I was five. He was up to get supplies for the Labrador.[2] We struck the end of a tropical storm, off Baccalieu. Oh, it really was bad, very bad! They tied my mother and myself into the bunks so we couldn't roll around. They rode out the storm, but there was a big motorboat tied on at the stern, and the rope broke and that was the end of her. We never saw her afterwards. So that was my first experience going to Trinity. Finally, we got down to Champneys

---

2   As is common usage in coastal Newfoundland and Labrador, Edgar uses the term "down" to refer to travelling north (from St. John's to Trinity) and "up" to refer to travelling south (from Trinity to St. John's).

Arm where everything is nice and calm, and the storm was left raging outside. Dad came down later by train.

Another uncle was Captain Nehemiah Day, who became captain of one of the coastal boats. We had a trip or two with him, from here to Trinity, later on. It's a nice trip from here to Trinity. You get on the boat at 10 o'clock in the morning and get off at five o'clock in the afternoon, with one good meal in the middle of the day. The meals were good. I didn't always keep mine though. No, I was seasick. It wasn't the roll of the boat, it was the smell. The smells used to get me. But the food was excellent. We'd have roast beef sometimes, salt meat and jigg's dinner sometimes, a little pease pudding.[3] Very good! The meals on the coastal boats were so good that my dad and Edith took the Labrador trip. They joined the boat at Lewisporte and went down the coast of Labrador and then back to Lewisporte by train. They had a marvellous trip because they went through every little place on the Labrador coast.

Nine times out of 10 you went by boat, which was a very pleasant trip. Ten o'clock in the morning and five o'clock in the afternoon. The last time I went down by boat, we had a couple of naval ships escort us right across Conception Bay and Trinity Bay. It was wartime, and there had been subs around. Occasionally, the boat didn't go into Trinity; we had to go to Catalina and take a taxi back to Trinity, Dad and I.

I remember I had the first bicycle that ever went down to Trinity and that area I guess. It was nothing for me when I first got there to have 30 or 40 youngsters coming around to have a look at my bicycle. I used to ride from Trinity down to English Harbour — it's only 10 miles. I can remember one night arriving a little bit late. It was dark enough for me to put on the carbide light that I had on the front of the bicycle, and as I was going across the road, the Beach Road, there was something in the road ahead of me and I honked my horn. Well, there must have been 40

---

3   Jigg's dinner is a Newfoundland meal that consists of salt meat (beef), cabbage, and root vegetables all boiled in one large pot; pease pudding is made by placing split peas in a cloth pudding bag to boil with the rest.

Lower half of Trinity showing part of the Lester-Garland fish merchant premises; Court House (1903) and Parish Hall (1899) at middle, right. (Trinity Archives, WW-S01-P07)

or 50 dogs in front of the stages there and the noise of the horn started them off barking. Between that and the rattling of their chains, it frightened the daylights out of me! They used the dogs for pulling wood, in the wintertime. There are no woods around English Harbour and Champneys, so they had to go a distance to get their wood and sled it back.

"The last sailmaker in Trinity."

Father had a sister who was married to the last sailmaker in Trinity. He was an Irishman, Paddy Egan. A real old Irish name. He came from Ireland, and was a Roman Catholic of course. That was a terrible thing! [jokingly] It was almost entirely an Anglican, Church of England community and Dad's sister marries a Catholic Irishman. He was a good fellow, and a fine sailmaker, too, Uncle Patrick. He used to make the sails for Ryans and others. He had a loft in the old house down in the Cove, where the shipbuilding place is now. It was great watching him. I used to spend hours down there with him sewing up sails and putting the grommets in them.[4] A great man.

They had two daughters, one of whom was bright as a button and the other, she wasn't quite with it. She could, you know, look after herself and go to the post office and get the mail and all that sort of thing, but she wasn't bright enough to take a job. But the other one, Katie, was given her chance when Uncle Jack opened Goodyear and House in Corner Brook. He immediately sent for her to come out, and he gave her a job and she became his right hand, really, for quite a while there. The other sister died down there, died early. Sadly, he [Paddy Egan] died fairly early, too, only in his early sixties. My aunt was left badly off and my dad used to pay the rent on her house down there [which is now the Campbell House Bed and Breakfast] for years. Five dollars a month, I think it was. In the latter years we used to stay there. We had every right to stay there I guess; we were expected to.

Trinity cricket team, 1896. St. Paul's Church in background. (Trinity Archives, WW-S1-P136)

---

4   A "ring or wreath of rope" (*DNE*).

Dad and I used to stay there with them because it was a good centre for trouting.[5] We'd take the ferry from right alongside on the North West Arm, which would take you right up to the foot of the hill going up to Goose Cove. We'd take the early morning ferry, nine o'clock, get off at the foot of the hill, and walk from there up to Southwest Pond and do our fishing [trouting], and get back at half past five for the last ferry back to Trinity, usually with a nice basket of trout, sea trout and mud trout. If we were lucky, we'd have salmon sometimes. The magistrate in Trinity had a little overnight cabin up there by the pond, and my dad used to get to use that sometimes. We'd go up and stay for a few nights and get the sea trout as they were coming up. Great!

We'd give most of the trout away. It's no trouble to give them away in Trinity. Yes, the Greens would take some and the Batstones would take some and old man Jenkins down at the Inn would take some. Oh yes, it was no trouble to get rid of them. I'm afraid we didn't bother too much with the limit in those days. You know, we used to take so many. We'd keep on going until we filled our basket and then we'd quit.

"Mr. House, your hot water is there for your shave."

Jenkins ran the inn down by the main wharf. He ran a very nice little establishment there, almost like an old English small inn. My dad and I stayed there a couple of times and he'd be up in the morning at half past seven. He'd knock on the door and say, "Mr. House, your hot water is there for your shave." He'd bring up the big pitcher of hot water so that Dad could have his shave before he came down to breakfast. He always wore a little white steward jacket. He looked the part and he was the part.

---

5   Trout fishing. As Smallwood recollects, "We never did call it trout fishing, except when we wanted foreigners to know what we meant, for how could you expect aliens and strangers to know that trouting meant trout fishing?" (Smallwood 63).

My dad was an excellent carpenter, long before he came to St. John's.
He picked it all up from his father. His father helped to build the
church down in Trinity in 1895 — he would have been about 28. My
father was a boy then, and helped out.[6]

I don't know what Edith and the girls did, really. When she was a little
older, she had everybody in for afternoon tea. Everybody had one,
and so she'd get asked out, too. She went berry picking. She went
trouting occasionally.

The blacksmith was a going concern and a place to go on a rainy day
when you couldn't get out to play — you could go to the blacksmith's
shop and watch him turning out. It was Ada Green's[7] grandfather,
and then her father, great friends of our family. In the summertime,
Mother and Father would always be asked up to the Greens' for dinner, and I'd tag along. The old shop is still there. One of the things that
they show off at Trinity now is the blacksmith shop.

---

6   Edgar seems to be confused here. Construction on St. Paul's Anglican Church in
       Trinity began on 20 March 1892 and was completed on 13 November 1894. Edgar's
       father George was born in 1876, so would have been 16–18 during construction.
       George's father was born in 1841, and would have been 51 at the time, not 28 ("St.
       Paul's"; St. Paul's Anglican; *St. Paul's Anglican*).

7   Ada Green Nemec was born in Trinity in 1925, and received her library science
       degree from McGill in 1948. She worked in libraries around the world, from the
       United States to Norway to Australia, and was librarian at Memorial, 1955–1964.
       She went on to found the library at the newly formed College of Fisheries (later
       renamed the Fisheries and Marine Institute of Memorial University of Newfound-
       land) in St. John's. Upon her retirement she returned to Trinity and became in-
       volved with the Trinity Historical Society. ("Citations"; "Ada Nemec").

"He died as he lived, placing his faith in Cod." — The Ryans[8]

When I was a boy, Trinity was bright and breezy. Yes, there was a lot of life in Trinity in those days. There were two or three big stores there and they were all prosperous. Ryans' was a big business, because the three brothers were all working together: one from King's Cove [Daniel], one from Bonavista [James M.], and one from Trinity [Edmund]. Motorboats came from English Harbour, Champneys, Bonaventure, to Ryan Brothers' in Trinity to get their supplies. Even when I bought the cabin down in Trinity in the 1950s, that store was still going. They used to have their own fleet, at one time, and they were big merchants. They sent their ships all the way over to the Mediterranean.

They used to meet every Wednesday afternoon in the summertime to go trouting out on the King's Cove Road. The one from King's Cove would drive by horse and carriage, and they'd all meet at this pond. To this day, there's a picnic spot in there called Ryans' Kitchen, where they used to make their fire and have their boil-up,[9] and afterwards smoke their pipes. One was a king of King's Cove, one was a king of Bonavista, and one was a king of Trinity. They were three big merchants, working together at both importing and exporting. Irish, fine people!

---

8   The Ryan business was started by Michael Ryan, a native of Kilkenny, Ireland, who settled in Bonavista in 1828. He began a fisheries supply business, which was greatly expanded by his son James M. Ryan to become one of the largest in the country. Eventually, branch operations were set up in King's Cove (1880) and Trinity (1902) and run by James's brothers Daniel and Edmund, respectively. The main business was supplying the inshore fishery, but they also outfitted schooners for the Labrador. Around 1910 James M. and Daniel moved to St. John's where they built huge mansions on Rennie's Mill Road. James then spent four years as a member of the Legislative Council before his death in 1917, after which the business was taken over by his wife Katherine (née McCarthy) and brothers. Business slowly dwindled throughout the twentieth century until the death of James and Katherine's son Herbert Ryan, the firm's last director, in 1978 (Poole vol. 4 "Ryan, Daniel A.," "Ryan, Edmund," "Ryan, James M.," "Ryan, Michael"; Riggs "A Successful" A10; Candow).

9   "A brew of tea, sometimes with a snack, taken during a rest from work in the country or on a vessel" (*DNE*).

Ryan Bros. staff in front of store, Trinity, 1910. (Trinity Archives, LG S3 p14)

Eventually, the Bonavista Ryan died, and the two brothers ordered a tombstone from a marble works in St. John's, Skinner's, or
Muir's, decided on the wording for it, and had it made. It was taken
down by coastal boat to Bonavista, and then into the cemetery in the
rectory. The brothers decided to go and check on it and see if they'd
done the thing properly, and at the end of the tombstone they had the
inscription, "He died as he lived, placing his faith in God." But unfortunately they had slipped on it and it said "He died as he lived, placing
his faith in Cod!" C-O-D.

The brothers looked at it and hit the ceiling; they wired the firm here
in St. John's and said to "have a stonecutter come down no later than
tomorrow and make the change on the inscription or we will not pay the
bill!" At that time Doug Fraser had a sea plane down on Quidi Vidi, and
so the marble works engaged him, and he landed in Bonavista harbour,
with the stonecutter. They took him into the cemetery and he made the
cut and changed the "C" into a "G." They took him by boat to the plane
again and then back to St. John's. He was only there a few minutes.

Mrs. Ryan, Mrs. Ned Ryan, was an Ottenheimer, Gerry Ottenheimer's mother or grandmother.[10] She was a fine woman. She did more work down there than the doctor did. Yes, the fellows would get a fish hook through their finger, they wouldn't go to the doctor, they'd go to Mrs. Ryan. As soon as they arrived, she'd say, "Oh, you poor fellow. You must have a little drink of rum to help you get through the operation." So she'd pour out a good tot of rum and then they'd file the barb off the hook and pull it out. They used to say that they'd get so hard up for a drink sometimes that they'd put a hook through their finger in order to get up to Mrs. Ryan.

A Trinity captain was on board the ferry from Port aux Basques for a long time, Captain Taverner. He was lost when the ship went down in the *Caribou* disaster.[11] He was a schoolmate of my Uncle Jack's, and Jack used to describe how Taverner was always whittling boats during

10   Edgar is confused a bit here. Edmund Ryan was the Trinity Ryan, and his wife, who Edgar is referring to, was Nora Bourke before marriage. Gerry Ottenheimer's grandmother was actually the wife of the King's Cove Ryan, Daniel. Her name was Margaret, née McCarthy, Katherine's (James Ryan's wife) sister. They had one child, Marguerite, who married Frederick Ottenheimer, and they were Gerry's parents. Gerald Ryan (Gerry) Ottenheimer was born in St. John's in 1934, and began his political career in 1966 as a Progressive Conservative in the House of Assembly, becoming leader of the opposition. In 1972 he became Minister of Education under Premier Frank Moores, and held key positions under Premier Brian Peckford after 1979. In 1988 he was appointed to the Canadian Senate. He died in 1998 at age 63 (Candow; "Ottenheimer" 1).

11   Benjamin Taverner was born in Trinity in 1880, and went to sea at age 14 as a deckhand. He gradually worked his way up and by 1928 was the captain of the flagship S.S. *Caribou*, a ferry carrying passengers and cargo between Port aux Basques and North Sydney, Nova Scotia. On 14 October 1942, the ferry was attacked and sunk by a lone torpedo from a German submarine. Only 101 of the 238 passengers and crew survived; Captain Taverner went down with the ship along with his two sons. A monument to the victims of the attack was later erected in Port aux Basques (Smallwood vol. 3 "Caribou, S.S."; Poole vol. 5 "Taverner").

the class while the class was on at school. Always making boats. So it was only natural that he went to sea. His family lived out at Taverner's Point, which is just beyond where they have the Ryan House. That was the last house out there, I think, Taverner's.

When they had the fish cured, the men would put it in their boats, motorboats, and go up to Trinity and sell it to the Ryans or Morrises, Ryans mostly. It used to be all done on credit. I remember even in the late twenties when Bishop Abraham was here and had a summer place over at Portland, Bonavista Bay, and the boys would be given five, 10, or 20 cents to go to the store. The children there were amazed because they had never seen money before. Everything was done by credit.

There was a road, but it was just a carriage road. There was one car there, an old Ford that we used to call a Tin Lizzie, with a one-armed driver. He had only one arm and he had the car adapted so that he could use it in Trinity. He took everybody everywhere. He'd take my dad and myself down fishing in the early morning, down halfway between Trinity and Catalina, dump us off and come back again at dusk and pick us up. Dad paid him a few dollars. A taxi, if you will. It was the only car in Trinity, I guess, at that time.

Rupert Morris was three or four years younger than me, but he was all go. Anytime we had a baseball or a soccer ball and Hal and Ed House or a few of us were around, Rupert would be out with us. That's where he learned to kick a ball. He became so good that when he came up to Bishop Feild for his Grade 11, he immediately made a place on the team as fullback. And he was good, very good.

Rupert's father, Fred Morris, had a big business in Trinity. He bought and sold and shipped quite a lot of fish. I can even remember going into Morris's shed with Margie first when we went to Trinity and saying, "Get on there now and I'll weigh you." She just tipped the kettle of fish, 112 pounds.

Trouting

Fred Morris acted as a supplier for a lot of the fellows from Champneys and English Harbour and so on. I had one famous trip with him with

Kel Marshall, Dr. Kel. He took us up to Pope's Harbour and we went by boat to Bonaventure. It was the most beautiful day. Kel took a bottle of rum, and Fred Morris had a heart condition, so going up to the pond we had to stop every hundred yards to have a little nip. We had a great catch that day, though. A fellow George from Pope's Harbour had a boat on the big pond, which you had to walk in quite a distance to get to, and then you'd get on this old motorboat and go up the pond to get to where the good fish were. Going up the pond, this fellow said, "The old engine, she's giving me all kinds of trouble." And just as he said that, she sputtered out. He worked on it for half an hour, and we got going again. Then she sputtered out again so he threw it overboard! Right out in the middle of the lake. He was taking us in to this good pond, but you had to cross one big pond to get to the good one. It *was* a good one too, really good! So we rowed the rest of the way, and then in the evening, we rowed back with a wonderful catch of fish.

If you go up to the headwaters of Salmon Cove River, Champneys River, the headwaters of that, that was a great place to fish. It meant a long trek, oh, about three miles I guess over the bogs and through the paths to get there, but it was well worth it when you got there. The sea trout would get that far, as well as an occasional salmon. The sea trout, oh, they were great! An odd nice, big mud trout, too. We'd come out with our basket full from there.

I remember on one occasion we turned into a little grove of woods, and there in front of us was a small bog about 50 or 60 feet

Edgar, trouting near Trinity, 1930s.

square, I suppose. It was yellow with bakeapples. Oh, the beautiful bake-apples, and just at that soft stage for picking. So my dad said, "We can't let them stay there." So he whisked off his basket and flushed it out, and we strung our trout on a "gatter," as they called it, a little bough to string the trout on.[12] So we filled our basket with bakeapples. We came back with a beautiful catch of fish and a basket of bakeapples, which my aunt promptly cooked, and then we had fresh cream because they had a cow there. We ate like lords that evening!

Now, the trout don't seem to run like they did at all. It was only a few years ago that Jordy [Edgar's son-in-law, George Squires] and I went in and got nothing. I don't think it's overfished. When there was a lot of fishing going on, there was a lot of food for trout at the mouth of the river. I think that's what used to bring the trout in from the sea. They got in the habit of going on up. What killed the sea trout in Trouty Pond was establishing the mill; woodcutting took place in the mill up at the pond. And sawdust and all that. The river became polluted.

I started to go in to Long Pond [near English Harbour] when I was only five or six years old. As soon as I could walk that far. That was a sure place for small trout. They weren't big ones but there were lots of them there. Oh yes, you could put on two or three flies and you'd quite often get two or even three at a cast. One cast!

The Halfway House was an outstanding place. There was a house halfway between Trinity and Catalina; it was right by one of the ponds, and in those days of travelling by carriage and by foot, people stayed overnight there at this halfway house. There were two or three very good ponds right alongside. I went down with Uncle Jack and Hal House one year. We camped down there, and had a ball, the three of us. We didn't know what to do with the trout. We had to give them away. There was no such thing as stopping when you got a dozen fish; you'd keep on going. Some of those trout at the Halfway House were good trout, too, large local trout.

---

12   Gad: "A pliable branch, often forked, passed through the gills of a trout or the toes of a seal's 'flipper' for ease in carrying; the quantity of trout or flippers so carried" (*DNE*).

It was a strange thing that, you know. My dad and I would go down to Champneys and they really didn't have too much food in the house. Here was this river right alongside with all kinds of sea trout and good mud trout, native trout. In the spring of the year, it seemed to be a tradition, all around Newfoundland, really, you'd get out the old bamboo rod and go in and get a trout. But they didn't keep it up. My father and I would go down and come back with a basket, a mixed basket of sea trout and mud trout, and maybe a salmon, too. They'd be delighted! Eat panful after panful of it. They had the worms; they had the hooks; they could have easily gone in and done the same thing.

The Garden Party in the parish hall was always a big affair. It was the usual thing, you know, afternoon teas, lunches by the ladies. Then they had the usual tables, handcrafts and sewing and so on and games of chance and rowing matches, too. They had two flat-bottom boats that were identical, just about, so they used to have a little regatta off the cove there, behind the parish hall. I don't remember now how they chose the teams. I think they were fishermen teams. It would probably be the Ryans against all comers.

Seabirds were hunted quite a bit out there. I went out with Roy Batstone, my cousin, one time looking for seabirds. I had never shot anything. I had some rifle practice with the CLB, and at Bishop Feild we had a rifle range, but those were only little light rifles. This was a big blunderbuss of a thing that Roy Batstone took out this day and he didn't tell me anything about the recoil. The first time I shot the thing, I went over backwards, head over heels into the bottom of the boat. He got some. He was a real sniper. He had been at it for a number of years I guess. Turrs, I suppose, were the main ones he hunted.[13] I didn't like them at all.

---

13   Turr: "Atlantic Common Murre" (*DNE*).

Conditions varied a great deal. Some people seemed to cope very well, while others needed help. Those were desperately poor times — the "dirty thirties" as they were called, the early thirties. We were very happy to be able to send down barrels of used clothing every fall.

I can remember one time, coming downstairs at my Uncle Will's, where there were four or five children, some a little older and some a little younger than I was, and I was singing some sort of a happy song at the top of my voice. One of them said, "You must be happy this morning?"

I said, "Yes, I'm happy!" I said, "Aren't you happy?"

He said, "Yes."

I said, "Well, why aren't you singing?"

He said, "I don't know anything to sing except hymns."

I said, "You're kidding, are you?"

He said, "No, that's all the songs I know."

Oh, 'twas sad. They didn't know any games to play either except the one they used to play with sticks and stones. I can't remember what the name of it is now.[14] I thought that was sad when he said I don't know any songs to sing except hymns.

We had a first cousin, Mary Freeman from Champneys West, who became a teacher. She came up to St. John's and came to live with us. She lived with us down in Winter Place for two or three years. Taught at the Model School, and then, somehow or other, she had a connection in New York, went up there, and the next thing we heard she was a secretary to a lawyer up there. She finished up by marrying him, a very fine fellow he was.

They came down one summer for a holiday and went to Trinity. On the way there, they said, "A drink would be nice," and so they stopped at the Welcome Inn, I think it was called, on the way to Trinity.

---

14   Probably a form of "tiddly," defined in the *DNE* as: "A children's game in which a stick, balanced on a rock or over a hole, is hooked or flicked into the air and struck with another" (566).

It was a hot day. They went into the bar there and asked for a screw-driver. The barman went out to the kitchen and brought them in two or three different-sized screwdrivers. He thought they had trouble with the car. But then when they told him what they wanted, he was able to make it for them. Yes, she did all right. She married well.

When I was a youngster, some of the Ryans' schooners used to go to Labrador. My Uncle Ben in Champneys West, Mother's brother, he had his own schooner. He went to the Labrador. Whatever he earned, he was on commission. Of course, they built their own schooners, I remember it happening between 1920 and '30 but I can't remember anything after that.

Most people built their own houses, and they were well built. There were good carpenters everywhere down there. The houses were well built and comfortable — certainly in the summertime. The beds were too comfortable with their feather mattresses! They saved all the feathers they could from the ducks and geese.

There were exceptions; you take the big house of Captain Fowlow up on the hill at Trinity. He had that built. Good Trinity carpenters built that for him, and I'm sure the doctor's house and others were built. Captain Fowlow was a successful sea captain. He built the house up on the hill that the Godfreys used to call the Aunt Hill. The Fow-lows were Ros's aunts[15] so the house became the Aunt Hill House. There's a great view up there.

My grandfather's house was somewhere near the old Ericson's, Batstone's store,[16] not far from there. He's down as a planter. That's the way he's recorded in the old records, which means that he had a boat and a small crew of men. So he must have had some waterfront, some-where down near Ryans' I guess.

---

15   Ros Godfrey, née Morris. Stuart and Ros Godfrey were great friends of Edgar and Margie.

16   Large, well-known store in Trinity originally built and operated by the Ericson family and later bought and operated by the Batstone family.

There was very little coal around. Ryans' would bring in one shipment of coal, I guess, each year, and that had to do all the people all around everywhere. No, it was wood, wood, wood that people burned.

I had a close call one day on the trestle bridge, I remember. I was on the trestle walking, about halfway across the trestle. I don't know who was with me, Doug Hunt I think, from Trinity. He said, "Oh my God, there's a train coming. We better clear off as fast as we can." We had to run off and I guess I tripped up and rolled half over the bank.

Edgar (left), late teens.

Often, if it was a nice day, someone would say, "Let's go out to Admiral's Island!" That's the one that's in the mouth of the harbour. There were blackberries on it. Two or three of the fellows would get together and row out to Admiral's Island and strip off and suntan and pick blackberries and have a swim. I nearly finished my days out there, too. I was at the bow of the boat with the grapnel and the rope from the grapnel.[17] I was to be the first one ashore, was to jump ashore when I got close. As I jumped, the rope tangled and I went down in about 12 feet of water. Still holding on. Luckily the rope was tied and they dragged me

---

17 "Light anchor to moor small boats and fixed or stationary fishing gear" (*DNE*).

up. Two of them came down to the stern and got me up in a hurry. I must say I was gasping.

So then we'd strip off. It was a beautiful day. You'd strip off and spread out your clothes and pick berries until your clothes dried. Admiral's Island! It goes back to the days when the fishing admirals came from England. When the first admiral from England arrived in the harbour in Newfoundland, he became the admiral of the fleet.[18]

---

18 Specifically, he became the admiral of the fleet in that particular harbour for the season, and got the best fishing rooms. He was also expected to act as magistrate. The system was inadequate and was phased out with the appointment of Newfoundland's first governor in 1729 (Smallwood and Pitt "Admirals").

8. Trinity: The Later Years

I had been going all my life by schooner and mostly coastal boat and train, but when the road opened up, that was a bit of an expedition, to go by car. It was a dirt road. We used to overnight at Goobies at my cousin's place, Cabot Lodge, on the way. The roads were dusty, and there were lots of loose stones. You had to watch it for skidding. They were narrow, too, in parts. There used to be a hill you'd come to and you had to blow your horn in case somebody was coming the other way. Yes, there were some very blind hills on that road down around Plate Cove. The roads weren't too bad, though; they were pretty good. The nice part of it was that you used to go through all those little communities that carried the English names: Jamestown, Charleston, Princeton, King's Cove.

"Sing-song every night."

Margie and I stayed at the Trinity Cabins to begin with. Bliss Murphy and I opened the first cabin. Rupert Morris prepared a cabin especially for us. He rushed it to get the two of us in there. I guess that was in 1949. And then, with the Butlers, Brenda and Ches and the children, we'd spend a couple of weeks a summer in one of the cabins down in the lower field. Very happy times they were, too! We'd have a nice little bonfire out in the centre of the field every night and cook up one thing or another. We'd have crab, a lobster boil. Clarence Powell was one of the people that used to go down there. We had a grand time. We'd toast marshmallows, and everybody would sit around the fire and sing songs. If we were lucky, somebody would play the fiddle or violin. Sing-song every night!

In 1950, the year after the Cabins opened, the CLB camped down there. And because I knew Trinity so well, Earl Best, who was the commanding officer, asked me if I'd be the adjutant at the camp. I drove down that year in a new car. It belonged to Earl Best — he didn't want to drive down so he asked me if I'd take his new car and drive it for him. He came down by train and took over from there. I had a very pleasant drive in a new Chev.

And so I used to get up every morning, put on my uniform, and go to the camp. The space it occupied belonged to Uncle Jake House,[1] who had just moved down from Bonaventure. He gave the CLB permission to use the space for their tents and everything. His house was only partly built, a little bungalow, and so he gave them permission to use it as a cookhouse. So all the meals were cooked in Uncle Jake's house. I got up early every morning and went over and took the boys, about 200 of them, for P.T. [physical training] exercises.

The next year, 1951, and every summer after that we went as a family, Margie and the kids and I. Mrs. Mews, who was the owner of the property that I now have, came back from London where she was living with her daughter and I was lucky enough to locate her and ask her if she'd sell the cabin and property, which she did. I think she was glad to pass it on to somebody that she knew would take an interest in it, because the cabin was built as a honeymoon cabin for her husband and herself in 1914, the first year of the war.[2]

Ericson's store in Trinity was owned by a Norwegian who fell in love with a girl at Trinity. He finished up making his place of residence there and building up quite a big business. When you were a youngster that was a thriving store. They had homemade ice cream, and I can remember Jan having a great big cone and going up on Gun Hill and coming down and wanting to go in for another big cone. I remember that particularly. She was most insistent.

---

1   As in many Newfoundland outports, the term "Uncle" was used by people in the community as a distinction of respect. Everybody, including our family, knew Jacob House as "Uncle Jake." He became a good friend of the family.

2   The cabin, which was called Glen Avon, was nestled in the woods above Glen Cove, near what used to be the Trinity Junction railway station and is now the location of the Trinity Fire Station.

The cabin, "Glen Avon."

Jan, Doug, and Edgar, c. 1955.

One year I had a barrel of books [examination booklets] packed up — history, I guess it was. It was sent by schooner down to Trinity. I took them up to the cabin and Margie and you and Jan used to go off down to the beach and have a swim and leave me up marking papers.

"Come down. I've got something to show you."

The person who did most of the carpentry work on the Trinity Cabins was Uncle Jake, along with three or four other men. Uncle Jake did a lot of work on those cabins. He almost built the swimming pool himself. My dad had talked about him and that he was a distant cousin, and so I think I just went in and introduced myself one day, and we struck up an acquaintance. And then the next year I went down, he said, "Come down. I've got something to show you." He had this lovely little boat, 13 feet long. He said, "That's yours!" He built it during the year and he gave it to me. Of course he used it himself when I wasn't around, but I thought 'twas really something. His wife, Aunt Hattie,[3] said, "Jake used to disappear for a couple of hours every morning." She said, "I didn't know where he was. He was down in his shed down behind building a boat for you."

Jake came from Bonaventure, originally. I guess he wasn't doing much with the fish up there. He was a fisherman, and he thought he could better himself if he went down to Trinity. You did what you did. He became known as Uncle Jake to everybody. His wife, Aunt Hattie, had her Grade 10 and became a teacher. Yes, she used to go to Kerley's Harbour, which got resettled, used to hike out to it.[4] She taught Grade 10 there and walked there from Bonaventure as long as the weather was good, and then she had to board at Kerley's Harbour a

3   Over the years our family slipped imperceptibly from calling her "Mrs. House" into "Aunt Hattie."

4   Abandoned as part of the government's community centralization or resettlement program, Kerley's Harbour is now accessible by footpath and is a popular tourist destination.

couple of bad months [in the winter]. When he was a boy, Uncle Jake used to go off to the Labrador fishery on a schooner.

Doctor's Point [in Goose Cove near Trinity] is called Doctor's Point because an Englishman, a retired naval doctor, bought the land and built a house on it. And he was a golfer, an amateur golfer, so he built a little golf course on it, too. This was in the early fifties, I guess. He came up from the south coast, where he'd been with his wife, a lovely looking girl, a real gypsy type. They lived on this boat on the south coast and then the vacancy for a doctor at Trinity suddenly came up. And so they moved up, and for quite a little while they lived in this little schooner at Goose Cove. I visited them there once. One time I wanted to inquire about some fellow being in the San and had gone back down there so I went up to visit him.[5] He was just getting ready to go up to Bonaventure in a Jeep, which had been provided by the people of Trinity and Port Rexton. They chipped in and bought a Jeep for him so that he could make visits.

Uncle Jake House and Aunt Hattie.

---

5   The sanatorium for tuberculosis patients in St. John's was commonly referred to as "the San."

When I went up, he was just getting his breakfast. He came up from down below. Came up and took this loaf of bread and broke it in half and got himself a cup of tea, and then he just ate the bread, not buttered or anything. Just ate the half loaf of bread and a cup of tea. That was his breakfast. He stuck people down there for the piping and supplies he needed for his little golf course and accepted the Jeep, and shortly after that he up and went off to Bell Island, Jeep and all. They couldn't do anything about it. They'd given it to him.

The house is owned by an American now. He comes down every couple of years and fixes the little house up. You could probably buy it for a song if you got hold of him.[6]

There used to be a nice, gentle little hill there [opposite Edgar's cabin] covered with some vegetation, cherries and blueberries and partridge-berries, and then they started to blow it away to get ballast for the railway. I remember the fellows doing it. One time, Jan was playing out in the front and suddenly this fellow came over and grabbed her up. "Come on, little maid, we're going to blast.[7] You have to get in out of this!" We had to put shutters up to cover the windows. They did it to get some ballast for the railway, that was all. I hope they clean that spot up, topsoil it [they never did].

Ros Godfrey's family owned all that land just beyond Uncle Jake's, and so they decided to build a little cabin there. Peter [Stuart and Ros's son] owns the property now, I guess. He was down last year once, I think.[8] Ros came from Trinity, a Morris, Rupert's cousin. Stuart worked with the government, though he'd never been to university. His background was Grade 11. He was all set to go to Memorial and

---

6   The house on Doctor's Point was subsequently torn down and replaced with a new house by its American owner.

7   Maid: "a woman; a young unmarried girl or daughter; frequently as term of address" (*DNE*). Short for maiden.

8   Peter Godfrey died in Clarenville just before Christmas 2010.

go on for a degree, but his father died in the pulpit, preaching. He had a heart attack and was dead before they got him to hospital. Stuart was the oldest in the family so he had to get out and go to work. He worked up to the point where he was Deputy Minister of Welfare here. And, without a degree, he applied for the job in Ottawa as Director of Welfare, I guess, in the city of Ottawa, and, without a degree but because of his good record here, he made it. He had some sort of falling out with Smallwood. I don't know what it was all about. We had a very good friendship with the Godfreys in Trinity. Several years of visiting back and forth, exchanging coffee and drink.

There were some summers I didn't go because I went up marking papers three years in Nova Scotia in the thirties, mid-thirties. Then sometimes you get caught up teaching summer school and one thing or another, but there's not many summers I haven't been down there some time or other. I wasn't as fussy as my father, though. My father just couldn't live if he didn't get to Trinity at least once.

Edgar, Margie, and Stuart and Ros Godfrey in Glen Avon.

"The economy depends upon summer visitors now."

There used to be six cows and no radios. Then there were six radios and no cows. That was the change! Trinity went downhill, you know, from a very prosperous period when they had the whaling factory over on the south side and schooners going down to Labrador. The factory was on the way out to the lighthouse, in that little cove out there. We used to picnic there. Part of the old foundation is still there, you can still see one of the old gateways of the factory. If you go around to houses in Trinity, you'll find that lots of the homes there have whales' teeth and whales' bones.

The decline was sad in a way, but it became a summertime place, a different kind of a place. The economy depends upon summer visitors now. I think, in some ways, Trinity died, and in other ways it revived, because a number of the houses down there were bought by St. John's people and only used in July and August. There are no empty houses in Trinity now as far as I know. I think that since they started

Trinity whaling factory in Maggoty Cove. (Trinity Archives, THS-PC82)

Glen Cove, Trinity, view near cabin.

the Trinity Pageant,[9] Trinity has picked up, and it's a busy spot in the summer now. It works both ways: you feel sorry in a way but then you feel glad that so many more people are getting down to see the beauty of Trinity, because it's a beautiful spot. No place, I think, on the east coast matches it until you get down to Notre Dame Bay. I can't think of any view to match that one over there [points to a painting showing the three arms of Trinity harbour]. And Gun Hill. And Doctor's Point in Goose Cove.

9   Since 1993, Rising Tide Theatre has presented live theatre each summer in Trinity. The Trinity Pageant, which is a movable event in which the audience follows the actors to scenes at historic buildings and sites, is the centrepiece of the program each year.

9. Education

Feild and Spencer were the two so-called "colleges" [in the Anglican system].[1] They were colleges when they started because they had Grade 12 Senior Associate, so to some extent they were doing some college work. That was a trend in 1892, to have high school colleges that went a year beyond Grade 11.

---

1   Bishop Feild College was an all-boys school, established in 1844 as the Church of England Academy by Bishop Edward Feild. It was one of the most prestigious schools in the country, attracting (in its earlier history) mostly middle- to upper-class boys from St. John's and the sons of outport merchants who boarded at Feild Hall (though most of the elite left the island for the later years of their schooling). However, by 1891 enrolment had declined from 100 to just 27 students. The appointment that same year of W.W. Blackall as Headmaster changed this situation dramatically and enrolment increased as the curriculum and extracurricular activities were broadened. See Chapter 3, note 2 (p. 104). By 1908 there were over 200 students at the College, and a new building was built in 1928.
     Bishop Spencer College was the sister school to Feild, also founded by Bishop Feild, in 1845, for girls. It took boarders throughout its history. The school underwent several name and building changes in the nineteenth century, eventually being established at the rebuilt Synod Hall in 1894. By 1918 there were 200 pupils, and the school was moved, for the final time, to the British Hall on Bond Street. After Miss Cherrington's appointment in 1922, enrolment increased to 330 by 1930 and extracurricular activities, music, and sports were expanded. With the opening of Bishops College in 1959, the top grades of both Spencer and Feild were sent to the new school. Spencer closed in 1972, with Feild becoming co-educational at the elementary school level. Doug was a student at Bishop Feild College from K-10, Adrian at Bishop Feild School from K-6, and Edgar's great-granddaughters Kate and Erin Cadigan were recent students at the school, representing the fifth-generation descendants of George House at the school. Edgar wrote a book in 1987 on the school and its founder, *Edward Feild: The Man and His Legacy* (Smallwood and Pitt "Bishop Feild", "Bishop Spencer"; "Bishop Feild"; Scammell).

A lot of the outport merchants and doctors, magistrates and so on used to send their sons in as boarders at Bishop Feild. There used to be about 30 senior boys from the outports. Quite a few of them joined up with the CLB. They benefited by a bit of discipline and drill. Some of them did very well, too.

The other main colleges at the time were just St. Bon's — St. Bonaventure's — [Roman Catholic], and the Methodist College, that changed its name, in 1929 I guess it was, to Prince of Wales. When Margie went there, she went to the Methodist College, but then later she taught at Prince of Wales College.

"We'd better go down and meet Miss Steed this morning."

I can remember when I first went to school; indeed, because I remember Miss Steed, who was a very lovable kindergarten teacher, so much so that we used to go to meet her in the mornings. She lived on King's Bridge Road. We'd know when she was coming up past Government House, and we'd leave the school and go down to meet her. A couple of us would always carry her books if she had any. Miss Steed was a very well-liked person. I remember just before Christmas there was a snowstorm. I said to one of the boys in kindergarten, "We'd better go down and meet Miss Steed this morning." So we went down and somehow or other she came the other way because of the snow, I guess, so we missed her. We got back and we were late. We were both crying our heads off. I can remember that so plainly.

The relationship between Bishop Feild College and Bishop Spencer College, for all the time that I can remember — that is from 1917 right up until they closed — was a very good one. The Principals always worked well together and there was an exchange of classes: the senior boys at Feild went over to Spencer for French, and the senior girls from Spencer came over to use our laboratory at Feild for chemistry. They used our Assembly Hall after we got the new school for practices for their Speech Nights. Speech Nights were a very important part of

Pyramid squad, Bishop Feild College gymnasium.

the curriculum, almost, in those days, because the Spencer girls prepared dancing and drill and stuff like that, and the Feild boys had plays and pyramid squads[2] and choir.

It was called Speech Night because that's the way it finished up, with speeches, but it was a prize-giving night where the boys that did well during the year received prizes from the Governor — it was the Governor in those days, not the Lieutenant-Governor. And there was always a play or singing part of the program, and some music; it was a big night. It was held in the auditorium at Feild in my time, usually about a week before Christmas.

"They were always referred to as the BBC."

Dr. Blackall started a lot of things at Bishop Feild — he came out from England to be Principal. He and his brother, who was a bit musical, as was Blackall, together wrote the college song, and he chose the light blue of Cambridge and the dark blue of Oxford as the two school colours. He was a gruff old fellow but he had a lot of good points. He became the Secretary of Education later on. Blackall, Burke, and Curtis, they were the three superintendents of education, on religious

2   Similar to the cheerleading pyramids seen today.

grounds in those days, and they were always referred to as the BBC. We always had several teachers from England, especially the classics teacher, the French, English, and Latin language teachers, and science. Nearly all our science teachers came from England. Most were good, I think; a few hopeless ones.

We had one teacher, a good teacher, very interested in the boys. He used to pay for us to go swimming down at the old YMCA pool. I remember how shocked my mother was when I told her that he had decided we'd swim in the nude because he didn't think it was good to get the dye from the swimming trunks into the pool. So when I came home and told mother that, she was very doubtful as to whether I should go anymore.

"Not only that but I'll be down to watch you."

Spencer had a hardwood floor, very well finished, and it may have been our imagination but we used to think that it had a bit of give to it in comparison with the marble floor over at Feild. It was very pleasant to dance on, and so when we got to Grade 11 the girls at Spencer with Miss Cherrington asked if they could have a dance and ask the boys at Feild. This would have been 1927, '28. She concurred immediately, much to their surprise, I think.

None of us knew how to dance. We had a problem. We went to Mr. Wood, the Principal, and asked if we could have the gym for half an hour, after basketball practice, three afternoons a week. Frank Stirling, one of our group, Joan's brother, was a good dancer; his sister had taught him, "and he'll teach us enough about dancing so that we won't make complete fools of ourselves," we said.

So Mr. Wood grinned and he said, "Yes, by all means." He said, "Not only that but I'll be down to watch you."

So, after basketball, 15 or 20 sweaty individuals would choose their partners to the tune of a foxtrot or a waltz on a little machine that somebody brought along, and we would try to learn to dance. I can still feel, feel and smell, as I danced around with Geoff Carnell,[3] who was 200 pounds, I guess, to my 160, and Mr. Wood looking down on us and getting a great kick out of it all.

The dance was a great success, and from then on there were regular Spencer dances. Eventually, the Feild boys decided that they had to have one, so they asked Mr. Wood and he said, "Yes, by all means," so we returned the compliment. Then Feild took it up in earnest to earn money for the Grounds. They earned a lot of money, particularly during the war, and they were able to tear up the mortgage when it was over. There was also the London Players,[4] who rented the hall for four or five months, and had a different play every week. I don't know how they did it. One week they were there every morning practising for the next week.

I remember when we were collecting for the new school [opened in 1929 at the present site on Bond Street], the committee roped in the Grade 11 boys and gave them a list of names of people who had pledged to give 10, 15, 20 dollars for a month. So we used to have to

---

3   Son of Mayor Andrew Carnell, Geoffrey C. Carnell (1915–87) became the director of Carnell's Funeral Home (see Chapter 5, note 24 (p. 134)) after serving overseas in World War II. He went into municipal politics in 1957, serving four terms on St. John's City Council. His son, Geoffrey Jr., succeeded him in the business (Cuff "Carnell").

4   The London Theatre Company was established when a group of actors and other theatre professionals, mainly from London and headed by Leslie Yeo, booked Bishop Feild's theatre in 1951. Twenty-six productions were put on in as many weeks ranging from Shakespeare to Tennessee Williams to a locally written review, *Screech*. Attendance was high the first few years, and then declined, perhaps due to television. The company continued until 1957, having produced 107 plays in St. John's. John Holmes, former actor with the company, provides an engaging essay on the group in *Newfoundland Theatre Research* (1993).

go around to all these businessmen. I met Walter Monroe,[5] and I had
to go to Mr. Goodland and Mr. Gray of Gray & Goodland and Mr. Job
— I had about 10 names I think, and I had to go every month. The
nursing superintendent at the General Hospital was on my list. They
were a pretty good bunch, some fairly generous folks among them.

"When you were 10 years old, you could join up."

The [Anglican] Church was behind the CLB, and I suppose it was
about training and marching and discipline and so on, as well as
camping, sports, etc. It must have had some effect because when
World War I broke out, the first half a dozen officers who were com-
missioned in the Newfoundland Regiment had been officers in the
CLB. They were NCOs [non-commissioned officers], and did very

Church Lads' Brigade on parade. (Courtesy CLB Archives)

---

5   Walter Stanley Monroe (1871–1952) was a businessman who served as Prime
      Minister of Newfoundland from 1924 to 1928 in a climate of mounting financial
      difficulties. A controversial taxation policy, which included eliminating income
      tax, led several members of his party to join the opposition. Monroe resigned as
      Prime Minister before his party lost in the 1928 election, and thereafter returned
      to his business interests (Cuff "Monroe").

well. In fact, you've probably seen that picture at the end of World War I where the two officers are marching across at the head of a regiment into Germany to sort of take charge of things there for a while, right after the Armistice. The two people at the head of it were two ex-CLB officers, Colonel Bernard and Major Raleigh. Raleigh came back to Feild afterwards, after the war, and so did Bernard, actually, for a little while. Bernard came back and he was teaching French, languages. They were officers in the CLB for several years after the war was over. We had a good strong company.

"We ate like lords for 10 days."

The CLB dates back to the 1890s and we had the two companies at Feild, C Company, the Senior Company, and the Junior Training Corps. When you were 10 years old, you could join up, so that's when I joined. By that time, Tommy Ricketts was back from the war and living with us, so I had sort of an incentive to get into it all. I enjoyed my years. I went out to the CLB Camp in Topsail for two summers while I was, oh, 14 or 15 years old I suppose. Later on when I became an officer, I went out a couple of years until finally I was in charge of the camp one year out there. It was hard work for 10 days, believe me. Oh, about 200, 220 boys under canvas for 10 days. It was quite a job.

Dad [George House] stayed on with it after the war, and he went out to the CLB Camp as late as the early thirties in Topsail. He was in charge of the camp one year. Stuart Godfrey was in charge of the meals in the officers' quarters, and we ate well. We used to get all sorts of stuff donated to us from Harvey and Company and Bowring Brothers and Job's. Yes, we ate like lords for 10 days, a lot better than the boys did.

We had a professional cook and he had to cook for as many as 200, especially on the Sunday of the week they were out there. That was a big day. A lot of people came in from St. John's, nearby. I can remember one Sunday, I was about 14 or 15 I suppose, being on duty at the cookhouse when we had extra people. The cook made fish 'n brewis and I can remember him now putting in a sack of "hard tack," as we called it, to soak and he used a half quintal. Soaking fish, rendering out fatback pork to make scruncheons.[6] Oh, disgusting, and the temperature about 85 or 90.

Just about everybody in the CLB band were lads in the companies at some time or other. They might have been buglers, some of them, and then they'd have taken an interest in the band and gradually worked into it. They became quite an outstanding group. They used to come out to the camps on special days, sports day and Sunday, always. They entered into a competition one year, went out to Vancouver; they came second in that type of band.

"He attracted people to him."

John Lewis Paton was the first President of the university [Memorial University College at the time], which started in 1925, I think.[7] Shannie Duff's mother was in one of his first classes.[8] He had been High Master at Manchester Grammar School, and was very well known as an educator throughout England. He made a name for himself before he came here. Quite a man!

---

6   Quintal: "a hundredweight (112 pounds)." Hard-tack: "thick, oval-shaped coarse biscuit, baked without salt and kiln-dried; ship-biscuit." Scruncheons: "Bits of animal fat or fish liver, especially after its oil has been rendered out." Usually pork fat. Fish and brewis: "codfish cooked with hard tack or sea biscuit" (*DNE*).

7   John Lewis Paton (1863–1946) was born in Sheffield, England, and studied classics at Cambridge, where he placed first upon graduation in 1886. From 1903 to 1924 he was High Master of Manchester Grammar School, and during that time participated in many other educational activities, such as being President of the Teacher's Guild. In 1924 he made a lecture tour of Canada, and from 1925 to 1932 was President of Memorial University College in St. John's. He contributed several works of scholarship on education, and after his retirement from Memorial returned to England and taught again during World War II, as Edgar relates (Carew).

8   Shannie Duff has been extensively involved in community volunteer activities, and involved in municipal politics since being elected to Council in 1977. She was mayor, 1990–93, and elected to Council again in 1997. After serving as deputy mayor of St. John's starting in 2009, Duff retired from politics in May 2013 (Dwyer 12; "Shannie").

I could go on all day about Mr. Paton. I got to know him before I went to Memorial because John Lewis Paton, being the man that he was, as soon as he got here he went around and walked all over the place. He used to go down to the waterfront and talk to the men that were in on the schooners. They'd come in the spring of the year to get their supplies and then come in the fall of the year with their fish to sell. So for Mr. Paton, that was a must, to go down and talk to the fishermen. In talking to one of the captains of one of the schooners, he said, "There must be something that the Memorial College can do for you people. What is it that we can do?"

So the old sea captain said, "Courses in navigation. Some of our fellows want to learn navigation. Is it possible to get navigation courses at night?" The next thing, there was a knock on our door. I went out and here was John Lewis Paton at our house on Winter Place. He had been told — I think the secretary of the NTA [Newfoundland Teachers' Association] knew — that my dad had taught navigation at one time. When Dad was growing up in Trinity, there were enough sea-going captains in those days, deep-sea captains, so that in the wintertime, when they weren't busy, you could learn navigation from them. And he learnt enough to be able to teach it privately. And so the next thing, Dad was up at Memorial a couple of nights a week for the rest of the winter, teaching navigation courses. That was typical of J.L. Paton.

He was a great classical scholar and he attracted people to him. Every Saturday night, he used to have about eight of the Memorial pupils in for dinner. His sister, who wasn't married, was a good cook and enjoyed doing it, so in the course of the year everybody at Memorial, in those days, had been at Mr. Paton's for dinner at least one night. If there was a play on, he'd take us all to the play afterwards or to a good movie. He always made sure that we were paired off at the end of the night so the girls had a male escort to take them home. Either streetcar or walking in those days. I know a couple of nights I seemed to strike the girl that lived the furthest away from me.

There weren't very many students at that time. The first year

Margie and I were there in 1929, there were only 111 students, and about 15 teachers on the faculty. You could only do the first two years of university.

Margie was very, very fond of J.L. Paton. She was in his class — he used to teach Latin and I think he taught some history, too. He used to always refer to your mother as "Lady Margaret." That's what he'd call her. He visited everybody. He'd visit anybody that was on the staff or in the student body. If anybody was home sick, Mr. Paton was there, usually with a bag of grapes.

He lived up on Newtown Road, by the old Memorial campus on Parade Street. The first trees that were planted there were planted on a Saturday morning. Mr. Paton got hold of some trees, as there were none around. I got some tools and some of the fellows and I went up and helped. We planted trees up on the west side of the building there. That was stony ground! We needed a flag pole. We said it would be nice to have a big flag pole and somehow or other, the word got around and somebody donated a huge flag pole, imported. I know it was floating around up in the dockyard for awhile before we got it up in place and that was the first flag pole. I've wondered since what happened to it. It would have lasted a long, long while.

His religious upbringing was Congregationalist. It's a branch of Methodism, really, but that didn't prevent him from attending other churches. If there was a communion service at the Anglican Cathedral, he used to tell us at the assembly sometimes. "While you're here, attend your own church. Attend your churches." This was to the outport boys, you know. He always went along to the Anglican Cathedral, especially when there were communion services. He didn't take part in the communion service, in the actual going to the altar, but he attended. He set examples for all the rest of us.

There was a Congregationalist church here — as you cross over Queen's Road there now, going west on Rawlins Cross, that gaily painted building, which is now a condominium, used to be a church. It wasn't as gaily painted then in those days. There was a small congregation here of Congregationalists, including the well-known Calver family.

This is a bit of an aside, but when I went to King's University [in Halifax], a chapel was attached to the building, Gower Lodge, and one of my friends and I decided that we'd join the little choir that they had there. Every Sunday, we'd go to this service in the basement of the gymnasium. I remember the very first service I went to and the preacher was Reverend Stanley Walker, who was the President, actually, of King's University at the time — the University of King's College. When he had finished his sermon, I said, "It's so much like J.L. Paton, there must be a connection somewhere." I made inquiries and I found out that he was a pupil of Paton's when he was at Manchester Grammar School.

J.L. Paton came here in '25 and left in '34. I remember that well because we had an Old Memorial Association and I happened to be president that year. We wondered what in the name of goodness we could give him as a parting gift when he left. Ern Maunder was a great builder of model ships, so he built a model of one of our famous vessels and that was presented to him. Sometime later, I got a letter back from England to say that he had had it glazed. It was occupying a prominent place in his and his sister's home. I've often wondered what happened to it in the end. It would be nice to get it back and put it in the Paton corner over in the library.

When he was over 80 years old, after he'd gone back to England, there was a shortage of teachers during the war, and so he went back to teaching. Yes, this was '42, in England. Margie and I heard this. We were out in Buchans at the time. Of course, sugar was short in England; candies were unknown in England, I guess, the first years of the war. So we got a five-pound bag of Hershey Bells and wrapped them suitably and sent them off. The next letter we got back from Mr. Paton said, "They arrived. Very grateful. They arrived in plenty of time. I was able to distribute quite a few of them to the boys that I was teaching." Teaching at 82! He said there were so many of the English teachers in uniform that they had to call on anybody and everybody.

There was a book written on him, a little booklet.[9] I have it over here somewhere as a matter of fact. I wrote chapter four. His philosophy was, I guess, one of Christian living and the love of the outdoors. He loved the outdoors. He hiked a lot. He encouraged everybody, the outport fellows, especially, to get into something and take part in something, and we did. I think there was nobody at Memorial, when I was there, that was doing nothing. Everybody seemed to have something. He gave a great example there.

"We'll never get to sleep with all these saints and martyrs gazing at us."

Edgar (kneeling) and friends.

The day I graduated from Memorial, I went to Harbour Main on a bicycle on the way to [New] Perlican. My friend Arch Garland's family had come from Perlican, and they still had the old house down there. He decided that on the last day of classes the two of us would take our bicycles and take a trip down to Perlican to have a couple of weeks down there in their summer house, go trouting and so on. So we started off, and as I was working at the time on the playground, I didn't get off until five o'clock. We started out, and found out that there was no way

---

9   *J.L.P.: A Portrait of John Lewis Paton by his Friends.* Edgar wrote a contribution in the booklet. It is a moving tribute to a man who obviously had a huge influence on everyone he interacted with. Among other anecdotes Edgar mentions J.L. Paton's custom of visiting any student who was sick with a bunch of grapes, and once giving his greatcoat to a needy boy on a cold day.

we'd get to Perlican in one night. We got as far as Harbour Main and decided we'd have to look for an overnight place there, so we made some inquiries and found that this family sometimes took people in overnight for a dollar for bed and breakfast.

That suited us so there we went. When we went up to our bedroom that night, the room was lined with religious pictures. We said, "Look, we'll never get to sleep with all these saints and martyrs gazing as us." So we took them all off and turned them backwards. That's the way we left them, so the next morning we jumped on our bikes and took off as fast as we could before we were discovered!

"We had our own little colony there."

I guess about three-quarters of the students that left Memorial went to Halifax. I knew a few people there, including an old form teacher, Reverend Gardiner, who was the minister at St. Paul's Church. He was my form teacher when I was in primary grade. I went to King's in 1931, and I went with one of the Phillips family from here who had been at King's. He was a couple of years older than I was so he took me

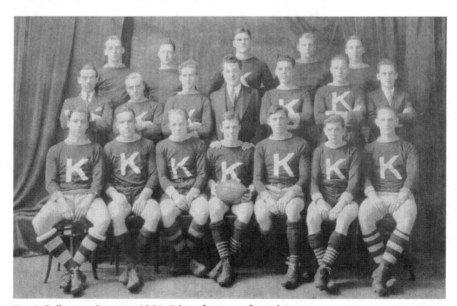

King's College rugby team, 1931; Edgar, front row (far right).

Dr. Elliott and his wife, with their daughter and grandchildren, and Edgar and Davey Tulk.

under his wing. King's was separate from Dal but they were closely associated. I took some courses at King's and some at Dal.

It was my first time out of Newfoundland. When we first got there King's wasn't ready so we had to stay down at the YMCA for a week while King's was being renovated. I stayed in residence for the first year, and the second year I stayed out with Dr. Elliott, an uncle of my roommate. My roommate was a Reverend Tulk's son from Portugal Cove, Davey Tulk, and we hit it off really well together.

There were nine of us that went from Memorial at that time, mostly to do engineering or medicine. We had our own little colony there. When Dalhousie started its first soccer team, there were 12 of us and 10 were Newfoundlanders, some quite good players from St. John's. We had a very good soccer team. The trouble was to find somebody to play.

I've got a picture of the team. Sir Richard Squires's son was one of

Dalhousie soccer team, 1932. Back row: W.E. Stirling (Physical Director), J. Malone, J. Gladwin, R. Cooke, G. Howell, F. Squire, A. Johnston; front row: R. Cousins-Hix, L. Petrie, C. Howse (Mgr.), E. House (Capt.), R. Squires, S. Parsons, R. Walton.

the players from here;[10] he was probably the weakest one on the team. We had a few very good players from Prince of Wales and Feild and St. Bon's that had gone to Dal. There was one fellow at Dal, Frank Squire, from Bell Island. He was a wrestler. He made his name for Newfoundland in the wrestling field.

---

10   Sir Richard Squires (1880–1940), one of the more notorious figures in Newfound-land political history, was Prime Minister of Newfoundland, 1919–23 and 1928–32. Born in Harbour Grace, he attended the Methodist College in St. John's before going on to Dalhousie University and graduating with a degree in law. He entered politics by way of Edward P. Morris, who ran the law firm Squires worked for, and his People's Party. Squires was first elected in 1909 in Trinity, and in 1919 won the leadership of the Liberal Party and the election to become Prime Minister. He was re-elected in 1923 but soon resigned under allegations of corruption. After pursu-ing his ambitions in other political spheres, he was re-elected again in 1928, and defeated in 1932 after a riot at the legislature that nearly saw him carried off by a mob. Squires went back to practising law and spending time on his farm until his death in 1940 (Poole vol. 5 "Squires").

Davey Tulk, Bill Collingwood, Jimmy Lahey, Edgar, Hal Taylor.

I started in medicine. Yes, I was pushed into it somewhat by my father and my sister, both of whom said whatever else you do, don't teach! It was so poorly paid. So they persuaded me to try medicine, but that wasn't my field. I switched after I failed a course in anatomy, I guess in my first year, by a few marks, though I did well in all the rest of it. I seized that as an opportunity to switch to something else. The professor wanted me to take a sub and carry on, but I felt otherwise.

I did end up with a Bachelor of Science degree, but that was accidental, because I started in medicine. I had enough subjects to spend another year and make up a degree in science, but actually in the last year, I didn't do any science; I did all arts. I did English and history, economics. That was the most enjoyable year I had, doing the subjects that I liked.

I took the first course in sociology that Dalhousie offered. The professor was going to New York that summer to do some sociological studies in the slums and wanted me to go along with him. I couldn't possibly do that, I thought, because I had a big job waiting on the playgrounds in St. John's and I had a place on the Feildians' soccer team. There was no way.

They used to have dances at the Lord Nelson Hotel in the afternoons, called *thé dansant* (dancing tea). They were for one hour, but usually lasted longer than that. They had a little three-piece orchestra, and any of the Dal and King's students who cared to could

Student days.

drop in. For 50 cents you could have an hour's dancing and a cup of coffee or a cup of tea or something. It was very pleasant, and a lot of people used to go — it was nothing to see 50 or 60 couples dancing there in the afternoon. You'd drop in on the way downtown or uptown. I met a couple of girls there that I took out afterwards. One was the daughter of one of the judges in the Supreme Court, sort of a stout girl. One evening, we were going to the V.G. [Victoria General] Hospital for a nurses' dance. I had to get a taxi to bring her there (I don't know where I got the money), but she was quite a stout girl, and when I opened the door for her to get in the car, the taxi man said, "That's all right, sir, I'll take it easy."

I said, "I'm in a hurry," as we wanted to get to the dance quickly.

The Furness Line, which Edgar took to Canada for university.

He said, "All right, but I'll take it easy over the bumps." He thought

Edgar, Margie, Davey Tulk. Woman on left unidentified.

Graduation; Edgar on left.

she was pregnant, because we were going to the hospital. She got a great kick out of it.

"Oh, they were good trips!"

We would travel from St. John's to Halifax by boat; you couldn't think of going any other way because it was too long by train. You'd get on the boat here in St. John's and you were in Halifax in 32 hours. Sometimes you went to St. Pierre, which was always a bonus because you'd pick up all the cigarettes you could manage for five cents a package. It was a Furness Withy ship; that was a big line with ships coming from England, Liverpool, and New York. They were busy because there were no planes until the mid-thirties. Oh, they were good trips! The

Basketball champions, 1936–37; Edgar, top left. (Courtesy Archdeacon Buckle Memorial Archive, Diocese of Eastern Newfoundland and Labrador)

meals were excellent, tops. I lost them on a number of occasions, though, as I wasn't a good sailor. The first time I was seasick, I wasn't out through the Narrows.

Margie went by train once, though; oh, she was beaten when she got to Mount Allison! The trouble there was you had to stop off at Clarenville overnight and wait for the branch train the next morning. You either got to a boarding house or you had to sit up in the station there all night, keeping the cockroaches company. Anyhow, that's the way she went on one occasion. I know because she had to take the train from here and a boat and then a train again and a branch train to get up to Mount Allison. Soon as she got there, she had to sit down and write an IQ test to see if they'd let her in. I guess she did all right. It was a long, tiresome trip.

The only other female student from Newfoundland I can think of at that time was her friend from Grand Bank, Jean Buffett; she got married in Corner Brook afterwards. And Grace Sparkes, who was a year or two ahead of us.[11] She was at Mount A. She's still going strong. Grace must be about 92, I guess. Her husband was Dr. Sparkes and he was one of the ones that used to play against you and your friends. You had a little bit of a league up there in the field behind the Old Colony Club when you were a youngster.[12]

---

11   See Chapter 2, note 13 (p. 96).

12   Dr. John Sparkes died in 1949 when Doug was only five years old, so Edgar's memory is likely incorrect here.

10. Teaching Career at Feild and Buchans

"Look, I need a teacher now, this September."

I was offered a job half an hour after I got home from Dal. Mr. Wood phoned me, and he said, "What are you doing? What are your plans?"

I said, "Well, I still recall the idea of taking teacher training."

He said, "Look, I need a teacher now, this September. Put off your teacher training. Come to Feild." So, rightly or wrongly, I went back that year and I stayed for two years and then in 1935 I did my teacher training. That was a smart thing to do because you got an increase in salary if you had your teacher training. And believe me, I needed it.

I had planned to go to the University of Toronto, but I got bad advice from my godfather, Mr. Samson. He said, "Why would you spend all that money to go to Toronto to take teacher training when we have a new man coming, the very last word in teacher training, to Memorial? We're starting a new curriculum in nearly all the subjects. He'll be introducing this new curriculum and it'll be a great chance for you to get right in on the ground floor." So very foolishly, I stayed back with this Lloyd Shaw, it was, first. Lloyd Shaw was not too bad but he didn't stay very long. The other fellow, Mr. Powell, was an absolute flop. The training got me a considerable increase in salary, but he was a hopeless teacher.

So I wasted a lot of time that year. The only thing that saved me was Mr. Wood coming to me and saying, "Look, I haven't been able to get anybody to do the games. Do you think you could manage to put some time in coaching hockey and soccer and so on?"

I said, "Sure, Mr. Wood, yes."

He said, "I'll pay you for it, you know."

I said, "That'll be very nice."

So I spent a lot of time after four o'clock in the afternoon at Bishop Feild. I also stayed with the CLB one afternoon a week. You had to pay for your teacher training, but it was, oh, practically nothing! I stayed with my mother. She almost insisted that while I was at the university I wouldn't pay any board, but I insisted. I gave her the grand amount of 40 dollars a month, I think it was. I thought 'twas fair at that time. I stayed there until I got married in '39.

The year that I was doing teacher training, I used to take seven or eight hours a week to go to the Model School to do some teaching in addition to the teacher training. The Model School was at the foot of Garrison Hill. It's the Cathedral Parish Hall now, but it was an elementary school at one time. There was another elementary school by St. Thomas' Church, one on Springdale Street, another one over at St. Mary's, and a Model School. They'd all feed pupils into Feild and Spencer. As they got up to Grade 7 — 7 or 8 — they'd come to Feild and Spencer.

I had filled in once at the Model School when Edith [his sister] was sick. She taught at Spencer, and Mildred Samson, our next-door neighbour, taught at the Model School. Edith became ill with erysipelas and all her hair dropped out as a result of a high temperature or something. And so Mildred Samson was moved from the Model School at Synod Hall over to Spencer and she didn't go back.

There was quite a little tower on that building and when it gave trouble, 1938, '39, they took it down, and I got enough bricks from it to make the chimneys for my house. These chimneys here are historical. I just knocked the cement off them and trimmed them off. (I didn't do what my father did, though, making his own bricks.)

"We had a grand time on weekends going around Nova Scotia."

In 1933, '34 or so, we used to go up to King's school residence in Windsor, Nova Scotia, take that over and mark our papers in the classrooms. We had what they used to call a common exam board — all the papers from Newfoundland and Nova Scotia were marked up in this central location. Before that, all the Newfoundland examinations were sent to England to be marked.[1] In marking the papers, we discovered one little school down in North Sydney where apparently the supervisor of the exams used to leave the exam and go to the next room and have a drinking party for Bob and himself, and the youngsters cheated right, left, and centre. They were word for word in some cases, and one of the stupid youngsters put down, "See diagram on page so and so." This was a dead giveaway.

There were a few of us from Newfoundland that used to go. Allan Fraser used to go up, and he was what they called Chief Reader, in charge of a group of history markers.[2] It was a pleasant four or five weeks because we were free at five o'clock in the afternoon and would make up a softball team, play tennis, that sort of thing. Altogether I guess there were as many as 50 of us from Nova Scotia and Newfoundland.

One year, Herb Cramm from Prince of Wales had a car and the four of us went up in his car: he and his girlfriend and Margie and I. We had a grand time on weekends going around Nova Scotia. They found a lovely boarding house in town there, in Windsor, very cheap, with a very burdened-down cherry tree. The cherries were just ripe so your mother and her friend were able to fill a whole basket. Delicious!

"As far as I'm concerned, the cane went out in the last century."

The discipline was quite strict in those days. Dr. Blackall [Headmaster, 1891–1908] used a strap, but he didn't have to use it too often. Mr.

---

1   See Chapter 3, note 1 (p. 103).

2   Allan MacPherson Fraser was born in Inverness, Scotland, 9 July 1906. Educated at the University of Edinburgh and Columbia University, New York, he was professor of history at Memorial University, 1928–53. From 1953 to 1957 he was member of Parliament for St. John's East, and he was radio commentator on international affairs for 30 years. He was also a champion tennis player; he was open singles champion of the North of Scotland in 1930, 1931, and 1933, and of Newfoundland in 1935 and 1936. He died in 1969 ("Distinguished"; "Fraser, Allan").

Wood [Headmaster, 1908–36] used a jam spoon, a wooden jam spoon. Mr. Hogg at Methodist College/Prince of Wales used a leather strap. Brother Strapp at St. Bon's used a leather strap. Mr. Wood used the wooden spoon so often he used to crack them off. In my years as Prefect, in Grade 11, one of my jobs was to go down to Martin Royal Stores on Water Street and buy a half dozen wooden spoons at a time because Mr. Wood used to crack them off every now and then. They would strap you on the hands, right in the middle of your palm. It would sting like the devil for, you know, a quarter of an hour or so but after that it would go away. "Oh," Mr. Wood said, "I'll never use a cane." And then Mr. Tanner [Headmaster, 1936–44], an Englishman, when he arrived in Newfoundland, succeeding Mr. Wood, introduced a cane.

That was 1936, I was on the staff. The first day that he wanted to use the cane, he invited me to come in and witness it. He said, "I always want to have a witness." He said, "I'm going to cane one of the boys for a misdemeanour."

I said, "Mr. Tanner, as far as I'm concerned, the cane went out in the last century. We don't use a cane in this country."

"Oh," he said, "I'll get somebody else." But he reported me to the Board for insubordination and the Board upheld me. That was the end of the cane. That was the last caning. The first and last.

"There was no end to activities in Buchans."

I started teaching at Feild in '33, and then I went to Buchans in 1941 for three years as Principal of the school there, which gave me the chance to go from a salary of $3,300 to one of $5,000, with a seven-room apartment and rent of $30 a month; I rented out my own house in St. John's for $45 a month. I made a few dollars on it — rented it to my best friend, Chancey Currie. Buchans was one of the bigger amalgamated schools [i.e., an amalgamation of all the Protestant denominations] around the island. I said, "This is a good chance for me to get some experience." It was a mixed school, of course, boys and girls. I've never regretted going. I think Margie was excited about it. The staff of

Buchans, 1940s. (From Red Indian Lake Development Association, *Khaki Dodgers: The History of Mining and the People of the Buchans Area* (Grand Falls–Windsor: Printed by Robinson Blackmore [n.d., 1993?])

Buchans Mining Company were highly paid people, and we were sort of accepted as members. We had a staff dance every Saturday night out there.

I guess there were about five or six hundred people in Buchans at the time.[3] The school was about eight rooms, and we had 12 teachers. Rather strangely, the Principal before me was Carl Howse, Claude Howse's brother. So we had a House coming after a Howse! I knew him well because we had marked papers together in Nova Scotia. Carl and I lived together at the Principal's house up in King's Collegiate. It was very good training for me, set the stage for my years at Bishop Feild.

---

3   See the discussion of Buchans in the General Introduction. Books on the town of Buchans and the Buchans mine include *The Buchans Miners* by Gary Cranford (1997), *Khaki Dodgers* by Ed Hamilton (1992), and *Riches of the Earth* by Derek Yetman (1986).

We made a number of good friends, nearly all of whom are dead now. In fact, there's only one here now, one of the mining engineers living here. I've forgotten his name now. We had some very good friends out there though, including Bill Dawe and Olive Dawe, who was Olive Field, a graduate of Memorial.[4] When I was first President of the first old Memorial's Association, she was my secretary. She married a chap from Buchans and we became very good friends out there. Bill was an accountant with the Buchans Mining Company. They're still alive and still go down to Florida all the winter, and spend the rest of the year in Nova Scotia, up the Valley.

The Bartletts were very good friends. He was the manager of Royal Stores in Buchans, which was quite a store during the war, because he saw the war coming and laid in all kinds of supplies in anticipation. It was so well stocked that the owner of Royal Stores, Campbell McPherson, when he came out to visit, would go to the store and lay out a lot of goods to bring back to St. John's with him, goods that weren't available here, for example, sugar, which was in short supply. In Buchans you could buy a sack of sugar any time. Flo, his wife, as far as I know is alive over in Harbour Grace, I think.

There was no end to activities in Buchans. Buchans has the best weather in the country [i.e., Newfoundland], I think. Never fog — no fog at all! A lot of sunshine and very cold in the winter, very hot in the summer, and no, the flies weren't bad. I don't know if the company sprayed or what but the flies weren't bad at all, unless you went out in the country. There was very good trout fishing within a few miles; the cross-country skiing was superb. On Saturdays, we'd put on our skis and take a tow rope and attach it to the tractors that were going off into the country to bring back logs of birch as pit props for the mine. The Dawes and the Bartletts and ourselves, just the three couples

4   There are two interview quotations from Olive Field Dawe in Malcolm MacLeod's 1990 book, *A Bridge Built Halfway*, a history of Memorial College. It appears she was a student in 1927. Both William and Olive are listed in the 1945 Buchans census as being 37; she was born in St. John's and he was born in Port de Grave. They both died in 2001.

Edgar, cross-country skiing, Buchans.

Margie, cross-country skiing, Buchans.

would go. So on a beautiful day, like today, actually — this is a real Buchans day, nice and bright and sunny — on a day like today, we'd hitch on to the tractors and get pulled 10 miles out in the country somewhere, out to where it was lovely skiing in the woods, where we'd be protected from the wind and the sun pouring down. And we'd go on up to a nice little clearing and have a rasher of caribou or moose, preferably caribou but not always; and then in the late afternoon when the last load was going back, we'd hitch on again and get towed back to Buchans, completely tired out, just able to stand.

The skiing in Buchans was mostly cross-country, fantastically good cross-country skiing, but the company there built a downhill ski run. They took the slag from the mill, piled it up tonne after tonne and finally they had a fairly high ski run, a couple of hundred feet high. You used your cross-country skis — I don't think anybody had two sets of skis. However, I had a special pair of Norwegian racing skis. On Winter Place there was a man named Harrsant, who was a Norwegian who came here and became a pharmacist. He lived just on the foot of the hill here. When he was leaving, I bought his Norwegian racing skis for five dollars. There were no houses down there, and so we used to go up on the hill, Robinson's Hill, and ski down toward the Feildian Grounds.

"Some vicious games!"

We played bridge with three or four different couples, including the manager and his wife. They were American. Socially it was sort of divided into three groups out there: the mines, the mill, and the mechanics. Together, they made a three-cornered hockey league. They took one of the big ore sheds and made a rink in it. It was quite a good-sized rink, too, with natural ice, of course, and we had a very good hockey league going there. Unfortunately, I made the mistake of saying that I had played hockey in St. John's and I'd done some refereeing in the school games and so on, so I got roped in as one of the referees. There was a mine captain, as well, who had played hockey at St. Bon's, and so we both became referees. They were a good bunch. Some vicious games! Sub-zero temperatures on the ice. The good thing was that, you know, most of these fellows had children at the school, so they couldn't be too hard on me.

Buchans Public School hockey team, with Edgar as coach.

One of the outstanding players was an Old Feildian, Ralph Collier. Ralph worked in the office, and finished up as the manager of Buchans mining town, and when he came back to St. John's he became the manager of Prince of Wales Arena [now Capital Hyundai Arena] when it was built.

There was a Catholic school, which wasn't very big, and the hockey players they had at the Catholic School were included with ours to make up a team. We played against Grand Falls. They'd come up to visit us and we'd go down to visit them, on the ore train.

"Buchans had more money flowing around than any other town in the country."

The miners lived just on the fringe of the town. They had their quarters and their dining room. I must say that for the most part, they were a very well-behaved bunch, mainly from fishing and logging backgrounds. Mining was straight money and good money in those war years. Buchans ore was very much in demand in wartime: lead, zinc, and copper and a little gold mixed in. They had some sort of a separator, where the metals were separated by water, the heavier gold going outside to be picked up. During the war years, Buchans had more money flowing around than any other town in the country. There was no road, so you had to travel by ore train. The ore train went right down through Botwood. It was no trouble to get a lift down and back at no cost.

There was a big staff house for the mining company — a lot of the men were single — a big bunkhouse and a big dining hall, which we used to get occasionally so I could show movies. I used to get movies in from St. John's, educational mostly. I remember one particular one done by a famous American sportsman, Lee Wulff, on fishing and the outdoors. I showed it down at the dining hall and we charged 50 cents each, which brought in quite a lot of money. Ignorant at the time as we were about the effects of smoking, we turned it all into cigarettes and sent it to the Buchans boys overseas. As a matter of fact a lot of them didn't smoke, but they used to exchange them for silk stockings to send home to their girlfriends, all that sort of thing.

Margie (third from right, top) and Edgar (front left) with friends, Buchans winter.

We had a fairly big apartment there and we entertained, and Margie got in with a bunch of card players. She played cards quite often in the afternoons, and then of course you came along [were born]. She had no dull moments after that! She had some good friends out there. We had a good social life there, quite a few dances. It was a great outdoor life and there were very good tennis courts. A few people there played fairly well too.

We really enjoyed our years in Buchans, very much so. Oh yes! We had all the amenities that they could give us. A dance every Saturday night at the staff house. Oh, they were very good to us. One of the managers of Royal Stores there was the chairman of the school board, and we got on very well. He was a man by the name of Courage. He had about five children at the school so he was interested. Buchans was one of the top schools in the country at the time; the company put a lot of money into it. When I was appointed, there was no office in the school. But when I went out from St. John's by the time I went to the school, there was an office. They had to build it on top of the school, and they put all the company carpenters up there. I had a lovely little office right up above the senior school and it was high enough for me to be able to look way, way down to Red Indian Lake.

The school was just two wooden buildings, eight classrooms; all hardwood floors and well built. The desks were made for the most part by the carpenter shops, made of local birch. Lovely job, too. They were all well-qualified teachers I had. The school went right up to Grade 11, but there were only six in Grade 11, I think, and so it was a little different teaching in the top grade, because you had to have them mixed in with the Grade 10s.

The wages were so high out there at the time that most of the boys, by the time they got to Grade 10, had had enough and went to work with the company. They used to have, at that time, war saving stamps to raise money for the troops overseas. I think Buchans had the highest per capita war stamps of any school around.

Walter Milley, Buchans postmaster, and employee. (Courtesy the Milley family)

Joe Smallwood as "The Barrelman." (Courtesy Memorial University of Newfoundland Archives)

Walter Milley was the postmaster.[5] Yeah, I knew him very well. I'd go up for mail at six o'clock, when the train had just come in. I'd go up to the post office and if the mail hadn't been sorted, Walter was working on it and he would say, "Why don't you go out and sit with Beulah and listen to the radio or talk to her while you're waiting," which I would. But at seven o'clock in the evening everything had to stop because if Joe Smallwood (Beulah's brother-in-law)[6] was around, everybody had to listen to Joe Smallwood and his *Barrelman* program.[7] If he was visiting Buchans, everything

---

5   Over 50 years later, Walter Milley's grandson, Cory, would marry Edgar and Margie's granddaughter, Vanessa.

6   Beulah's sister was Clara Smallwood (née Oates), born in Carbonear in 1901. Clara was a gifted singer and pianist, and while visiting Corner Brook in 1925 met Joseph Smallwood. They married later the same year. Never a prominent public figure, Clara died in 1994 at the age of 94 (Riggs "A Woman").

7   Airing on the Broadcasting Corporation of Newfoundland (BCN) beginning in 1937, the 15-minute show consisted of "The Barrelman" (Smallwood, until 1943) telling anecdotes and tales illustrating the culture and positive attributes of the Newfoundland people in a historical context. Michael Harrington took over hosting the show when Smallwood departed, and the show ended when he left in 1955. The program made Smallwood a household name throughout Newfoundland ("Barrelman"). For a good overview of broadcasting in Newfoundland in the decade before Confederation, see Jeff A. Webb, *The Voice of Newfoundland*, 2008.

had to stop so that he could listen to himself. He never missed it! He [Smallwood] told stories of Newfoundland history. He always came up with something and he always listened to himself.

The first moose I ever saw was up in the tennis courts. I told the youngsters at the school, "I've never seen a moose."

They came to me one day all excited: "Mr. House, there's a moose up in the tennis courts. The gate blew to on him and he's stuck in the tennis courts. If you want to see him, come on!" So there I saw my first moose. We opened the gates and the youngsters drove him out of Buchans.

"I couldn't eat a bite."

Ern Bartlett was manager of Royal Stores [in Buchans] and a great friend. He was an officer in the CLB and he'd been to camp out at Topsail CLB Camp. So we became great friends, and one day he said, "Let's go off and see if we can shoot a rabbit." Rabbits had come down from the hills, and there'd been a few showers of snow, enough for them to turn white. They were perfectly white — they were hares, really, Arctic hares.[8]

So I said, "Sure Ern, I'd love to." So off we went. By and by, sure enough, there was a rabbit right out in the path in front of me.

Ern said, "You go ahead now. I've shot many rabbits so you go ahead." So I went ahead and I shot the poor little rabbit and he went head over heels for about 20 feet. We skinned him and Margie cooked it. I couldn't eat a bite. I just could not bring myself to eat that poor little fellow that was sitting in the path. That was the first and last time I went rabbit shooting.

---

8   "Rabbits" in Newfoundland are actually snowshoe hares, an introduced species.

"No, it's a beautiful night. I'll walk up."

There were no taxis in Buchans. The only car was owned by the man-ager and you wouldn't dare ask them for the use of it, so I had a dog team booked to get your mother to the hospital in case there was a stormy night. The dog team was owned by Don Jamieson's sister's husband.[9]

There were a few dog teams. There were a few families of Mi'kmaq people who had come to Buchans from down around Port au Port; they were half Mi'kmaq and half French.[10] They used to go around the west coast, and then they'd go cross-country by dog team to Buchans to get work. They'd bring the dog teams with them. It was a common sight on Saturdays to see a dog team or two going off in the country and bringing back a caribou or a moose, or some rabbits. We used to get pulled out on Saturdays sometimes. We'd get a dog team some-times that was going out to pull us out into good skiing.

The night that you were born, it was twelve below, the most beau-tiful night, clear as crystal. And when the time came, your mother said, "I think I'd better get up there" [to the hospital].

I said, "All right, I'll see if I can get some way to get you there. I'll get Jim Oakley's dog team."

She said, "No, it's a beautiful night. I'll walk up." Which she did — and actually wanted to go for a walk when we got there, too! I soon whisked her inside and went home. In the morning I had the good news that you had been born and everything was great. That was on Ash Wednesday, death morning. The Roman Catholic teachers who were liv-ing above us all went to Mass and said a prayer and lit a candle for you.

9   See Chapter 5, note 1 (p. 125).

10   The Port au Port Peninsula on the west coast is the centre of French Newfound-land. Mi'kmaq people, who had close relations to the French, began to settle there and in Bay St. George in the late eighteenth century, arriving from Cape Breton. Doug Jackson's 1993 book, *On the Country*, is an engaging history of the Mi'kmaq in Newfoundland. References to a migration to Buchans could not be found (Bar-tels; Jackson).

The next few months, before we came back to St. John's, I had a choice of seven babysitters. The girls in the apartment upstairs all wanted to come down and babysit you. We lived in an apartment house. The Principal and his wife and family were in one apartment, and the other teachers, the female teachers of the school, lived together in one large apartment. And so I had a choice of six or seven babysitters. You were well pampered for four months before we came back to St. John's. You were christened John Douglas House, but we already had Uncle Jack House, John House, in Corner Brook. He was still alive. We said, "No, we don't want another John. We'll call him Douglas."

Margie and baby Doug.

"One of the plums."

Then Mr. Wood retired as Principal of Bishop Feild in 1944,[11] and I had nerve enough to apply for it. I wasn't expecting at all to get it because I thought that they'd appoint another Englishman. Mr. Wood wasn't English, but he was English-trained. He was the son of Canon Wood of Canon Wood Hall. His father got him into Cambridge, and he finished his education at Cambridge and in Paris. He did a whole summer of French over there, and so he taught French in the top grades at Feild.

---

11 Edgar's memory is at fault here. As documented in the book that he authored, *Edward Feild: The Man and His Legacy*, Ralph R. Wood left in 1936 and R.E. Tanner, an Englishman, was Headmaster of Bishop Feild College from 1936 to 1944 (House *Edward* 68).

But for the first time, they decided to have a Newfoundlander trained in Newfoundland. I did come in for a bit of an interview, out in the old Principal's office at Feild. My father had been teaching there for 30-odd years, and my sister had been at Spencer teaching for 17 years, I think, so between us, we had about a hundred years plugged in at the two places. Of course, Margie was a teacher, too, but she had to quit as soon as we got married. You weren't allowed to teach after you got married. It was an unwritten law, and nobody thought of breaking it. Today, if you took away the married teachers, there wouldn't be many left.

Bishop Feild College was recognized as a good school. The Chairman of the School Board at Buchans, when they gave me a going-away party, said, "You know, we've been very lucky to have Mr. House here. He has a university degree, as has his wife, and he's going to take one of the plums of the teaching profession in Newfoundland, Bishop Feild College." "One of the plums," he said.

11. Headmaster, 1944-52

What attracted me about the job? Well, I suppose I liked working with boys to begin with. I worked on the playground and I was in the CLB and so on. It was a bit of a boast as well, I suppose, after my father had been teaching at Feild from 1900 until 1935, a long time there. He was all for it. He was scared to death that I was going to go to Prince of Wales, because the Headmaster position at Prince of Wales became vacant when Mr. Cochrane (whom I knew well and liked very much) became ill and wrote me while I was at Buchans. He asked me if I'd be interested in succeeding him, and he said, "If you are, I'll recommend it to the Board."

I went and told my dad that I had a chance to go to Prince of Wales, and he said, "Don't you dare!" He couldn't stand the thought of me going to Prince of Wales. Anyhow, he didn't have to persuade me too much because the position at Feild came open at about that time.

It was exciting, very exciting, because it was 1944, which was the 100th anniversary, 1844–1944, so it was a big year to begin with. There were a lot of special events, church services and dinners and one thing or another. We had two good football teams and won both the junior soccer championship and the senior soccer championship. That meant something. It was a great start.[1]

I didn't get paid much more, but enough to make it worth my while. We had two children to look after, their education and all. I didn't have to use any of my savings for that at all though, in the end. You got a scholarship and Jan got the government grants for her

---

1   In a letter of congratulations to Edgar on the centenary, the Headmaster of St. Bon's thoughtfully wrote: "To you it must be a great joy to find yourself in this memorable year the Headmaster of the college whose name is woven in the fibres of your heart."

training. But on the whole, I don't know if I was as well off because in Buchans, I had a cheaper apartment, and I had rented my house in St. John's to one of my friends, so all in all, I wasn't as well off, I don't think; but there was a little prestige, I suppose. As you looked around at that time, the early forties, I would say there weren't more than 30 teachers on the whole island that had a degree. It was only the Principals of the big schools like at Grand Falls, Corner Brook, Buchans, and all the St. John's schools, that had degrees.

Football champions of 1949: Edgar, top row, right; Ches Parsons, top row, left. (Courtesy Archdeacon Buckle Memorial Archive, Diocese of Eastern Newfoundland and Labrador)

I took over from Tanner in 1944, and I went out to see him the first day I got back [from Buchans]. He said, "I'm leaving some money in a bank account, the sports bank account. You'll have lots of money to get a new set of uniforms, a few soccer balls and so on, which you'll need in September." Oh, I thanked him very much. I felt great about it. He was no sooner out through the Narrows and heading back to England than the bills started to come in from Water Street. Some of the stores down there heard he was leaving and they sent their bills in a hurry. It added up to over $400 he owed! For sweaters and soccer balls, rugby balls for the school. I had to go to the Board of Directors and they bailed me out.

"The first thing I did was persuade the Board to let me have a games teacher."

In terms of directions for the school, academic work wasn't too bad, but I certainly wanted to pull them up in sports if I could a little bit.

So the first thing I did was persuade the Board to let me have a games [physical education] teacher. I couldn't afford to get a fully qualified man with a degree from England; we didn't have the money for it. And so I looked around at all the Old Feildians that were around, and I picked out Ches Parsons as being the most all-around person I could find.[2] He was a very good athlete, running and so on. He was a clerk in a store down on Water Street, Harris and Hiscock, and I persuaded him to come to Feild as games teacher. I actually went down to the store and talked to them and stole him from there; sent him up to the States in the summer, New York, for a course. He turned out to be a very good bet, as well. Later on, in the fifties, he went to Nova Scotia and really made a name for himself. He comes home every year to see his wife's people and dropped in to see me last summer.

So that's the first time we had a full-time games teacher. That's one thing I wanted to build up a fair bit. I wanted to improve the science teaching in the upper school. I got the Board to give me a grant to order equipment for the chemistry lab, which they did. We finished up with a very good chem lab, which was used also by the girls at Spencer. It was even used on Saturday mornings by three or four of the nuns from the convent.

I wanted to get music on the program. When I was going there, we had a Mr. Stirling who was the organist at St. Thomas' Church. But it was rather useless because he only used to come once a week. So I wanted to get a special teacher for music, and for art as well, and I was able to do both. The music teacher became a permanent teacher, there all day, every day. He taught, and was able to play for special occasions, prayers in the morning and such.

---

2   Chesley Parsons was born in St. John's in 1924, and sold newspapers at Rawlins Cross as a boy in the 1930s. He attended Bishop Feild College, where he was heavily involved in sports. He also worked as a messenger and delivery boy. In a *Telegram* article, the story of his hiring by Edgar is that he was walking down the street and Edgar stopped him and asked him if he wanted the job. "I couldn't get home fast enough to tell my mother I had a new job," he says (Sweet A17). He worked at Feild from 1946 to 1952 and then moved to Dartmouth, N.S., where he had a long and successful career teaching physical education in high school. He died on 13 January 2014 ("Parsons, Chesley").

"The third time was lucky."

I had an art teacher who was only part-time. He was one of the best artists we had in the country, Harold Goodridge.[3] He had been teaching in India at the time of the war, teaching a class full of very wealthy Indian boys. In the fall of the year, he used to arrive there, and they would send a bunch of servants in for his family. He would take a house and they'd live in this house and go to this English school. He came to become the official artist for the Indian Navy. One of the Goodridge family. He did some very good work. I was lucky enough to get that picture over there [on the wall of his living room], a picture of Goose Cove, from him.

Goose Cove, by Harold Goodridge.

---

3   Harold Belfield Goodridge (1901–89) is one of Newfoundland's best-known artists. He was born in St. John's in 1901 but grew up in England. As Edgar notes, he was the official artist for the Indian Navy, in 1942. In 1944 he returned to Newfoundland and taught geography at Memorial University College until 1960. Upon his retirement he became a full-time professional artist, and several of his murals hang in the Confederation Building in St. John's. He was awarded an honorary Doctor of Laws degree by Memorial University in 1977 (Cuff "Goodridge"; "Profile: Harold").

I went to ask him if he'd do a painting of Bishop Feild because there was nothing in the hall. Nothing in the school at all really, except a picture of the Bishop. I said something about his life, and Goodridge said, "Oh yes, I'll try to do something." So I gave him the book on Bishop Feild that I had and he went off. I met him some time later and he said, "I've been through that book a couple of times and I cannot get any sort of an inspiration at all from it."

I said, "Well, keep it and have one more try anyhow." And so the third time was lucky. Going through it, he found a paragraph there that described the Bishop serving communion at an Indian burial place, in a little fishing settlement in Notre Dame Bay which no longer exists. He had to serve communion in the twine loft of this fishing hut. He [Bishop Feild] describes the smell of the fish and the cod oil and the people. The poor people coming up in this twine loft and having to use the barrel as an altar.[4] That's what he used to do his picture of Bishop Feild, and it's a very good picture.

I'm a little bit worried about the picture because it's in a school now which has no interest in the Anglican Church really.[5] I'd like to see it in a place where it would be better looked after and seen by people that should see it. It's not seen by anybody now. I made a move to have it placed at Queen's College or better still in the Anglican Cathedral I think. To be seen by people.

I guess the art classes went on for a couple of years. They had to be held after school, because we couldn't work them in. A limited number of boys were interested in it, some of whom turned out very

4   More details about Bishop Feild's experiences in Newfoundland are contained in *The Diary of Edward Feild in 1844*, edited by Ronald Rompkey.

5   The picture hangs above the library in Bishop Feild Elementary School. The school discontinued its official affiliation with the Anglican Church after 1998 with the abolishment of the religious denominational school system in Newfoundland. The denominational system started in 1843, when churches took over from charitable institutions in the administration of Newfoundland's schools (Downer 5). It continued until the late 1990s, when, after two referendums, Newfoundland and Labrador's citizens voted to dismantle the system and make the schools public (Higgins "The Collapse").

Harold Goodridge presenting painting of Bishop Feild to Edgar.

well. Harold Goodridge was interesting, you know, a very interesting man. He built that little house down on Winter Avenue, on the right-hand side next to Emerson's old big house, opposite O'Leary's, and lived there for a number of years.

Kindergarten for the boys was over at Spencer, but then we had these two rooms that became available, so I suggested to the directors that we make it a Carnell Memorial Kindergarten. We named it in memory of Geoff Carnell Senior's mother, the present Geoff's grandmother,[6] because she had been President of the Feildian Ladies for a long while and a wonderful woman. So I collected around $2,500, I guess, in memory of Mrs. Carnell, and we opened up the Carnell Memorial Kindergarten.

---

6   See Chapter 9, note 3 (p. 193).

"Look, I'll take them myself, that's a challenge."

It was the latter part of the war, I guess, and I had to cope with the "American invasion." There were a lot of boys at Pepperrell,[7] and I must have had about 40 at one time. I had to take the end of the corridor upstairs and make a classroom of it, a spare classroom, for the American students from the base. We had to use the stage at one point, too, as a classroom.

As I was coming out of prayers one morning, there was a [Chinese] man there who I knew because I had laundry done at his place, and he said, "Mr. House, I've got some boys here that I'd like to enter into the school in early September. They'd like to go to school." I looked up. There they were, 12 of them, up to about 20 years old. The 20-year-old fellow had been in the Chinese Army. They had all just arrived here in St. John's right from China.[8]

Anyhow, he said, "They don't know any English whatsoever." I just couldn't do it. I didn't have the space at all.

---

7   See Chapter 5, note 31 (p. 140).

8   The Chinese began arriving in St. John's in the 1890s. After they set up several laundries and began to arrive in slightly greater numbers, a backlash ensued against them resulting in the 1906 Chinese Immigration Act, which imposed a $300 head tax on new immigrants from China (Newfoundland followed Canada in this initiative). Chinese immigration continued at a slower pace, and the first Chinese restaurants were opened about 1920. Chinese women were not permitted into the country. Confederation in 1949 led to the repeal of the Immigration Act, making it easier for Chinese immigrants to come to Newfoundland and allowing women to immigrate as well; however, China's status as a closed state greatly restricted emigration until after 1976, the year of Mao Zedong's death (Sparrow 27). That same year the Chinese Association of Newfoundland and Labrador was formed, with Dr. Kim Hong as the first President. The National Household Survey (2011) listed 1,645 people of Chinese origin residing in Newfoundland (0.3 per cent of the population). For more on the early history of the Chinese in Newfoundland, see Robert Hong's 1986 dissertation, "To Take Action without Delay," and Krista L. Li's 2010 dissertation, "Knights of the Flatiron." John Sparrow's 2007 essay, "From Sojourning to Citizenship," presents a summary of the history of the community up to 1967 (Smallwood "Chinese Community"; Canada 6).

I spoke to Jack Courage, who was head of Adult Education at the time, and told Jack my problem, and he said, "Look, I'll take them myself, that's a challenge." 'Twas early September, and he said, "I'll take them now until Christmas, and by the first week in January, they'll know enough English to be able to start at Bishop Feild College."

I said, "Fine!" And so he took them for four months, and did a marvellous job. He taught them every day, from September up to Christmas. I don't know how the rest of his work suffered; I'm sure it did a bit, but it was a personal thing with him. He was so dedicated, to the extent that they were so grateful at Christmastime that he was presented with silk ties, silk shirts, and all kinds of presents from these lads. He did a great job in teaching these fellows English, and they knew their maths already.

Gradually, as the Americans got transferred here and there, I'd say, "No, I won't replace that spot." I thought the Chinese had preference over the Americans, as they were here permanently. By the time January the first came, I had another 10 desks vacant, ready for them. Anyhow, I took them in and they all did well!

Joseph Lee painted that picture out there in the dining room [in Edgar's house]. I met him one day and I said, "Look, I was up at the art exhibition at the university and I saw the lovely painting you have up there."

He said, "You mean 'Gently on the Strong and Fragile'?" That was his title for it, the birds on the birch [bamboo].

I said, "Yes, I really admire it." The next morning he gave it to me. He arrived at school with it. I was delighted! He brought a number of students here.

Kim Hong [one of the Chinese students] became a doctor.[9] He went off to medical school with John Collingwood, they were good friends.[10] He was a protégé of Bliss's, and he and Bliss were quite close.[11] He was the one that discovered that Bliss had trouble. Bliss asked him over to Brigus one weekend, and when they were approaching Brigus, Bliss was swerving, so Hong got him to have a checkup the next day and he found he had a bloody cancer. Kim Hong stayed a very loyal Feildian.

The Chinese had many laundries and restaurants throughout the city. They were meticulous as far as paying their school fees was concerned. At that time, we were charging four dollars a month for tuition, and an extra 40 cents that went towards scribblers and exercise books and pencils that were given out once a month.

One time the father of a student came to me and said, "Mr. House, don't worry. Don't worry, I'll be in next week." He said, "We have a big game this weekend. I'm very lucky. If I don't win a couple of thousand dollars, it'll be a strange thing to me."

I said, "A couple of thousand?"

He said, "Yes, we play for big money. It's nothing to win a couple of thousand dollars on a Saturday night."

So I said, "Fine!" I took it with a grain of salt, but boy, he was up next week with the full amount that he owed. He could have paid more. He pulled out a roll, a wad of bills.

---

9   Dr. Kim Hong, M.D., D.M.R.T. F.R.C.P.(C), left his home in China at age 13 and arrived in Newfoundland in 1950 to work with his grandfather at John Lee Laundry on Gower Street. He enrolled in Grade 1 at Bishop Feild at age 13 with little English, and graduated with honours in 1958. Dr. Hong graduated from Dalhousie University School of Medicine in 1965 and became a specialist in radiation oncology. He was very active in the provincial Chinese Association from its founding in 1976 (Kim Hong 32–33).

10   Dr. John Collingwood went on to become a well-known general practitioner for over 30 years in St. John's.

11   Dr. Bliss Murphy; see Chapter 1, note 16 (p. 85).

234   AN EXTRAORDINARY ORDINARY MAN

"The Rosenbergs, the Levitzes . . . "

It seemed that most of the Jewish boys in St. John's went to Bishop Feild.
A few went to Prince of Wales but by far most of them went to Feild,
and I suppose that's the way I got in contact with them. The Rosen-
bergs, the Levitzes, they were a good group. There's a book on them
actually.[12] I think there's something like 17 very well-known names.
They fitted in very well with everyone else. Some of them were good
athletes, good scholars, and one of them won the Bishop's prize for religion. There was quite a laugh from the audience when they announced
that the Bishop's prize for divinity was won by so-and-so Rosenberg![13]
They didn't have to go to prayers, but this fellow had gone.

There were several Jewish families around our neighbourhood [on
Glenridge Crescent] — the Wilanskys, the Sheffmans, the Shulmans.

---

12   Edgar is referring to *Listen While I Tell You* by Alison Kahn (1987). Wholesaler
and retailer Israel Perlin was the first prominent Jewish businessman to move to
the island, which he did in 1891. Soon he and his brother Frank brought in relatives and acquaintances to work as peddlers in the outports, and eventually these
peddlers set up businesses of their own on Water Street. By 1936 there were 24
Jewish businesses in St. John's. Eventually religious services were held and a synagogue and cemetery built; however, the cohesion of the community was ham-
pered by the difficulty in finding a rabbi to permanently locate in Newfoundland.
By the time of the writing of Kahn's book, most of the community had moved
away to other parts of Canada or the U.S., and it appeared to be dying. However,
with in-migration and immigration to the province due to education and employment in the growing economy, the congregation at Beth-El Synagogue is
alive and well today with around 20 families. In addition, a less formal group
called the Jewish Community Havura was formed in 2006, and now consists of
about 40 members (Smallwood "Hebrew"; "The Atlantic").

13   Possibly Horace, who went on to become a general practitioner in Burgeo, on the
south coast of Newfoundland and, eventually, Ottawa.

Menjie Shulman was an interesting character.[14] The first time I saw him I was shaving up in the bathroom upstairs, I looked out the window and here was this fellow walking across from the house where he lived, walking across to Maurice Wilansky's standing on his hands. He walked all the way across to the carport on his hands.

"That's that John Crosbie."[15]

For a couple of years, while they were getting a room ready at Feild, the boys and the girls attended kindergarten together, at Spencer. There was no playground there, just a little schoolyard down in front of the school, and this is where, at recess time, the kindergarten youngsters used to go out and play. Now among them on this occasion was a young fellow, five or six years old, and it was a hot day, and the two Ediths, Manuel and House,[16] were leaning out the window of the second floor looking down at them at play and suddenly out came a string of awful curses, language that you wouldn't hear at the waterfront. Edith said, "Listen to that!"

Miss Manuel listened and looked down, "That's that John Crosbie," she said. "I'll fix him." She went down, took him by the ear, pulled him indoors, and that was it. Edith never did find out what she did to fix him!

---

14   Menjie Shulman was an American who settled in St. John's and became well known as a broadcaster for VOCM radio, promoting several successful bluegrass bands including the Hillbilly Jewels. A brief memoir of his time in Newfoundland radio is contained in McNeil and Wolfe, *Signing On: The Birth of Radio in Canada* (36–37; McGrath).

15   Edgar respected and appreciated John Crosbie's successful political career. But he liked to reminisce about some of the boyhood foibles of famous former students such as Crosbie and Joey Smallwood. John Carnell Crosbie was born in St. John's in 1931. He went on to become one of Newfoundland and Labrador's and Canada's best-known politicians, serving in several cabinet positions in both the provincial and federal governments. In February 2008 he was appointed as the twelfth Lieutenant-Governor of Newfoundland and Labrador. He wrote a best-selling memoir entitled *No Holds Barred: My Life in Politics* (1997) (Cuff "Crosbie"; Knott 3).

16   See section below on teachers at Bishop Spencer College.

I remember John Crosbie [at Bishop Feild] particularly because he was such a bad writer — his handwriting was disgraceful. I can remember one time taking an essay that he'd written, and I said, "Crosbie, obviously you borrowed your father's shoe brush to write that with." They were interesting years, at Feild.[17]

"You never knew what the outcome was going to be."

I always claim that I started Bob Cole[18] on his career. I was approaching the Grade 11 class one morning after prayers — I was a little bit late getting there — and this boy was up on the platform broadcasting

---

17   A patriotic poem by John Crosbie was reprinted in the 1947 issue of *The Feildian Magazine*:

NEWFOUNDLAND UNFETTERED

(By JOHN CROSBIE, formerly of B.F.C.)

For years they fought to make their country free,

They were the men who fought for what was theirs.

They always loved and knew their foe, the sea,

For there they fished, and learned through all its cares.

But now they did not have the right to hold

An office, and their vote was held in fee.

Because an unpaid debt had left them sold

Into a crown domain, with no man free.

But now are rising men who love their land,

Who soon will try to govern once again,

Their native country, belov'd Newfoundland

Led by these men 'tis hoped to break that chain

Of bondage. Up true Newfoundlanders! Rise!

And fight once more to win proud freedom's prize.

— From the St. Andrew's College school magazine.

18   Robert Cecil Cole was born in St. John's in 1934. He was the primary play-by-play announcer for *Hockey Night in Canada* on CBC television from 1980 to 2008, and continues in that role on a reduced basis. He was inducted into the Hockey Hall of Fame in 1996 as the recipient of the Foster Hewitt Memorial Award for broadcasting excellence, and in 2007 received a Gemini award for best sports play-by-play announcer (Vincent 24–27; "Bob Cole"). In December 2014 Bob Cole was named a Member of the Order of Canada.

a game that the Feildians had played against the Guards the night before. He was doing such a good job of broadcasting with a hockey stick with the tape side up by his mouth as the microphone that I didn't go in. I stopped at the doorway and listened. When they finally realized I was there, he was very embarrassed. I said, "Cole, there's no need for you to be embarrassed. You're doing a much better job than was done last night by the regular broadcaster." So he laughed, and I might have sown the seeds. Shortly after that he came with another boy and asked if they could borrow the tape recorder that I had been given by the Feildian Ladies, probably the first tape recorder in any school in the country. I said, "Yes, by all means."

He said, "We want to try it after school and see how we sound. We'll record some of the plays that are in our literature reader." So that was Bob Cole's start. He'd play through a piece they'd recorded, and he'd say, "Gee, that sounds awful. I can do better than that." Then they'd play it through again, and correct their mistakes. Eventually, he went into broadcasting, VOCM at first.

At a dinner several years later, Bob Cole was making a speech or replying to a speech or something. He said, "I can see Mr. House now in a soccer game, running up and down the line encouraging us to shoot more or pass more." He said, "I can see him now running up and down with his flannels and Harris tweed coat with patched pockets. He always seemed to have a Harris tweed coat with patched pockets. I suppose he owned a suit but I don't think I ever saw him with it on!"[19]

"What can I do for you gentlemen?"

Around 1950, the time of Confederation, we introduced the new teachers' salary scale. At that time a teacher's salary was so low that I don't know yet how Dad managed to put me through university for two years. I have no idea. And so about 1950, Allan Bishop, who was a whiz at mathematics, drew up a new salary scale for teachers for the

---

19   See the Foreword by Bob Cole for his comments about Mr. House and his time at Bishop Feild.

whole island, and it was a good one, very cleverly done. He didn't ask for too much and he didn't ask for too little.

One afternoon, about four o'clock, I made the arrangements to take our new salary scale up to the Colonial Building and present it to Joe Smallwood, the new Premier.[20] So at four o'clock this afternoon after school, Brother Knight, I think it was, from St. Bon's, and Mr. Partner, the Principal at Prince of Wales, and myself, the three of us, went up to meet with Joe Smallwood and present our new salary scale and pension scheme. When we went into Joe's office, he motioned us to come in, although he was on two phones — he was handling two phone calls at the same time. Typical Joe!

He motioned to us to come in and sit down. When he finished his calls, he said, "What can I do for you gentlemen?"

I had this document there that we had prepared. I said, "Mr. Smallwood, we have a new salary scale and pension scheme to present to you, because teachers' salaries are ridiculously low and so is the pension."

He said, "Oh, yes!" He put his hand in the drawer and pulled out this thing. He said, "Would it be like this?" He passed it over to me and it was identical to what I had in my hand. Figure for figure. He said, "I took that home last night. I looked it over. I see nothing wrong with it at all. I'll go along with it. We'll give you the increase that you want in your salary scale and government will also increase your pension scheme. Thank you very much." More or less dismissed!

We discovered that Sammy Hefferton had leaked the whole thing up to him, ahead of time.[21] It was ridiculous, you know, what he did. Anyhow, that was the end of Sammy Hefferton as far as we were

---

20   Edgar was President of the Newfoundland Teachers' Association at the time.

21   Samuel James Hefferton was born on 28 March 1896 in Newtown, Bonavista Bay, and educated at Memorial University College, the University of London (U.K.) and Queen's University in Kingston, Ontario. Between 1942 and 1949 he served as president of the Newfoundland Teachers' Association and was elected Liberal member for Trinity North in 1949. Between 1949 and 1959 he held variously the portfolios for Education, Municipal Affairs and Supply, Health, and Public Welfare. He died in 1980 (Grenville).[

concerned and that was the end of Sammy Hefferton's year at Feild. He went into politics, and became the Minister of Welfare with Joe Smallwood. He and Allan Bishop used to go home together every day, because they lived in the same part of the city and they were almost inseparable. After that, Allan Bishop never spoke to Sam Hefferton. They used to play cards, he and their wives. They used to go back and forth. He never spoke to him afterwards. But the scheme was immediately adopted by Joe Smallwood with no hesitation at all. Overnight, teachers' salaries improved greatly. I always give Joe credit for that; he didn't hesitate at all to put it into effect.

"I changed the habits of the nuns."

I was teaching chemistry in Grade 11 and I had just fitted out the lab with a year's supply when one of the nuns from Mercy Convent phoned me and said, "Mr. House, we want to introduce chemistry to our Grade 11 girls. They haven't got a science lab. Would you be willing on Saturday mornings to give us some instructions?"

I said, "Fine, Sister, yes, come down."

They had a little accident there one morning. In those days they wore these black habits and big celluloid, starched fronts. One of them leaned over a Bunsen burner a little too far and the celluloid caught fire. Oh, it went straight up around her hair. I grabbed a lab coat and smothered her and brought her down to the General Hospital. She got a great kick out of it. She lost some of her hair but she was laughing all the way. She was back next Saturday, too. That was the end of the celluloid, though; from then on they got linen. So I can say I changed the habits of the nuns!

I guess we did it for about three months. It was only on Saturday mornings but at the end of three months, they felt they knew enough to introduce chemistry next year to the Grade 11 class. Later, I was very happy to get a chemistry teacher from England, because I didn't like chemistry, didn't like teaching it. So then I could swing over to teaching history and English, especially English, which is what I enjoyed.

"He was a really, really good fellow."

Good teachers were few and far between. In my time as a pupil, Llewellyn Colley, who came originally from Port aux Basques, was one of the best teachers that I've ever had and I was very lucky I had him in Grades 4 and 5 and 6. As I moved up, he moved up. Yes, I was very, very fortunate. He was a splendid teacher. Llewellyn Colley. He also lived at Feild Hall, which was almost exactly where St. Thomas Parish Hall is now, and so he was responsible to some extent for the homework that the boys did down there, supervising their evening homework and that sort of thing. He was a really, really good fellow.

I had an Englishman there doing classics, Lewis Baxter. He came out to teach at Feild in about the mid-thirties, I guess. We became very good friends, to the point that when he was going back to England, the year Margie and I were being married, he came to me and said, "Edgar, I'm sorry. I'd like to be able to give you a nice wedding present but I just can't afford it. I have so many expenses going home but I've got a couple of chairs — the Morris chairs that were made by Sylvia Wigh's father.[22] They're good chairs. I'd like to give you two of them for a wedding present." I was delighted! One of them I sent down to Trinity, and it's still there inside the door [of his cabin] as you go in. The other one I used yesterday upstairs in my den. They'll last forever, solid oak.

Lewis fell in love with Felicity Partridge, who was an English teacher on the staff at Spencer. She went out to teach in New Zealand

---

22   Sylvia Wigh, born in England in 1913, was one of the best-known figures in New-foundland theatre. She spent her childhood at boarding school in England, coming to St. John's for holidays, where her father had an antiques business. Eventually she stayed in St. John's and finished her schooling at Bishop Spencer, going on to Memorial College and then Columbia University in New York in 1939–40. Heavily involved in theatre all the while, she taught for seven years at Bishop Feild, and was one of the original members of the local theatre company, the St. John's Players. She also wrote about theatre, fashion, and books for the *Evening Telegram* beginning in 1954, as well as producing radio and television segments. She died in 2005, aged 91 (Stacey "Theatre"; Patey).

and he went out to teach in Hamadan, Iran, working partly with the oil company and partly teaching the American boys who were there in the oil field. They finished up in London.

We had a Miss Edgar who was very knowledgeable about flowers and plants. She was a very good teacher of nature study, so good that Mr. Paton heard about her because he was also very interested in flowers and plants. He sort of befriended Miss Edgar and had her up there for dinner sometimes.

"God, give us men!"

When I brought Ann Chatwood in to teach kindergarten, I had to wait for her. She was over in London taking her course in kindergarten work, and wouldn't be ready until the end of October. So I got Miss Purchase, who had retired from the Model School, to take over the new Carnell kindergarten room that we had made, and she held the fort for September and October until Ann got back. She was very good. I always remember Ann and Gwen Woodley [another primary grade teacher] coming to me a little time after prayers one day. They were nearly laughing their heads off at prayers that morning. It was the morning that they started work. Ann said, "You started off with a lovely speech of introducing us and welcoming us to the staff and you really laid it on thick. Then you announced the hymn for the morning, 'God, give us men!'" She said, "Gwen and I could hardly keep from laughing out loud the whole time the hymn was being sung." Gwen was a good teacher.

I knew that Ed Press, "Dim" Press, who played soccer with me, the Old Feildians, was an excellent woodworker. His father was a cabinetmaker and Dim, as we called him, had picked up the trade. He was an excellent carpenter and cabinetmaker. He was working on Water Street at the time, but I picked him up the same way that I picked up Ches Parsons. I took him out of his job on Water Street and put him into the manual training room. By and large, he did a very good job. I had to get the approval of the Board for hiring decisions, but they usually went along. I had an advantage in that the secretary of the Board was my father, so I'd always talk things over with him first.

Dim Press did a good job there. But I remember one day, I was in my office there, and a knock came to the door and I said, "Come in." Dim Press opened the door and he had this boy in his arms, struggling, struggling. He took him in. He was really in a bad way. He was a very, very clever boy, but he wasn't going to do any woodwork. No, he was going to do Latin while everybody else was doing woodwork. So Dim had to carry him into my office and by this time the youngster was hysterical. So I did what somebody had told me about — you slap the person hard in the face and it sobers them up; and it did, it took him right out of it.

There were no boarders as such by the time I came back; there were some outport boys, but they lived with family or friends or boarded somewhere else. I don't remember exactly when the old Feild Hall closed.[23] I know that a number of well-known people went there. I remember George Earle and Isaac Mercer, the lawyer, and Ralph Anderson.[24] There were some well-known people that went through Feild Hall, including Joe Smallwood. It was just by St. Thomas' Church, just west of where the Canon Wood Hall is now. It should never have been pulled down. They had a fire, but it could have been saved. I think it could have been restored, but they decided it was cheaper to pull it down, I guess.

The old college faced Colonial Street, but for the new building, it was the playground that faced Colonial Street, and every ball that went over the wall landed on the other side of the street. Football, basketball, tennis ball, softball, whatever kind of ball it was, it was seized by an old lady who lived across the street. She'd run out and

---

23   In 1933; see Chapter 6, note 13 (p. 156).

24   See Chapter 1 , note 15 (p. 82) about George Earle; Isaac Mercer was a well-known lawyer in St. John's; R.S. Anderson succeeded Edgar as Headmaster at Bishop Feild College, serving from 1952 to 1965 (House *Edward* 117).

grab it and go in and that was it. Couldn't do anything about it. She was a bit crazy. When she died, I got a call from her lawyer. He said, "Mr. House, there's a lot of footballs and one thing or another down in the basement of this home. If you want to send the boys over you can get it all back." So we went in, and . . . oh, it was amazing. All kinds, softballs, tennis balls, baseballs, basketballs, soccer balls, the whole works.

"She left the imprint of her personality and knowledge on the school."

My sister, Edith, was at Spencer for 17 years. With several dozen other teachers, all of whom were spinsters and all of whom we thought would remain spinsters for the rest of their lives. But suddenly when Edith was 39, she hooked up with Wilf Furneaux and they were married just after Margie and I were.

Wilf and Edith Furneaux.

Another Edith, Edith Manuel,[25] was a very interesting person. I knew her quite well. She taught kindergarten at Spencer — she wasn't really suited to teach kindergarten, but she was an excellent adult education teacher. She used to teach at night at Memorial. I met her somehow when she was

---

25 Edith Mary Manuel, L.L.D. (1902–84), a native of Twillingate, obtained a Master of Arts and Science degree from Columbia University, New York. She afterwards taught at Spencer for 30 years and was very active in the Girl Guide movement. She was awarded an honorary Doctor of Laws degree from Memorial University in 1978 (Cuff "Manuel"; "Dr. Edith").

doing chemistry at Memorial, and I helped her out on a couple of occasions with some of the experiments she was doing. We were always good friends, a great person.

Miss Cherrington was an unusual woman.[26] She left England with the idea of teaching in Canada but she did the thing properly. She went to Vancouver and didn't like the rain there, so she came back to Toronto and wasn't impressed. Then she saw an ad in one of the Toronto papers for a Headmistress for Bishop Spencer, an old school in St. John's. She applied for it and got it, in 1922, and she stayed until 1952. Thirty years. She left the imprint of her personality and knowledge and everything on the school. She left it there in exactly the same way that Dr. Blackall left his imprint on Feild, 50 years earlier.

"Edgar, you're a chemist, why don't you make some wine?"

In 1933, I went to Feild as a chemistry teacher. I came home one day and I had a lot of blueberries there. Mother said, "Edgar, you're a chemist, why don't you make some wine?" So I went down to an old Feildian, Glen Stafford. He had wholesale drugs, pharmaceuticals, and he let me have this lovely oak keg. I paid for it and took it home, spotless. I got four gallons of blueberries and sugar, a couple of pounds of raisins, a couple of bananas. At the end, I got a bottle of Newfoundland rum, potent stuff in those days, and added that to it (I didn't tell my mother of course, or father).

I put it all in and let it work. When the time came, around the end of November, I bottled it off. Shortly after I had it bottled, Mother said, "Edgar, I'd like to give Miss Cherrington something for Christmas. How about a bottle of your lovely blueberry wine?" We had used a couple of bottles for a party that Edith and I threw together at our house one night. I had seven in and Edith had seven, 16 of us all

---

26   Violet M. Cherrington, C.H.L. (Hons.) M.B.E., served as Headmistress of Bishop Spencer College for 30 years, from 1922 to 1952, as Edgar notes accurately. She was also a member of the Council for Higher Education and involved in the Girl Guide movement (Cuff "Cherrington"; "Violet").

together, and we drank blueberry wine until it came out of our ears. Everybody got gagged and we had a great party.

"A bottle of that for Miss Cherrington for Christmas would be lovely," she said, so I very carefully got a bottle ready. She wrapped it up with Christmas paper and ribbon, and a couple of days before Christmas I delivered it at Spencer Lodge, the residence for the outport girls. A maid came to the door, took my bottle, and that was it as far as I was concerned. She didn't know what it was, really, and put it on top of the warm oven in the kitchen. A quarter of an hour later it exploded, all over the wall, the ceiling, all over the place! The poor girl sat down and cried. When Miss Cherrington came in, she told Miss Cherrington and Miss Cherrington sat down and laughed. She said, "Thank goodness!" She said, "I've been after the Board of Directors to get that kitchen re-modelled, repainted, redone and now they've jolly well got to do it!" She wasn't at all put out by it. No, she was quite a woman. As I say, she started at Vancouver and then Toronto, finally finished up at St. John's, Newfoundland, after trying out a couple of other places.

She was Principal of Spencer when I was Principal of Feild for quite a few years. We had a very good relationship, which started when I was a boy at Feild, aged 17 or 18, and she wanted a basketball net and post laid for Spencer Lodge. So she asked my dad, who was working at Feild at the time, if he could do it for her. He came to me and said, "I've got a job for you. I don't know anything about basketball. You get the post, dig a hole, get some cement and cement it in. Get the right height and make a backboard, get a ring made, and I'll do the net for you. I'll knit the net." He could knit quite well. So we did that. Miss Cherrington was very grateful. She paid me well. I remember that. She paid me quite generously for it. It was her idea that the girls coming in from the outports could spend their spare time out having a shoot, passing, and so on, and in that way they might catch up to the town girls who had all the advantage. Of course, she was right.

One of these was a girl Fitzgerald, Dr. Fitzgerald's daughter from Trinity East. Her name was Doreen but she was invariably called Deen. Nobody ever called her anything except Deen. At one point, the music teacher at Spencer had a combined choir, the older Feild boys and the older Spencer girls, called the Mixed Choir. Deen was a member of this. One night they had a practice at the Cathedral for a church service. She went along early and went into the big Cathedral and sat down up in the middle and waited for the others to come. While she was there, this big tall man came in dressed in a clerical robe. He came up and said, "Oh, good evening, I'm Dean Reison of the Cathedral."

She said, "I'm Deen Fitzgerald of Spencer College." He was quite taken aback.

Partridge-Berry

There were two teachers at Spencer, one for art (and she was very good too) and the other for phys. ed., who met on the boat, because the teachers from England had to come by boat in those days, the early thirties. No planes. They met on the boat, shook hands, and introduced themselves: "I'm Partridge."

"I'm Berry." There was nothing remarkable about it to them. It was only when they got on the staff that Edith and all of the rest of them said, "Oh, Partridge-Berry!"[27]

"Too many people knew me."

One downside to being Headmaster was that there weren't enough hours in the day; you were bothered by every little detail. I think one of the troubles was that I knew too many people or too many people knew me. Bill Smith would lose his cap and his mother would ring me up and say, "You know, that's scandalous, it's disgraceful. He lost his cap in school and he can't find it. It's a new cap I just bought," and so on. This phone call would come perhaps when I was at a staff meeting.

I didn't have any secretarial help. Allan Bishop was the senior master, and though he was never designated as Vice-Principal, if I

---

27   See Chapter 1, note 10 (p. 79), regarding partridgeberries.

were away or sick or anything, he'd take over. He was a brilliant mathematician. I spent half my time as Principal teaching, just about. Yes sir, you had to! Every school Principal in those days managed to give himself five or six free periods, but the rest of the time was teaching. So any Principal duties that had to be performed had to be done after school and Saturdays, evenings. It was a tough job.

12. Politics and Joe Smallwood

Sir Richard Squires and the 1932 Colonial Building riots

Politics wasn't talked about that much at home. My dad was interested but mother couldn't care less. He never liked Sir Richard Squires, first nor last, any more than I did.[1] He was crooked. He got caught, of course. Disgraced! The two boys, Sir Richard's, were contemporaries of mine at Dalhousie. They're both dead now. One died very early and the other died not too long afterwards; he developed tuberculosis, and never did recover.

I remember the riots out at the Colonial Building in 1932[2] because

---

1   See Chapter 9, note 10 (p. 203).

2   The riot outside the Colonial Building happened on 5 April 1932. It took place amid widespread unemployment and poverty in the wake of the Depression, as well as accusations of financial corruption against Prime Minister Richard Squires. About 10,000 protestors gathered outside the legislature, and some forced their way inside, doing approximately $10,000 of damage. Squires barely escaped. In the wake of the riot the House was prorogued, elections were held, and Prime Minister Squires was defeated by Frederick C. Alderdice's Liberal-Conservative-Progressive Party 25 seats to 2. See Doug Letto, *Newfoundland's Last Prime Minister: Frederick Alderdice and the Death of a Nation* (2014).

     In the *Evening Telegram* story of 6 April 1932, Edgar's memory of Rev. W.E. Godfrey's role as rescuer is confirmed. He was a representative of a citizens' committee presenting a petition to the government, but when the unrest began he appealed to the crowd and "announced that he would take 40 law-abiding citizens within the building on a special errand." He proceeded inside and managed to get Squires and others out of the building and away from the mob.

     For an overview of contemporary news articles on the riot, see *The Story of the Colonial Building* (a booklet by the NL Provincial Archives); a detailed analysis of the social, political, and economic conditions surrounding the riot can be found in Chapters 6 and 7 of Patrick O'Flaherty's *Lost Country* and in Gene Long's 1992 dissertation "William Coaker and the Loss of Faith."

Stuart Godfrey's father helped Sir Richard to escape. He happened to be on the street, and this big crowd was trying to break in the front door of the Colonial Building, in which Squires had taken refuge. Mr. Godfrey was a clergyman at St. Thomas' at the time — he was the rector, an assistant. He had the good sense to get in, somehow, and get Squires out the back door. I suppose he had a clergyman's collar on and everybody sort of gave way for him. He got Squires across the street and into the front door of a house on Military Road that had a back door on Bannerman Street. He went in the front door and out the back door, the crowd chasing. He escaped through the playground at school, Bishop Feild.

"Do what the police do."

I have a very good reason to remember the Commission of Government.[3] On the day they were installed, they had a special Guard of Honour from the police and the CLB. Because Bishop Feild was quite close to the Colonial Building, they decided that the Guard of Honour should come from C Company. And so I was in charge of a Guard of Honour of about 16 boys, I guess, CLB lads, with orders that when I got there, we were to take orders from the Chief of Police, which we did. They were all in their special uniforms and we lined up there; I remember that occasion rather vividly. Unfortunately, the police in their arms drill did things a little differently from what we did. The police were on the west side and the C Company was on the east side, and after the Chief took over, he gave an order which we weren't used to at all with rifle drills. He ordered, Stand at Ease, when we were actually at the Slope. We had never done that. We had Order Arms first and then Stand Easy. So I just turned on the corner of my mouth and said, "Do what the police do." We got away with it.

I think a lot of people were relieved at the time the Commission of Government came in. Things were really desperate, especially in our outports. We had several weak governments, crooked and weak.

---

3   See Chatper 5, note 28 (p. 137).

We had a crooked government under Sir Richard Squires, a weak one under Alderdice. The leadership just didn't seem to be there at the time. I must say that some of the commissioners that came out were very able people. So I think it was a relief to some extent, although there were a lot of people that were up in arms about the idea of losing our identity to some extent. There was a lot of uncertainty and divisiveness. In certain families, the son would be on one side and the father would be on the other, and the wife would be on one side. It caused a lot of trouble, making up one's mind.

Inauguration of Commission of Government, Newfoundland Hotel, St. John's, 16 February 1934. (Courtesy The Rooms Provincial Archives, E 23-29)

Memories of Joe Smallwood

I can't describe Joe Smallwood at all. He was a man of many, many parts, so brilliant in some ways and so stupid in others, especially in money matters. He didn't know the difference between a dollar and a million dollars. He was a man of vision, though; he was really something. I suppose I can say I had more than a passing acquaintance with him.

When Joe was going to Bishop Feild, his grandfather decided it was too far away over on the South Side for him to go back and forth, and so he put him in Feild Hall, which was a hostel for outport boys. Although he was a townie, he went to Feild Hall, which was down by St. Thomas' Church, and went to Feild from there. The prestigious position at Feild Hall was Hall Captain, which Joe desperately wanted to be. The first week or so they were there, they were working up toward the election. Joe borrowed a typewriter from Mr. Pike, who was in charge of Feild Hall, and took it right to the north side of Kent's Pond. There's a clearing there on the north side; I know the clearing now. He sat down and composed his first election talk, to become Captain of Feild Hall.

When he had finished typing it, he stood up and gave the speech a couple of times. All of the time, he was witnessed by my brother-in-law, Wilf Furneaux, and one of his friends who had been in for a walk that afternoon. Going up the side of the pond, they heard the typewriter, and so they snuck up and just watched the whole proceedings. They watched it all and didn't make a sound. When Joe finished, he took his typewriter under his arm and made his way back to Feild Hall, ready with the speech to give that night. But he didn't win the election! It was the first election he took part in and he lost. I heard the story from Wilf, and I told it later on to Joe. Joe didn't like it. Oh, he was ready to cut my throat!

When I was at Buchans, '41 to '44, Joe used to come up quite a lot on weekends, when he had the pig farm near Gander, to see his sister-in-law, and that's when I got to know him really. He got all the swill from the American and Canadian bases, so it didn't cost him much to get some supplementary food and fatten them up. When they were fattened up, they'd have them killed and sell them to the base or the bases, both the Canadian and American. So he had a recycling plant. But if a couple of the American airmen were going on leave up to Buchans for a few nights, Joe would get a ride with them and go back with them.

Smallwood's great speech on the British Empire

On one occasion, he gave the greatest speech that was ever given on the British Empire. When he was up visiting his sister-in-law in Buchans one weekend, Empire Day was coming up. And so I had the nerve to go up and ask if he would stay on for an extra day and speak to the school on Empire Day, and he readily agreed. He had nearly two days to prepare for it, and he obviously did some preparation. He gave one of the finest speeches — I say this and I mean it — he gave one of the finest speeches ever given by anybody on the British Empire, the British Commonwealth. He loved the Empire.

The talk was outdoors, on the playground. I didn't have a place big enough for them all inside, so we had to go to the playground, and I got chairs from the mess hall and wherever I could get them. It was a beautiful day, cold, but it was a beautiful day. They all wrapped up — that's one thing about them, the children of Buchans were well off in those days and they dressed for the climate. About 220 youngsters, from kindergarten to Grade 11, sat for 20 minutes while Joe Smallwood spoke to them about the British Empire and the Commonwealth. It was a fantastic job. Unfortunately, it wasn't recorded. He didn't have it written out. I'd love to have had that. A few of the parents came around who lived close by and all the teachers, of course. It was a great outdoor speech.

Leading up to Confederation, there was a lot of questioning of what was going to happen in Newfoundland and all that kind of thing. Yes, it was a tough period because sometimes families were almost split up. I can remember one particular occasion. In our ignorance, the Feildians used to have what we called "smokers." These were evening meetings, get-togethers, when we'd have a special speaker and a card game, and perhaps supper; but on this occasion, I had decided to ask

Joe Smallwood to be a speaker. The next thing I had a call from Ches Crosbie:[4] "Is it true, that you're having Smallwood as your speaker?"

I said, "Yes, we've asked him to speak."

He said, "Look, I'd almost take my boy away from Bishop Feild College for that!" He didn't.

Smallwood gave a good talk and we had somebody that knew about it send us two cartons of cigarettes from the Imperial Tobacco factory close by. They heard we were having a smoker so they advertised their ware. It was my job to introduce Joe at the dinner. In my introduction, I mentioned that he'd been at Feild, and having a name like Smallwood, the boys gave him a nickname, "Splits."[5] He didn't like that at all. Oh no, he was ready to chew me up.

"A little place like Newfoundland, stuck out in the ocean by itself, needed help."

Confederation wasn't much of an issue at Feild. I think most of the fellows were Confederates. I was all for Confederation, very much for it. I had a few years at King's/Dalhousie, and I travelled around Nova Scotia and got to love it; I still do. And I managed a few motor trips up to Montreal, and further sometimes. So I loved Canada, right from the start. I think most people wanted Confederation, most people that really thought about it. There were some people who were so patriotic they couldn't see beyond the Union Jack. I think any people who did any real thinking knew that it was the only course for us to follow. A little place like Newfoundland, stuck out in the ocean by itself, needed help.

Chancey Currie [Edgar's friend] was an Anti-Confederate, and so was his father. I remember he had a country place out in Holyrood. It

---

4   Chesley Arthur Crosbie (1905–62) was a prominent St. John's businessman who favoured economic union with the United States. He was the only member of the delegation to negotiate the Terms of Union with Canada who refused to sign the agreement on 11 December 1948 (Smallwood and Pitt "Crosbie").

5   See Chapter 1, note 11 (p. 79).

was taken over by one of Joey's industries.[6] Chancey had a summer house in Holyrood up on the hill just behind where Joe was putting his factory to make rubber boots. He was going to have every fisherman in the country in Newfoundland rubber boots. Of course, that fizzled out like his chocolate factory over at Bay Roberts. And like his veneer part plant at Octagon Pond. That could have worked, though. If we had had a good supply of birch at the time, I think that could have worked out, but we didn't have veneer and that was it.

At the opening of that plant was a Rotarian who had been a woodsman with the AND [Anglo-Newfoundland Development] Company, and he grabbed the first piece that came off, the first sheet of veneer. He brought it along to a Rotary group meeting that night. At the end of it, I asked him what he was going to do with it. He said, "I'm going to throw it away."

I said, "Give it to me and I'll take it to Bishop Feild and I'll show it to the boys as an example of one of Joe Smallwood's new industries." So I took it down and I showed it to the boys in Grade 11, and at recess time, brought it back to the common room. At the time we had this woodworker, Ish Humber, who could do everything. I said, "Ish, some time when you have nothing to do, see if you can use some of that in a veneer picture for me." So he did those two pictures there out in the dining room [points to the pictures]. They're both made from the first piece of veneer. That light, light birch, that's the first bit of veneer that came off at the Octagon plant. He did another one that I gave to Stuart and Ros Godfrey for their wedding anniversary, a lovely one. I guess those are historic pictures now.

"Won't it be wonderful to have a Lord?"

He had his pig farm in Gander up until the end of the war. I don't know when he acquired the big property over on Roaches Line.[7] It

---

6   The Superior Rubber Company operated from 1953 to 1956 before failing badly (Letto 42–46).

7   Roaches Line is in Conception Bay, about 50 km west of St. John's.

was a very big piece of property, and there was this big chicken farm, eggs everywhere. His eggs were sold to stores all out around the area. I remember buying his eggs two or three times driving through Roaches Line; the service station there used to sell them.

I visited the farm on one occasion, an historic occasion, actually. I was on the Board of Regents at Memorial for a couple of terms when we were choosing a new president for the university. In the early sixties this was, and Joe Smallwood had been at a dinner in London where he'd sat next to Lord Taylor. He was quite impressed. He said to himself, "There's the man now to head up the university. Won't it be wonderful to have a Lord?" And so he told him about the university, for which they were trying to appoint a new president, and asked him if he'd be interested. And the outcome was that he brought out Lord Taylor and his wife, Lady Taylor, at the expense of the Newfoundland government. Lord Taylor looked things over and decided to take the job. That's how he got Lord Taylor here.[8]

We actually had a meeting with Lord Taylor over at Joe Smallwood's ranch house, and that's when we made the decision. It was the strangest meeting. We gathered in Joey's library, surrounded by 8,000 books or more. There weren't enough chairs for everybody, but we managed somehow to squat around. Lord Taylor got on the floor in the middle of the room and we all sat around in chairs and chesterfields and so on; he sat on the floor. That's where he did all his talking from, the floor. He impressed us quite a bit, enough for him and his wife to be asked over. The Regents decided to go along with it. He had his points. At that time, we were interested in the possibility of a medical school, and Lord Taylor had a medical background. We thought it would be a very wise move to have somebody like that. But Mose

---

8   Stephen J.L.Taylor (1910–88), who became a life peer, Lord Taylor of Harlow, in 1958, was an English physician and educator who served as President and Vice-Chancellor of Memorial University from 1967 to 1973 (Cuff "Taylor").

Morgan was really the President at the time.[9] He did all the work and made all the big decisions.

The group [Committee of the Board of Regents] that I headed up made the recommendation that we have a medical school. Ian Rusted was one of us, Doug Eaton, and several others.[10] We met regularly, every two weeks. We finished up our last meeting saying there's no way Newfoundland can afford to have a medical school, but there's no way Newfoundland cannot afford to have a medical school. So we recommended to the Board of Regents that they should have a medical school, which they implemented. Thank goodness! Newfoundland would be a much poorer place today in medical terms if we didn't have the Health Sciences Centre.

9   Moses Osbourne Morgan (1917–1981) was from Blaketown, Trinity Bay. A Rhodes Scholar, he went on to become Department Head, Dean, Vice-President, and then President of Memorial University, 1973–81, succeeding Lord Stephen Taylor (Cuff "Morgan"). He and his wife, Grace, became good friends with Edgar and Margie.

10   Dr. Ian Rusted (1921–2007), O.C., was the first Dean of Medicine at Memorial University. He was born in Upper Island Cove and studied medicine at Dalhousie and McGill, returning to practise in Newfoundland in 1952 ("Biographical Sketch).

Dr. J. Douglas Eaton (1925–2007) was Director of Physical Education and Athletics at MUN, 1954–63. He later became Dean of Men and Vice-President (Student Affairs and Services). He volunteered extensively with sporting groups and the Red Cross, Scouts, and St. Andrew's Church. He was inducted into the NL Sports Hall of Fame in 2004 ("MUN Physical").

13. TB and the Lung Association[1]

"I had two children to educate."

Frank O'Leary[2] was the President of Rotary and he was also President of the Newfoundland Tuberculosis Association [in the early 1950s]. He dropped up to see me one afternoon after school, about four o'clock, and said that they were going to advertise for somebody to direct the rehabilitation program for tuberculosis. We were having six or seven hundred men and women come out of our sanatorium every year, and more than half needed help with rehabilitation into society. He advertised and I rang up about it, but before I had a chance to have an interview, he came up to the school and offered me the job with a considerable increase in salary over what I was getting as Principal of Feild. Seventeen hundred dollars' difference, actually! I had two children to educate then, so I accepted quickly. I started in '52, and then stayed with the TB Association for 25 years.

I was very happy to make the change; it broadened my world.

---

1   During his retirement, Edgar House wrote a book about the eradication of TB called *Light at Last: Triumph over Tuberculosis in Newfoundland and Labrador, 1900–1975* (1981). In 2005 it was republished in a revised edition by the Lung Association of NL.

2   Frank O'Leary, O.B.E., K.S.G. (1894–63), was a successful businessman, community developer, and philanthropist. He sponsored *The Barrelman* radio program and also founded the O'Leary Newfoundland Poetry Awards. During World War II O'Leary initiated a "one per cent scheme" as a fundraiser for the war effort, whereby all full-time employees would give 1 per cent of their salaries, which was a huge success. He later initiated a similar scheme to raise funds for the Memorial Stadium. After World War II O'Leary campaigned for a return to responsible government and became president of the Responsible Government League in 1947. (Cuff "O'Leary"; Poole vol. 4 "O'Leary").

There were annual meetings of the Canadian TB Association, and every year I attended them in a different province, so I got to see all of Canada. Quite often I would take my holidays after the meeting. It might be in Alberta or B.C. or anywhere. Quite often Margie came along with me so that we could have a holiday afterwards.

The last year I was at Feild there was a rehabilitation workshop arranged in Nova Scotia lasting about 10 days. That was my first exposure to rehabilitation. I enjoyed it very much, to the point where I've never regretted doing it. Then, I was appointed at the end of that year, although I didn't actually take up the position until school finished in June. I did a lot of reading about rehab. There were a lot of books that were helpful and reports from other provinces, what they had been doing.

The 1950s were desperate times in Newfoundland as far as TB was concerned. We had by far the highest number of TB patients per capita in Canada and we needed the highest number of beds. There were sanatoriums here in St. John's, one for the men and one for the women, in Corner Brook, and in St. Anthony.

"He had friends in every port."

There were quite a lot of communities that weren't accessible by road, and there was something about the *Christmas Seal* that attracted people.[3] There was no trouble to get them on board for their X-ray. Captain Peter Troake[4] was better known in Newfoundland than Joe

---

3   The *Christmas Seal* was a 111-ton Fairmile vessel that was built in Massachusetts. It was purchased by the Newfoundland Tuberculosis Association in 1947 and provided services to small coastal communities in Newfoundland and Labrador from then until 1970. In addition to X-ray and BCG testing for TB, the *Christmas Seal* also conducted diabetic testing and surveys of persons with disabilities (House *Light at Last* 105–10).

4   Peter Troake, C.M. (1908–97), was a mariner from Twillingate. He served in World War II in the Newfoundland Forestry Unit in Scotland, and commanded many Newfoundland sealing vessels. He commanded the *Christmas Seal* from 1950 to 1970, and was awarded the Order of Canada for his work. His autobiography, published in 1989 by Memorial University of Newfoundland Faculty of Medicine, is entitled *No One Is a Stranger* (Currey 27–28).

Residents of Brookfield, Newfoundland, watch the arrival of the MV *Christmas Seal*. (Photo by Chris Lund, 1960. Courtesy of the Lung Association of Newfoundland and Labrador.)

Smallwood! He had friends in every port. The vessel was picked up in New York as naval surplus, and she did a remarkable job for a large number of years. Not only in tuberculosis testing; she did diabetic testing, too. They would do a patch test, BCG [Bacillus Calmette-Guérin], and a lot of people were picked up on that. If they were positive, they went and got the X-ray.

There was a mate and a seaman, a cook, the X-ray technician, and quite often a nurse. They didn't have a big crew. Sometimes they'd have somebody looking out for handicapped people. We had a fellow, Bill Lane, one year who was looking for handicapped people all over the south coast. He himself had a frozen spine, that's what they used to call them, to the point that he couldn't bend his spine at all. He had to sleep lying flat all the time. When Captain Troake heard that he was coming on for a month down on the south coast, he said, "Look, we can't take him. There's no way we can take him, handicapped like that. He'll never get up and down and get his meals and so on."

Bill Lane heard him say this. He said, "Captain, can you swim?"

"No, I can't swim."

He said, "All right, sometime if you fall in, I'll jump in and save you. I can swim." Even though he had a frozen back, he could swim. So that decided it . . . he took on Bill Lane.

"The barbers used to practise on the cooks and the cooks would practise on the barbers."

Most of the patients, both men and women, had led a very active life, fishermen, loggers, and that sort of thing, and so most of them were advised after their session at the San not to go back to their previous hard work, which meant a lot of them had to change their occupation. I had to do a lot of thinking to devise ways and means for some of these fellows and girls to improve their education. We trained cooks and barbers, and many of them boarded on the *Christmas Seal*. We used the cook on the *Christmas Seal*, a very accomplished cook, to do the teaching. It worked out very well. The barbers used to practise on the cooks and the cooks would practise on the barbers. As well, the barber students used to get their practice on the patients at the Waterford Hospital; they were very glad to accept them in there.

A number of fellows who were at the San showed that they had very skilful hands, and we set up a leather craft class. We brought in a man from Saint John, New Brunswick, I think it was, to teach the leather class. Tying flies, that was another occupation. One man became a full-time fly-tier, selling to The Sports Shop afterwards, and did quite well. The watch repairing was probably the biggest success. I brought in a watch repairer from Moncton, I think it was. We ran a class and provided watch repairers for Grand Falls, Deer Lake, Corner Brook, Grand Bank, oh, quite a few places, and here in St. John's, of course, as well. I think there were nearly 20 who set up in watch repairing in various places. Some of them did very well, too.

I had one group of about 12 women. While they were at the San, they expressed an interest in commercial [i.e., secretarial] training, so

— I blush when I think of this now — I hired a room at the BIS Hall and bought 12 used typewriters. We set up a commercial class, including teaching of English because some of them only had about Grade 8 or 9. I had a very good English teacher. Anyhow, we trained about a dozen of these women, and one man, and before they were finished, they were nearly all placed. On Water Street, mostly, and at Pepperrell, a few of them.

One man did a painting of our cabin. He was working with his father turning out lumber for a sawmill, and somehow or other he developed TB. It was TB of the spine of all things, a difficult one; there was all kinds of TB in those days. So when he came in, they put him on what they call a striker frame, which meant that he was lying down all of the time, strapped, really, to this frame. He had to spend so long face up and so long face down.

I had this slide of the cabin, a coloured slide, and took it in to him one day and said, "Look, you're quite a good painter. I know that because you've been taking lessons here. If I put that slide in a projector and project it up on the wall in front of you there while you're lying on your stomach, could you paint it?"

He said, "Yes, sure, why not!" So lying on his stomach on a striker frame, he painted that picture of the cabin.

I checked on him afterwards, and I said, "You're very good at art. I'll get you a job at Ayre & Sons in the advertising department or somewhere."

But, "No, thank you, sir," he said, and he went back to logging with his father.

"The priest here wants a man."

I did a lot of travelling, mostly by car. It paid off, I think. I remember one particular occasion when I spoke to the Lions Club down in St. Lawrence. When I got there I went to see the manager because I was early. He said, "Oh, gee, I forgot you were coming. We've got a wedding on here at St. Lawrence tonight. Everybody at the Lions Club is asked to the wedding after dinner."

"What can we do?" I said.

He said, "I know what we can do. I'll give you five minutes between the first course and the second, and five minutes between the second course and when they take the dishes off. Then I'll give you five minutes to finish up." That's exactly what happened. I had three speech opportunities, dividing the speech I had written into three different parts.

At the end of it he said, "What can we do for you now?"

I said, "You can find jobs for some of the people that I have training in St. John's."

He said, "For instance, what?"

I said, "Well, you haven't got a shoe repairman here in St. Lawrence at the present time."

"No," he said, "we haven't."

"Fine," I said, "I'll send you out a shoe repairman."

"Have you got a barber here?"

"No, he's not really a barber. Not a regular barber."

"All right," I said, "I'll send a barber out to you." Anyhow, I finished up by getting five jobs altogether. They all fitted in very well, too.

The last one amused me a little bit. He said, "The priest here wants a man."

I said, "What do you mean?"

He said, "There's always a man in the community who is always referred to as the priest's man. He does all the odd jobs for the priest, janitorial work and so on. Father So-and-so is looking for a man now."

I said, "Boy, I've got just the right man for that." So I sent this fellow out. He was really accepted out there. The priest was delighted. He finished up becoming a wharfinger. These places had to have a man down on the wharf who looked after the arrival of all the boats and the departures of the boats. Kept everything tidy and in good repair, so he finished up as a wharfinger. Paid a little more money than the priest did, I guess.

"On the floor, you fellows, for your meal!"

I was the speaker for the day once at the Stephenville Lions Club, as well. When the Lions come in, they're always supposed to have their special Lions cap on and their pin. A bit different from Rotary. There were a lot of Americans there because it was close to the base. As a matter of fact, the president was an American, an American serviceman. They were a fun-loving group. On this particular day, two fellows came in late. The president jumped on them immediately and said, "On the floor, you fellows, for your meal!" They had to take the tablecloth off their table, and dishes and everything, put them down on the floor, and the two of them had to sit on the floor and have their meal! That was their punishment for being late. But it wasn't enough. He said, "Before you do that you have to go to the piano and sing 'Sweet Adeline.'" So they sang "Sweet Adeline" and they had to sit down for the rest of their meal on the floor.

Travels across the province.

I didn't pick the cheapest lodgings while travelling. No, the Board said when you're travelling around don't do it the hard way. At Grand Falls, I stayed at the Staff House, at Corner Brook the Glynmill Inn. I went to Labrador, too, to the main settlements, including a little trip to Mud Lake. They had an Eskimo [Inuit] population there. That was interesting.

On one occasion, I was going down with Claude Howse.[5] He offered me a guest room at the hotel in Labrador City, plus a car to take me around. Claude was the big shot down there then, at that time. His father was a United Church clergyman and he moved from place to place. He was at Grand Bank, and oh, three or four different places, but he and I went to Memorial at the same time and we became very good friends. Eventually, he lived down here on Winter Avenue. I think he was on your paper route.[6] Claude knew the surface of Newfoundland probably better than anybody, before or since. He was

---

5   See Chapter 5, note 29 (p. 138).

6   Doug delivered the *Daily News* in his neighbourhood as a boy.

a prospector and surveyor, and he covered the island from one end to the other and then went to Labrador working with the company [the Iron Ore Company of Canada]. He was a natural, because nobody knew the surface of Newfoundland better as far as the ore was concerned. He did most of it on foot.

"You can see immediate results for your efforts."

The most enjoyable thing about rehabilitation as compared to teaching is that you can see immediate results for your efforts. In teaching you have to wait, sometimes for years, before you can see it. If you train a man in shoe repairing and set him up out in Botwood or somewhere and take a visit there a few months later, and see that he's making a living and supporting a family, it's a good feeling. That was true in many, many cases. I went back year after year to follow up on some of them. You'd get to know them well. I had a dual purpose every time I went out: to check on the people that were already out and, hopefully, find openings for others that were coming out. Some of them had extra training, too, especially true of shoe repairing and watch repairing.

"She'll blow off the track."

After Walter Davis left, I had to take over as Executive Secretary.[7] I was doing two jobs for quite a little while. I had the overall job of looking after the X-ray work, planning the trips for the *Christmas Seal*. We still had a bus on the road in those days too, an X-ray bus.

There's a famous place on the west coast, the Wreckhouse, where the winds are so high that the people that lived there used to phone Port

---

7   Like Edgar, Walter Davis (b. Freshwater, Conception Bay, 1919) was a schoolteacher before becoming involved with the Tuberculosis Association, of which he was the Executive Director, 1945–56. During his lifetime he also became known as a peace activist and activist for children's rights, travelling all over the world from Ceylon (Sri Lanka) to Northern Ireland. He received the first Newfoundland Human Rights Award in 1988. Davis died in July, 1993 (Cuff "Davis"; Bennett "Province's").

aux Basques and say, "Look, don't let the train go out today. She'll blow off the track."[8] And it did, it happened a couple of times, blew right off the track. One time, going through the little settlement where the Wreckhouse was, the bus blew right over! Smack over on its side. They got a crew and uprighted her and none of the X-ray equipment was hurt in any way whatsoever. She was able to carry right on with the X-rays. It was amazing! Luckily, she was empty of people at the time.

"One of the most soft-spoken persons that I have ever known."

Rex Matthews came back from World War II just at the right time, when we were looking for a couple of X-ray technicians. He and another chap, Fred Fitzgerald, applied and we sent them down to Bliss Murphy at the General Hospital, and he gave them the training they needed in X-ray work. He turned out to be a top-notch employee. We had a public relations person, Rosemary Fitzgibbon, and she was very, very good at it. She was a Memorial graduate, from the old College. She was the daughter of one of St. John's favourite and best-known characters, Joe Fitzgibbon.[9] He'd been a city councillor for years. He was one of the last of the St. John's characters. Oh, he really was something. He became a town councillor on a couple of occasions but he really was the last of the old kind. He was an Irishman, really. Although

---

8   The Wreckhouse or Wreck House is located about 11 kilometres north of Cape Ray on the southwestern corner of Newfoundland, and was named for the destructive winds that funnel from the Table Mountains and used to blow trains off the tracks. In the 1930s, Wreckhouse resident Lauchie MacDougall was contracted to "sniff" the wind and inform the railway whether it was safe to proceed or not (Poole "Wreck House").

9   Joseph M. Fitzgibbon (1881–1960), a highly successful auctioneer, first served on City Council in 1925, and was elected to the House of Assembly in 1928. Beloved for his wit and storytelling ability, he was an attentive and sympathetic politician. "His neighbours weren't limited to those on his street," remembers the *Telegram*'s Jack White. Fitzgibbon Street in St. John's West End is named after him (Jack White 7a).

he was born in St. John's, he was as Irish as they come; he could make up a story so quickly.

Sally Coady worked in the rehabilitation part of the program. She was a Coady from Burin, a very well-known merchant family out there. She had been an adult education worker. She looked after the women's side of the sanatorium.

As for the board members, I remember particularly Frank O'Leary, who was president for a while, who was followed by Josh O'Driscoll. He was a very good chairman of the Rehabilitation Committee. Took a lot of interest. A war veteran.

The one person that I remember most was my old friend, Dr. Miller, one of the most soft-spoken persons that I have ever known. At a Board meeting with 10 or 12 people around this big table, if Dr. Miller spoke everybody, everybody became completely quiet and just listened. He always had something worthwhile to say. Yes, he was renowned for that at all the meetings, the government meetings and all the rest. A very soft-spoken man, and yet he had a terrific knowledge of Newfoundland medical conditions, outports and everywhere. He became the Deputy Minister of Health, Leonard Miller. The Centre down there now has his name on it.[10]

"They were miracle drugs."

Thank God they struck streptomycin, and PAS [Para-Amino-Salicylic] and INAH [Isoniazid]. These three drugs came along at about

---

10   Leonard Miller (1906–78) was born in St. John's and educated at Dalhousie, Harvard, and later Vienna. Miller began private practice as a medical doctor in 1930 before moving to the Department of Health and Public Welfare, and continued in government for the rest of his career. He had a key role in forming the province's Child Welfare Association and in establishing Newfoundland's cottage hospitals in the 1940s. The old General Hospital on Forest Road in St. John's was renamed the Dr. Leonard A. Miller Centre in his honour in 1978. The Miller Centre complex, a centre for rehabilitation and a long-term care facility, now includes Southcott Hall, the present home for the Centre for Nursing Studies, and the Caribou Memorial Veterans Pavilion, a residence for war veterans (Smallwood vol. 3 "Miller"; "Dr. Leonard").

the same time [in the 1950s]. That spelled the end as far as TB was concerned. They were miracle drugs. Finally, we were able to close the sanatorium here, and the Corner Brook one turned into a general hospital. I was involved in the Association for nearly 25 years, '52 to '76, and in my time, they were able to close down the hospitals at Twillingate, Corner Brook and St. Anthony, and St. John's, finally, until there was nothing but a chest unit of six beds up at St. Clare's hospital. Finally there was only one patient in it. That was all due to the discovery of the three miracle drugs that worked together. Lots of patients were able to go home after two or three months and continue their drug treatment at home with no risk to their families.

Eventually some of the other chest conditions had exploded in numbers, emphysema and asthma. Smoking was very much part of our mandate, anti-smoking. There was still work to be done on TB but not to the same extent, of course. And so the association changed from the TB and RD [Respiratory Diseases] Association to the Lung Association. But the British Association never did take on the name they planned to take. They were going to call it the British Association for the Suppression of Tuberculosis and Respiratory Disease. Anyhow, when they put it together to form an acronym, it spelled out BASTARD! They actually came almost to the point of accepting it.

I might have worked at the head office in Ottawa, but my family turned me down. Your mother was against it. When we put it up to you and Jan, you were both against it. No uncertain terms! Well, I wasn't too fussy about it anyhow. I have no regrets at all.[11]

---

11 In his oration introducing Edgar to receive an honorary degree from Memorial University in 1993, Shane O'Dea says, "While he would never claim that he eradicated TB in Newfoundland, no one would ever speak of its eradication without thinking of him" (O'Dea 16).

14. Rotary and the Rotarians

"What meeting are you going to tonight, Dad?"

I joined in 1950. I'd reached a point where at lunchtime one day, you said, "What meeting are you going to tonight, Dad?" I started to think about it and realized that I'd been to a meeting four nights that week, so I said, "That's enough! I'm going to get out of some of this stuff." It was nearly all school or church things I was involved in. Newfoundland Teachers' Association, the Council of Higher Education, etc. So I decided to join Rotary, and it was the best thing I ever did. I enjoyed every year of it and it's up to 50 years now. I'm still enjoying it. We had an historic meeting last week: we have two girls in the Caribou Group now, and we had our first meeting at one of the girl's homes. That made history.

I think the big thing that was important to me when I first joined was that it put me in contact with people who were not involved in education or church. Yes, it's a very mixed group. There were people from all different professions; that's the way you get in. I went in representing education.

I had a hint from John Ayre. John Ayre was one of the directors of Ayre and Sons, and he always seemed to be there greeting customers and showing people around and things and being nice to people. So somehow or other in conversation with him one day (I knew him because he played football, I guess, or rugger), he asked if I'd be interested in joining the Rotary Club. He said, "We only have one member of the club now representing education." That was Allan Fraser, who was a professor of history at Memorial, and also the most outstanding tennis player in Newfoundland.[1] He had been runner-up for the

---

1   See Chapter 10, note 2 (p. 211).

Scottish International Championship before he came here. Nobody here could touch him at all. He went to Nova Scotia to tournaments and cleaned up. "But," John said, "we have nobody at the high school level." He told me the fees and I talked to Margie and I agreed to join: the best thing I ever did because it gave me some variety. Rotary gave me a much wider range of friends.

"Thank God you've joined the right club."

At my first Rotary meeting, I was brought to one of the tables by John Ayre and sat with Charlie Bell and Edgar Hickman. Next to me on my right were John Ayre and Dick Steele.[2] I was fascinated by the conversation that Charlie Bell and Edgar Hickman were having, and then during the conversation, Charlie picked up his fork and one of the prongs of the fork was twisted. So without breaking off in his conversation in any way, he put his hand in his vest pocket, pulled out this little pair of pliers and straightened up his fork, and folded up his pliers and put them back in his pocket again as if it was an everyday occurrence! Later on, when I got to know him, I asked him about it and he said, "Oh yes, I've always carried a pair of pliers ever since I was an engineering student." He said, "You'd be surprised at the number of times that I've had occasion to use them." He told me that just a few weeks before, he had been up to New York with Randy [his son], and Randy got a sparable[3] in his shoe. And so on the sidewalk of New York, hundreds of people passing, off went the shoe and out came the pliers, and he took the sparable out of the shoe and went on.

After the meeting, I went back to school at two o'clock and I was wearing a Harris tweed jacket with patched pockets, and as I've said I was sitting next to Dick Steele on one side and John Ayre on the other. When I went to write something on the blackboard, I felt something

---

2   John Ayre, Charlie Bell, Edgar Hickman, and Dick Steele all were prominent business people in St. John's at the time.

3   A "sparable" is an "Ordinary shoemaker's nail which has worked its way through the heel or sole of a boot or shoe" (*DNE*).

hard in my pocket. I put my hand down and pulled out a spoon with Newfoundland Hotel marked on it! I thought I better try the other side and sure enough, it was a fork, Hotel Newfoundland. These fellows had poked the stuff into my pockets during the meal. So next week I had to sneak back with them and put them back. Margie loved it. She thought it was a great joke and so much so that she said without hesitation, "Thank God you've joined the right club."

"'That really was the spark plug that got the thing going."

The President when I joined Rotary was Frank O'Leary. We used to make bets as to how many times he'd say "Ah" during his speeches. We were up to 47 at one point. He was a very fine man though, Frank O'Leary. You can thank him for the Stadium [Memorial Stadium]. The first Stadium, oh yes! The Lions Club started out fundraising for the new stadium, on King's Bridge Road, and they hadn't gone very far when they ran into difficulties. So Frank O'Leary took over and started this campaign on Water Street of having scores and scores of employees give one per cent of their salary every month and put it into a fund. That built up. That really was the spark plug that got the thing going.[4] He had a lot of very good lines of tinned, bottled goods, and packaged goods, wholesale. He was down just opposite the War

---

4   Memorial Stadium operated from 1954 to 2001. After the Prince's Rink burned down in 1941, the city was without a stadium for hockey and large events, and the $300,000 needed for the project seemed out of reach. However, as Edgar mentions, the Lions Club got involved and began selling shares in the Stadium company, promoting it at "street dances and water carnivals." The building's foundation was completed in 1951, but another $500,000 was needed to complete the project. F.M. O'Leary (see Chapter 13, note 2 (p. 257)) then stepped in and "called a giant meeting of 120 city organizations," and, as Edgar says, it was his campaign to get employees to pledge 1 per cent of their salaries that finished the project. O'Leary was later nicknamed "Spearhead" for his efforts. In the end 7,000 workers signed up, but everyone in the city was involved, even schoolchildren selling lemonade. It was a colossal effort of proud citizen engagement. After much controversy and despite the opposition of most citizens, the Stadium was converted into a Loblaw's supermarket in 2005 (Souvenir booklet; Craig Jackson A3; Bouzane A1.)

Children's Parade to raise funds for Memorial Stadium and a notice by The Great Eastern Oil Co. of its participation in the 1% campaign. (Courtesy Centre for Newfoundland Studies)

Memorial on Water Street. He and Gerald Doyle were the two best-known agents, food agents.

Bliss Murphy joined with four others in 1949, and they almost called themselves the 49ers. Then they changed the name to the Caribou Group. One of them went down south at the time. He was manager of a tobacco company here at the time when Bliss was fighting cigarette smoking. Yes, he was transferred down to Kentucky or somewhere.

The Victorian Order of Nurses

I was very much involved in that — the very first job I had in Rotary. Frank O'Leary, President of Rotary, came to me and said, "Do a little survey and see whether there's any need in St. John's for the Victorian Order of Nurses." So I did; I talked to the Public Health people and they all agreed it would be a good thing for St. John's. The Victorian Order of Nurses is a very old order of nurses, originally from England, which spread to Canada. Instead of calling a public health nurse, which you can't always get, you can be more independent and ring up a Victorian Order nurse to come to your home. They charge a fee, but if the person is not well-to-do, then they just forget the fee or cut it down to what they can afford. It was very strong in some of the cities in Canada.

So I did a survey and I found that it could work here. We sent away and got the first nurse down, Kay Mattiford, a very fine woman, retired now, I think. She did an excellent job in setting up the Order, and Rotary took part of its radio auction money that year and bought a car for her, with "Victorian Order of Nurses" on the side of it. She did a great job. She was from Toronto, and she became one of the top people nationally after she left here.

We set up a small Board. I was Chairman for the first year or two, and then I passed it over to a remarkable character, Hughie Cole. He was retired from the AND Company, living on Circular Road.[5] He was a ball of fire, a great fellow. His son was Harvey Cole. I think there are seven nurses now. They've grown, they're in Corner Brook and Grand Bank now, too, I think.

Volunteer work at the Waterford Hospital

I immediately got into the work at the Waterford Hospital, which at that time had about 700 residents. It was a big, big hospital, and we used to bring in movies and arrange bingo parties, picnics, and we'd buy gifts for everybody in there and give them out on Boxing Day, Christmas gifts. They were all gifts that had been picked out by the staff in the hospital. We'd give them carte blanche. They knew that Bill Smith would like a tie, Tom Jones would like a tin of tobacco, and so on. All the presents were tailored to the wishes of the residents. We nearly always got a cut price for the presents from the merchants. We matched them all. Seven hundred and fifty people at the start, down to three or four hundred later. We went in on Boxing Day morning and gave out the gifts personally to each one of them.

They'd unlock the locked wards and I went in there with Bliss one

---

5   Anglo Newfoundland Development Company. The AND Company was directed by the English newspaper publishers Alfred and Harold Harmsworth. They established a pulp and paper mill at Grand Falls in 1907 (Poole vol. 4 "Pulp"). Hugh Henry Wilding Cole was superintendent of the AND Company, 1912–47, leaving for two years in 1917 to serve overseas with the Newfoundland Foresters. His headquarters were in Badger, where he was known as "King" Cole (Cuff "Cole").

year. Bliss used to read out the names, and I'd pass the gift to Bill Smith or whoever it was. Wish him good health in the New Year or something like that. I can remember this old fellow looking up at me and saying, "My sir, I only hope I live to be as old as you are." Bliss got a great kick out of that.

In the afternoon we'd always have a very good concert. Some of St. John's best artists would give up the time to go in Boxing afternoon. All on a volunteer basis, of course. It was our group, the Caribou Group, that did that. Other groups do different things. We started it because [Dr.] Harry Roberts was in our group, and his brother Charlie was the superintendent of the hospital. The very first thing we did was bring in the CLB Band, back in 1945 [before Edgar joined Rotary]. That was the first record we have of a visit by the Caribou Group to the Waterford.

"All in all, it was a good bit of rehabilitation for them."

After the war, when the big central laundry down at Pepperrell became available, all the Waterford Hospital laundry was sent down there. The result was that a building at the hospital became vacant, and I brought it up to the boys. I said, "Look, there's a great chance there to make a workshop for the better patients that are carpentry-minded and so on, and turn it into a nice workshop for their rehabilitation treatment." So that's what we did. We spent a lot of money in fixing up a very fine workshop for the men, and there were as many as 30, I suppose, working in there at a time. Some of them had carpentry skills before they went to the hospital as patients. They turned out some very fine bookcases, cabinets, and tables and one thing or another, and sold them. The money went to the patients, but it became the Caribou Rehabilitation Workshop. And the tools were all provided by the Caribou Group. We spent a lot and Maurice Wilansky donated a couple of power tools that he had. All in all, it was a good bit of rehabilitation for them.

One of the things we decided to do was get the Newfoundland driftwood from around the lakes and get the residents to clean it up,

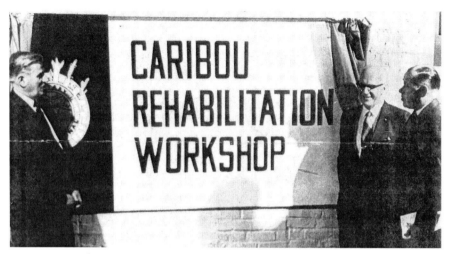

Opening of Caribou Rehabilitation Workshop at Waterford Hospital. Edgar, second from left.

polish it and varnish it. It went very well — there's a piece down in the cabin at Trinity. Most of the driftwood was obtained by Maurice. He took his boat and went down to the southern shore, towed his boat up to three or four different ponds up there and came back with a boat-load of driftwood suitable for ornaments. The patients would spend hours cleaning it and sanding it and the rest of it. It worked very well.

We ran the canteen at the hospital for years. We used to clear about $5,000 a year, which we used for the patients' benefit: movies, picnics, trips on the *Scademia* [a small schooner that offered cruises around St. John's harbour], all that kind of thing. Yes, we used $5,000 no trouble. We hired somebody to do it, but we always had two members from the group, businessmen, to go in once a week and check on everything. I went in two years with the manager of the hotel and we used to check all the goods, and make sure that there was no stealing going on or pilfering. The profits were pretty good.

The Rotary Auction

The Rotary Auction [an annual radio auction] was going strong long before I joined. That was the big event every year, and St. John's was better off as a result. We supplied the money for quite a lot of things, especially the park off Thorburn Road, the Sunshine Park and Lodge, and many other things. Somebody had to do the recording as the bids came in. You had to do the write-ups and the broadcasting. It was all part of it. We've always been lucky in getting people to do the broadcasting, finishing up with John Fitzpatrick,[6] and he's still at it.

We were very much involved in the Iris Kirby House for battered women and their families. That's been a Godsend. It's been going strong ever since it opened on Waterford Bridge Road.

We've collected eyeglasses for Dr. John McNicholas [Doctors Without Borders] on a couple of occasions. I think we've donated money to his work in the Dominican Republic, too. John still comes in at the last minute. He came in yesterday, it must have been half past one. We were all finished our meal. And he just takes a couple of rolls and his dessert. He doesn't get his meal at all.

Changes in Rotary

Our club has grown from 80 members when I started in 1950 to 150 now. There are 10 or 11 groups in the club now. Each group has some particular thing that they look after, so its interests have grown a lot in the last 50 years. There are more clubs in the city now, too, three clubs. There are well over a million Rotarians worldwide.

I have gone to other Rotary Clubs when I've been away working with the Lung Association, particularly. I've gone to many clubs from Halifax out to Vancouver and London, England. Jim Campbell and I went to one of the big London clubs, and at this particular club, you were assigned to a table with all the visitors from various countries assigned to different tables, two to a table. When your name was called, when Jim Campbell and I had our names called, everybody at the table

---

6   John Fitzpatrick was a local auctioneer, head of Fitzpatrick's Auctioneering, which
     he started in 1978. Highly regarded by his peers, he was a tireless volunteer, active
     in Rotary, the Stella Burry Centre, Iris Kirby House, and many other local charities
     and organizations. John Fitzpatrick died on 7 July 2014 (Howells).

got up and clapped and shouted and made as much noise as they could. And that's the thing that happens there. Each table where there are guests tries to make more noise than the one before. They're not very "dignified" Englishmen, not the reserved Englishman stereotype.

"They gave me a standing ovation!"

Yesterday marked my fiftieth year in Rotary. So they had a huge big cake there, and I had to go up and cut it. Dennis Knight was the President. I said to him, "You're taking a chance on this."

He said, "How come?"

I said, "Well, on a previous occasion at a birthday party, I was asked to carve the roast. This was Bliss Murphy's sixteenth birthday. His mother decided that in honour of the occasion, she'd buy a 16-pound roast, which is quite a roast. Anyhow, she invited six of us and Bliss's sister and the girl next door, so we had eight of us sitting down to dinner. And when Mrs. Murphy came in with this huge roast, she said, 'Edgar, you're in first year at university now, and no doubt you're doing some biology and you're cutting up this and that. You should be able to carve the roast.'

The Caribou Group, 1993. Back row: Colin Patey, Ian Wishart, Robert Andrews, Armand Agabab, Jim Strain, John Hicks; front row: Harry Roberts, Phonse House, Edgar House.

"'Oh,' I said, 'I'd be glad to, sure. I've carved it at home.' So I took the big carving knife and the steel and very professionally I started to rub the knife over the steel and sharpen it up a little bit. It slipped and took my thumb there [indicates]. Blood all over the white linen table-cloth. I was mortified. Dr. Murphy heard the commotion so he rushed in. He grabbed my hand and staunched the blood. Took me down-stairs to his surgery and did a job on my thumb. No stitches; he did a wonderful job of taping it. When it cured, you could hardly see the scar there, but I really bled.

"That was only the start of the night. Later on, we went out to the billiard room and started playing billiards. Bliss's sister, Ethel, was over on one side of the table and went to pass the cue to me, and in doing so struck the big bowl light up over the table. It smashed in a hundred pieces all over the surface of this beautiful billiard table. Of course, we were both mortified. The doctor rushed in and he started to laugh. He said, 'Thank God, I've been going to get that billiard table covered for the last two or three months. Now, I've got to have it cov-ered!' He was a good sport about it."

So that was my tale of woe before I cut the cake at Rotary. But it went very well, and they had a good crowd there. That's when they gave me the Fiftieth pin. And they gave me a standing ovation! Vanessa [Edgar's granddaughter] was there. I was delighted that she came along. She was actually a guest of Heidi Windsor's, but Heidi had to sit at the head table and Vanessa sat with me down at the Caribou Group table. It was great! I think she enjoyed it. She enjoys most things, I think.

Conclusion

After a long and satisfying career, Edgar stopped work with the Lung Association in 1976 and spent the last 30 years of his life in a contented, but by no means idle, retirement. He turned to writing local history, and had three books published: *Light at Last: Triumph over Tuberculosis in Newfoundland and Labrador, 1900–1975* (recently reprinted); *Edward Feild, The Man and His Legacy, With Extended Reference to Bishop Feild College*; and *The Way Out: The Story of Nonia, 1920–1990*.

He continued his community involvement as well, especially with Rotary. His grandchildren can remember twisting the leaves

Edgar receiving portrait of Glen Avon from NONIA (the Newfoundland Outport Nursing and Industrial Association) after publishing *The Way Out: The Story of NONIA* in 1990. Margie in foreground, Premier Clyde Wells on left, and artist Carl Stephenson to Edgar's left.

off dried silver dollar plants with Pop and Nana to sell to fundraise for St. Thomas' Church. An expert woodcarver, he would often borrow our ornaments and sculptures and make perfect replicas of them in his workshop. He enjoyed watching his children and grandchildren progress and grow up. He and Margie took several trips to Florida, where they enjoyed swimming in the ocean.

Edgar and Margie with Grandchildren, c. 1985.

Edgar kept going to Trinity in the summertime for as long as he could, right up to the last few years of his life. Part of him was anchored in that beautiful place; it was a counter to the more bustling

Marie Giannou, Margie, George Giannou, and Edgar. Florida, c. 1970s.

pace of life in St. John's, and he still felt deeply connected to the area through his parents having both been from there.

From Trinity and Champneys, via Change Islands, George and Mary House had moved to St. John's as a young, excited couple and dove into city life with alacrity. George taught at Bishop Feild with I.J. Samson and became heavily involved in the community, and Mary became busy as a housewife and mother, gardener, knitter for her family and community, and bridge player. Edgar grew up as an outstanding athlete and scholar, and upon returning from getting his B.Sc. in Canada he immersed himself into teaching and community involvement with the full enthusiasm of his father. Positive and ambitious, he took the opportunities that came his way, such as moving to Buchans, and taking the job as Headmaster at Feild, fully enjoying the different

Margie and Edgar, c. 1990.

paths that he took in life. He especially enjoyed the many interactions he had with the boys under his tutelage and the men and women he helped rehabilitate from TB, gaining satisfaction from the positive changes that education and rehabilitation could make. He married a dynamic, bright, and light-hearted woman and had a thoroughly satisfying family life.

Edgar's life was not what you would call dissatisfied or angst-filled! Nor was it a passive one — he was always striving for new ways to challenge himself or make a difference in his community, which he did. As his son-in-law, Jordy Squires, put it, Edgar was an "extraordinary ordinary man," and he lived his life with integrity and humour.

The latter part of Edgar's life was not without sorrow, however. Margie developed Alzheimer's disease in the late 1980s, and it was incredibly difficult for Edgar to come to terms with. He wouldn't accept that her memory was fading away, and couldn't understand when she forgot people's names, or small things throughout the day. As is the case with the disease, she slowly deteriorated over the years. The last few years of her life and up until her death in 2000 were perhaps the one low period in Edgar's life; his lifelong love, companion, and friend was lost to him.

Edgar and great-granddaughter Erin Cadigan, 2000.

It was hard to rally from that, but rally he did, and the last few years of his own life were relatively happy ones. His grandchildren were a source of joy and stimulation to him, and it delighted him to have visits at 20 Portugal Cove Road from his great-grandchildren when they started to arrive.

He continued to enjoy attending the meetings of the St. John's Rotary Club as part of the Caribou Group. He found renewed pleasure in the company of others, and took a keen delight in recounting stories of the past to any visitors he had. When he eventually required homecare, his attendants grew immensely fond of him, with his quirky, charismatic personality and rich cache of stories and history.

For his many, varied services to his community, Edgar received formal recognition through honorary life memberships in the Newfoundland Teachers' Association (NTA), both the Newfoundland and Canadian Tuberculosis and Respiratory Diseases Associations, the Feildian Athletic Association, and the Caribou Group of the Rotary

Edgar receiving honorary Doctor of Laws degree from Memorial University President Art May, 1994.

Club of St. John's, where he was also made a Paul Harris Fellow. In 1994 he was awarded an honorary Doctor of Laws degree by Memorial University, and in 1995 he was honoured with the Bishop's Award of Merit from the Anglican Church. His athletic prowess was recognized in 1999 when he was named to both the St. John's and the

Newfoundland and Labrador soccer halls of fame. In 2004, the new computer lab at Bishop Feild School was named The Edgar House Legacy Learning Centre in his honour.

But it was the informal recognition that Edgar received, the smaller acknowledgements of the way in which he touched people, like the following excerpt from a letter that he had saved, dated 8 January 1949, that most typified his modest, purposeful life:

> Dear Edgar,
> I want you to know that I heard your friendly and complimentary reference to me at the Rotary Club the other day. Several friends telephoned me about it too. I've been laid low for 3 years now, pretty much out of things and it is nice to be remembered in this way. I appreciate it most sincerely. (from Ted Meaney)[1]

This is a good example of Edgar's character and philosophy, passed down from such figures as his father, his schoolteachers, J.L. Paton, and others.

He continued to live in his house, the same one that he and Margie had bought and renovated in 1938, right up until a couple of weeks before he died, which happened peacefully. His death came in 2006, at the age of 94.

In his obituary for *The Telegram*,[2] Senator Bill Rompkey, a former federal cabinet minister and Feild student, wrote with fondness and admiration of his former teacher, remembering the "confidence in his gaze and hint of a smile about his eyes" as he inspired the students in sports and academics. Rompkey remarked that, at the dedication of

---

1   Edward Meaney (1917–49) was a TB sufferer who dedicated himself to fighting the disease in Newfoundland. While still in hospital he started a magazine, *The Happy Warrior*, to further his cause. Upon his release he continued the magazine and made public appearances. Tragically, his TB returned and he died in 1949, but not before becoming the main driving force to establish the TB Association in Newfoundland (House "Light at Last" 78–80; Smallwood vol. 3 "Meaney").

2   "A Man Who Made a Difference," *The Telegram*, 6 Aug. 2006.

the computer lab, "It was clear that those of us who had been Feildians still kept a special place in our memories for a spirit we could not define or describe but which was, nevertheless, real and abiding." The flags at the NTA flew at half-mast at the news of Edgar's death.

The funeral took place at St. Thomas' Church, which had been Edgar's church for the latter half of his life. It was massively attended. Prominent among the mourners was a large group of grey-haired men, Edgar's former students at Bishop Feild. Perhaps the most moving moment of the service was when, as his coffin was carried down the aisle of the church, these former students spontaneously burst into the college song, to see their old Headmaster off. *Non moritur cujus fama vivit*, "He does not die whose fame lives on," was the motto of his old school. Edgar would have smiled.

Bibliography

Abbott, Bill. *Herder Memorial Trophy*. St. John's: Breakwater Books, 2000.

"Ada Nemec Biographical Note." *Trinity Historical Society*. Trinity, NL: Trinity Historical Society, 2004. Accessed online 24 Mar. 2014.

Adams, Fred. *Fred Adams' St. John's*. St. John's: Creative Publishers, 1986.

———. *St. John's — The Last 100 Years*. St. John's: Creative Publishers, 1988.

"About Shannie." *Shannie Duff Deputy Mayor*. Shannie Duff, 2010. Accessed online 2 Dec. 2011.

Alexander, David. "Development and Dependence in Newfoundland, 1880–1970." *Acadiensis* 4, 7 (1974).

Andrews, G.H. *St. John's City Directory, 1924*. St. John's: St. John's Directory Co., 1924, 356.

Andrews, Gerald W. *Heritage of a Newfoundland Outport: The Story of Port de Grave*, rev. ed. Carbonear, NL: Transcontinental, 2006.

Andrews, Ralph L. *Integration and Other Developments in Newfoundland Education 1915–1949*. Edited by Alice E. Wareham. St. John's: Harry Cuff, 1985.

———. *Post-Confederation Developments in Newfoundland Education 1949–1975*. Edited by Alice E. Wareham. St. John's: Harry Cuff, 1985.

"Annual Totals." *The Feildian* 29, 3 (1923–24): 91.

Atkinson, Robert. *The Life Story Interview*. Thousand Oaks, Calif.: Sage, 1998. Accessed online 4 Sept. 2013.

The Atlantic Jewish Council. The Atlantic Jewish Council, 2012. Accessed online 14 Mar. 2014.

"Arthur Scammell, Dead at 82." *The Evening Telegram*, 29 Aug. 1995.

Baggs, C.R. *St. John's Business Directory*. St. John's: Allied Newfoundland Publications, 1948, 10.

Baird, Moira. "Bowring Coming Back Big." *The Telegram*, 25 Aug. 2004, D1.

———. "Provincial R&D Corps Unveiled." *The Telegram*, 14 May 2009, D1. Accessed online 9 May 2014.

Bartels, Dennis A., and Olaf Uwe Janzen. "Micmac Migration to Western Newfoundland." Paper presented to the annual meeting of the Canadian Historical Association, Victoria, 1990.

"Barrelman Radio Program," coll-028. Finding aid by Gail Wei in CNS archives, MUN 1992.

Bennett, Bernie. "Former Lieutenant Governor John Harnum Dead at 85." *The Telegram*, 1 Mar. 1996, 8.

———. "Flashback: Adrian Miller." *The Evening Telegram*, 17 Oct. 1981, 15.

———. "Like Father Like Son: Doug House Centre Half for 1st Feildian Title Team Since Dad's Champ." *The Daily News*, 26 Sept 1961, 11.

———. "Province's Leading Peace Activist Dies." *The Evening Telegram*, 27 July 1993.

Bennett, Tara Bradbury. "The Sports Shop Burned Again: This Time, Thieves Do Damage to Downtown Business." *The Telegram*, 8 June 2004, A4.

Benson, Bob. "A Lifetime of Achievement: Grace Sparkes Will Be Missed." *The Telegram*, 16 Mar. 2003, A12. Accessed online 16 May 2014.

"Biographical Sketch: Dr. Ian Rusted." *The Early Days of the Medical School at M.U.N.* Memorial University of Newfoundland. Accessed online 5 Jan. 2012.

"Bishop Feild College." *Newfoundland and Labrador Heritage*. Memorial University of Newfoundland and the C.R.B. Foundation, 1997. Accessed online 6 July 2013.

Blake, Raymond B. *Canadians at Last: Canada Integrates Newfoundland as a Province*. Toronto: University of Toronto Press, 1994.

Blishen, Bernard R. "A Socio-Economic Index for Occupations in Canada." *Canadian Review of Sociology and Anthropology* 5, 1(1967): 41–53.

"Bob Cole." *Bios, CBC Media Centre*. CBC, 2013. Accessed online 6 Nov. 2013.

Bottomore, T.B., and Maximilien Rubel. *Karl Marx: Selected Writings in Sociology and Social Philosophy*. London: Watts, 1956.

Bouzane, Bradley. "Nays Turn Out in Force." *The Telegram*, 6 Oct. 2004, A1.

Brock, Kathy L., and Keith G. Banting, eds. *The Nonprofit Sector and Government in a New Century*. Montreal and Kingston: McGill-Queen's University Press, 2001.

——— and ———. *The Nonprofit Sector in Interesting Times*. Montreal and Kingston: McGill-Queen's University Press, 2003.

Brookes, Chris. *A Public Nuisance: A History of the Mummers Troupe*. St. John's: ISER Books, 1988.

———. *Not Fit for It: How Newfoundland Gave up Elective Democracy in 1934*. St. John's: Battery Radio, 2004. Compact Disc.

Broom, Leonard, and Philip Selznick. *Sociology: A Text with Adapted Readings*, 5th ed. New York: Harper and Row, 1975.

Browne, Gary, and Darrin McGrath. *Soldier Priest in the Killing Fields of Europe*. St. John's: DRC Publishing, 2006.

Browne, John. "Rugby Alive and Well in Newfoundland." *The Telegram*, 3 July 1994, 10.

————. "Plenty of Problems to Tackle." *The Telegram*, 13 July 2013, B4. Accessed online 23 May 2014.

Bugden, Richard. Letter. *Atlantic Guardian* 8, 3 (1951): 9.

Burke, Maurice. *Memories of Outport Life*. St. John's: Creative Publishers, 1985.

Button, E.P., and A.R. Thomson. *St. John's Classified Business and City Directory*. St. John's: Manning and Rabbitts, 1932, 30.

Canada. Statistics Canada. *Newfoundland Census 1901*.

————. *Newfoundland Census 1911*.

————. *Newfoundland Census 1921*.

————. *Newfoundland Census 1935*.

————. *1945 Population Census District of Grand Falls: Buchans*. Accessed online 27 Mar. 2014.

————. Statistics Canada National Household Survey: Data Table. "Religion (108): Newfoundland and Labrador." Statistics Canada. Accessed online 14 Dec 2014.

————. Statistics Canada National Household Survey. "NHS Profile, Newfoundland and Labrador, 2011." Statistics Canada, 2011. Accessed online 25 Sept. 2013.

————. Statistics Canada National Household Survey. "Population and Dwelling Counts Newfoundland and Labrador, Census Metropolitan Area (CMA) and Census Agglomerations (CA)." Statistics Canada, 2011. Accessed online 2 June 2014.

Candow, James E. *A Short History of James Ryan Limited*. Halifax: Parks Canada, 2005.

Carberry, Fred. "A History of Football in St. John's." Memorial University of Newfoundland, 1973.

Carew, S.J., ed. *J.L.P. A Portrait of John Lewis Paton by His Friends*. St. John's: Memorial University of Newfoundland Paton College, 1968.

Carnell's Funeral Home. Accessed online 4 Oct. 2011.

Carter, Fred. "The Generosity of a War Hero." *The Telegram*, 11 Nov. 2004, A11.

Cave, Joy B. *Two Newfoundland V.C.s.* St. John's: Creative Publishers, 1984.

Chen, C. Peter. "Newfoundland in World War II." World War II Database. Lava Development, LLC. Accessed online 12 Aug. 2014.

Chiaramonte, Louis J. *Craftsman–Client Contracts: Interpersonal Relations in a Newfoundland Fishing Settlement*. St. John's: ISER Books, 1970.

"Citations of Faculty Members." *Memorial University of Newfoundland Gazette*, 8 June 2000, 13.

"City Council." *The Evening Telegram*, 4 June 1910, 5.

Clarke, George W. *Can Any Good Thing Come out of Crocker's Cove?* St. John's: Harry Cuff, 1992.

Clarke, Sandra. "Language in Newfoundland and Labrador: Past, Present and Future." *Journal of the CAAL* (Canadian Association of Applied Linguistics) 19, 1–2 (1997): 11–34.

———. *Newfoundland and Labrador English*. Edinburgh: Edinburgh University Press, 2010.

———. "Sociolinguistic Patterning in a New-World Dialect of Hiberno-English: The Speech of St. John's, Newfoundland." *Perspectives on the English Language in Ireland*. Edited by John Harris, David Little, and David Singleton. Dublin: Trinity College, 1986, 67–81.

CLB website. "A Company #119 C.L.B. has the honour of being first C.L.B. Company in the Colonies (1892)." www.theclb.ca/index.php/history. Accessed online 18 Aug. 2014.

Climo, Jacob J., and Marian G. Cattell, eds. *Social Memory and History: Anthropological Perspectives*. Walnut Creek, Calif.: Altamara Press, 2002.

Cole, Doug. *Elliston: The Story of a Newfoundland Outport*. Portugal Cove, Newfoundland: ESPress, 1997.

Cole, Sally. *Women of the Praia: Work and Lives in a Portuguese Coastal Community*. Princeton, N.J.: Princeton University Press, 1991.

Collier, Keith. "Churchill Park Garden Suburb." Newfoundland and Labrador Heritage website, 2011. Accessed online 17 Nov. 2013.

———. "Six Decades of Expansion: St. John's Suburbs and Surrounding Communities." Newfoundland and Labrador Heritage website, 2011. Accessed online 16 Oct. 2013.

Colton, Glenn David. *Newfoundland Rhapsody: Frederick R. Emerson and the Musical Culture of the Island*. Montreal and Kingston: McGill-Queen's University Press, 2014.

Conveyance document. Glenridge Crescent to Charlie Hutchings from the Winter Estate. 1942.

Cranford, Garry. *The Buchans Miners: A Mining and Hockey Legacy*. St. John's: Flanker Press, 1997.

Cullum, Linda, and Marilyn Porter, eds. *Creating This Place: Women, Family, and Class in St. John's, 1900–1950*. Montreal and Kingston: McGill-Queen's University Press, 2014.

Cuff, Harry, ed. *Take a Deep Breath: Reflections — Lives Touched by Tuberculosis*. St. John's: Harry Cuff, 2003.

Cuff, Robert H., ed. *Dictionary of Newfoundland and Labrador Biography*. St. John's: Harry Cuff, 1990.

"Blackall, William Walker."

"Carnell, Geoffrey Conrad."

"Cherrington, Violet."

"Cole, Hugh Henry Wilding."

"Crosbie, John Carnell."

"Davis, Walter H."

"Goodridge, Harold Belfield."

"Jamieson, Donald Campbell."

"Manuel, Edith Mary."

"Monroe, Walter Stanley."

"Morgan, Moses Osbourne."

"O'Leary, Francis Martin."

"Sparkes, Grace Margaret."

"Taylor, Stephen J.L."

"Winter, Marmaduke."

"Winter, Thomas."

Currey, Rev. John E. "Remembering Capt. Peter Troake." *The Downhomer* 11, 7 (1998): 27–28.

Danson, Barney. "Newfie Screech Was Maligned." Canadian Press Clipping Service, 13 June 1973. Letter.

Davis, Ryan. "The Newly Veiled Face of Mummering: Reinventing Tradition and Conserving Culture." *Newfoundland Quarterly* 104, 3 (2011): 43–47.

Dawe, William Albert, and (Field), Olive Florence. Stonepics Database, NF135/SCP01.

"Distinguished Flying Medal." Veterans Affairs Canada, 28 Jan 2014. Accessed online 22 Apr. 2014.

"Distinguished Newfoundlander Allan M. Fraser Dies." *The Fisherman's Advocate*, 21 Nov. 1969, 10.

"Dominion of Newfoundland." *New Zealand History.* New Zealand Ministry for Culture and Heritage. Accessed online 12 Aug. 2014.

Downer, Don, and Jody Bull. "Newfoundland's Denominational Education System: Stages of Development, the Constitution and Legislative Changes." Paper presented at the annual conference of the Canadian Association for Studies in Educational Administration, June 1996.

"Dr. Edith Mary Manuel, L.L.D." Twilingate Museum and Craft Shop. Accessed online 12 Jan. 2012.

"Dr. Leonard A. Miller Centre." Eastern Health Newfoundland and Labrador. Accessed online 3 Aug. 2013.

Dwyer, Mark. "What She Said." *The Newfoundland Herald*, 12 Feb. 2000, 12–13.

Dyer, Gwynne. "A Triumph for Left over Right." *Winnipeg Free Press.* Accessed online 30 Aug. 2009.

"Early History of the CLB." The C.L.B. Accessed online 4 Jan. 2012.

Faris, James C. *Cat Harbour: A Newfoundland Fishing Settlement.* St. John's: ISER Books, 1972.

Farquharson, Danine. "London Theatre Company." Newfoundland and Labrador Heritage. Memorial University of Newfoundland and the C.R.B. Foundation, 1997. 2001. 10 Nov. 2011.

"Fictive Kin." Adoption.com. 2013. Accessed online 7 May 2014.

Fitzgerald, John, ed. *Newfoundland at the Crossroads: Documents on Confederation with Canada.* St. John's: Terra Nova, 2002.

Fizzard, Kelleher, et al. *The History of Education in Newfoundland 1727–2000.* St. John's: Faculty of Education, Memorial University, 2007.

Flynn, Paula. "Don Randell: Mistaken Fiddling Dichotomies." *Newfoundland and Labrador Studies* 22, 1 (2007). Accessed online 12 Jan. 2012.

"Fraser, Allan MacPherson, M.A." *Newfoundland's Who's Who,* 1952, 37.

Freund, Alexander, ed. *Beyond the Nation? Immigrants' Local Lives in Transnational Cultures.* Toronto: University of Toronto Press, 2012.

Furlong, Wallace. *Georgestown: An Historic Corner of Old St. John's.* St. John's: Flanker Press, 2004.

Galgay, Frank, and Michael McCarthy. *Olde St. John's: Stories from a Seaport City.* St. John's: Flanker Press, 2001.

Gerth, Hans, and C. Wright Mills. *From Max Weber: Essays in Sociology.* New York: Oxford University Press, 1946.

———. *Character and Social Structure: The Psychology of Social Institutions.* London: Routledge & Kegan Paul, 1953.

Gluck, Sherna Berger, and Daphne Patai. *Women's Words: The Feminist Practice of Oral History.* New York: Routledge, 1991.

Godfrey, Stuart R. *Human Rights and Social Policy in Newfoundland, 1832–1982.* St. John's: Harry Cuff, 1985.

Goodley, Dan, Rebecca Lawthom, Peter Clough, and Michele Moore. *Researching Life Stories: Method, Theory and Analyses in a Biographical Age.* London: Routledge Falmer, 2004.

Gorham, Beth. "Old-fashioned Businesses Buckling Under." *The Evening Telegram,* 6 June 1992, 30.

Grattan, Patricia. *City Seen: Artists' Views of St. John's, 1785–2010.* St. John's: Winter Place Projects, 2011.

Grenville, Nancy. Samuel Hefferton papers COLL-018, Archives and Special Collections, Queen Elizabeth II Library, Memorial University, St. John's, 1981. Accessed online 17 Aug. 2014.

Gwynn, Richard. *Smallwood: The Unlikely Revolutionary.* Toronto: McClelland and Stewart, 1968.

Hall, Michael, et al. *The Capacity to Serve: A Qualitative Study of the Challenges Facing Canada's Nonprofit and Voluntary Organizations*. Toronto: Canadian Centre for Philanthropy, 2003.

Halpert, Herbert, and G.M. Story, eds. *Christmas Mumming in Newfoundland*. Toronto: University of Toronto Press, 1990.

Handcock, Gordon. *The Story of Trinity*. Trinity: Trinity Historical Society, 1997.

"'Happy Memories': Water St. Institution and Historical Business Closing Up Shop after 108 Years." *The Independent* 4, 45 (2006): 13.

Harding, Robert James Allen. "Glorious Tragedy: Newfoundland's Cultural Memory of the Battle of Beaumont Hamel, 1916–1949." M.A. thesis, Dalhousie University, 2004.

Harris, Julie. "Colony Club Restaurant, 64 Portugal Cove Road, St. John's, Newfoundland." Agenda paper. Ottawa: Historic Sites and Monuments Board of Canada, 1987.

Hebbard, Gary. "Cancer Centre Named after Crusader for Patient Care." *The Evening Telegram*, 27 Jan.1993, 3.

Higgins, Jenny. "Labrador West." Newfoundland and Labrador Heritage. Memorial University of Newfoundland and the C.R.B. Foundation, 1997. Accessed online 4 Oct. 2011.

———. "The Collapse of Denominational Education." 13 May 2014.

———. "Fort Pepperrell, St. John's." 10 Nov. 2011.

High, Stephen, ed. *Occupied St. John's: A Social History of a City at War, 1939–1945*. Montreal and Kingston: McGill-Queen's University Press, 2010.

"History: Rugby on the Rock." The Rock: Official Website of the Newfoundland Rugby Union. 2011. Accessed online 24 June 2013.

"History." Prince of Wales Archives. 4 Jan. 2011. Accessed online14 Nov. 2011.

Holmes, John. "The London Theatre Company." *Newfoundland Theatre Research: Proceedings*. Edited by D. Lynde, H. Peters, and R. Buehler. St. John's: Memorial University of Newfoundland, Department of English, 1993, 81–87.

Hodder, L.L. *Brief History of the Society of United Fishermen*. St. John's: Society of United Fishermen, 1973.

Horwood, Harold. *A Walk in the Dream Time: Growing Up in Old St. John's*. St. John's: Killick Press, 1997.

House, Edgar. *Edward Feild: The Man and His Legacy*. St. John's: Jesperson Press, 1987.

———. *Light at Last: Triumph over Tuberculosis in Newfoundland and Labrador, 1900–1975*, 2nd ed. St. John's: Lung Association of Newfoundland and Labrador, 2005.

———. *The Way Out: The Story of NONIA, 1920–1990*. St. John's: Creative Publishers, 1990.

House, J.D. *Lectures on Newfoundland Society and Culture*. St. John's: Division of Part-Time Credit Studies, Memorial University, 1978.

———. *The Challenge of Oil: Newfoundland's Quest for Controlled Development*. St. John's: ISER Books, 1986.

Hong, Kim. "My Life in Newfoundland." *Reflections of the Chinese Community on the Occasion of the 30th Anniversary of the Chinese Association of Newfoundland and Labrador 1976–2006*. St. John's: Chinese Association of Newfoundland and Labrador, 2007, 32–33.

Hong, Robert G. "To Take Action without Delay: Newfoundland's Chinese Immigration Act of 1906." Dissertation, Memorial University of Newfoundland, 1986.

Howells, Laura. "Friends Fondly Remember John Fitzpatrick." *The Telegram*, 8 July 2014. Accessed online 14 July 2013.

"Howse, Dr. Claude Kilbourne, M.Sc., Ph.D." Obituary. Mackey's Funeral Home. 4 April 1996. Accessed online 4 Feb. 2014.

Hunt, Rev. Edmund. *Aspects of the History of Trinity*. Edited by Percy Janes. St. John's: Harry Cuff, 1981.

Hunt, Robert. *Corner Boys*. St. John's: Flanker Press, 2011.

"In Memory of Wing Commander Arthur James Samson." Canadian Virtual War Memorial. Veterans Affairs Canada. 14 Mar. 2014. Accessed online 15 Apr. 2014.

Kahn, Alison. *Listen While I Tell You: A Story of the Jews of St. John's, Newfoundland*. St. John's: ISER Books, 1987.

Kendall, Victor, and Victor G. Kendall. *Out of the Sea: A History of Ramea*. St. John's: Harry Cuff, 1991.

Kennedy, Frank J. *A Corner Boy Remembers: Growing Up in St. John's*. St. John's: Breakwater Books, 2006.

Knight, Dennis. *The Place: Recollections of an Outport Childhood*. St. John's: DRC Publishing, 2010.

Knott, Greg. "Crosbie Appointed Lieutenant Governor." *The Telegram*, 21 Dec. 2007, 3.

Jackson, Craig. "Councillors to Reject Stadium Report." *The Telegram*, 14 Jan. 2005, A3.

Jackson, Doug. *On the Country: The Micmac of Newfoundland*. St. John's: Harry Cuff, 1993.

"The Jeweller St. John's Knows." *The Evening Telegram*, 10 Aug. 1995, 14.

"Join in the Celebration: Big Parade Planned for This Morning." *The Daily News*, 12 Nov. 1918, 3.

"John Louis Paton." Celebrate Memorial History. Memorial University of Newfoundland. Accessed online 2 Dec. 2011.

Letto, Doug. *Chocolate Bars and Rubber Boots*. Paradise, NL: Blue Hill Publishing, 1998.

———. *Newfoundland's Last Prime Minister: Frederick Alderdice and the Death of a Nation*. Portugal Cove-St. Philip's, NL: Boulder Publications, 2014.

Li, Krista L. "'Knights of the Flatiron': Gender, Morality, and the Chinese in St. John's, Newfoundland, 1895–1906." Dissertation. University of New Brunswick, 2010.

Long, Gene. "William Coaker and the Loss of Faith: Toward and Beyond Consensus in the Suspension of Newfoundland's Self-Government, 1925–1933." Dissertation. Memorial University of Newfoundland, 1992. Accessed online.

———. *Suspended State: Newfoundland before Canada*. St. John's: Breakwater Books, 1999.

MacEachern, Daniel. "St. John's Rejects Heritage Designation for 130-Year-Old House." *The Telegram*, 25 Nov. 2014, A1, A4. Accessed online 1 Dec. 2014.

Mackenzie, David. *Inside the Atlantic Triangle: Canada and the Entrance of Newfoundland into Confederation 1939–1949*. Toronto: University of Toronto Press, 1986.

MacLean, Colin. "Mummers on Parade." *The Telegram*, 17 Dec. 2012, A1.

MacLeod, Malcolm. *A Bridge Built Halfway: A History of Memorial University College, 1925–1950*. Montreal and Kingston: McGill-Queen's University Press, 1990.

Maggo, Paulus. *Remembering the Years of My Life: Journeys of a Labrador Inuit Hunter*. Edited with an Introduction by Carol Brice-Bennett. St. John's: ISER Books, 1999.

"Magistrate." "Twillingate Celebrates." *The Evening Herald*, 11 Nov. 1918, 7.

"Main Street Jamboree." Hillbilly Music Dawt Com. 2009. Accessed online 5 Jan. 2012.

Malone, Greg. *Don't Tell the Newfoundlanders: The True Story of Newfoundland's Confederation with Canada*. Toronto: Alfred A. Knopf Canada, 2012.

Martin, Wilfred B.W. (with the assistance of Eileen Martin). *Random Island Pioneers*. St. John's: Creative Publishers, 1990.

Martin, Willis P. *Two Outports: A History of Dildo—New Harbour*. St. John's: Flanker Press, 2006.

Matthews, Ralph D. *"There's No Better Place Than Here": Social Change in Three Newfoundland Communities*. Toronto: University of Toronto Press, 1976.

McCourt, Frank. *Angela's Ashes: A Memoir of Childhood*. London: HarperCollins, 1996.

McGrath, Darrin. "K of C Memories Still Sharp." *The Telegram*, 12 Dec. 2007, A1. Accessed online 10 June 2014.

McGrath, Robin. "2009 Index of Jews in Newfoundland." Memorial University of Newfoundland, 2009. Accessed online 5 Jan. 2012.

McNeil, Bill, and Morris Wolfe. *Signing On: The Birth of Radio in Canada*. Toronto: Doubleday, 1982.

Mead, George Herbert. *Mind, Self and Society*. Chicago: University of Chicago Press, 1934.

Mellin, Robert. *Newfoundland Modern: Architecture in the Smallwood Years, 1949–1972*. Montreal and Kingston: McGill-Queen's University Press, 2011.

Memorial University of Newfoundland. *J.L.P.: A Portrait of John Lewis Paton by his Friends*. St. John's: Paton College. N.d.

"Meritorious Service Awards Recognize MUN Pensioners." *The Communicator*. Accessed online 16 Jan. 2012.

Miller, Adrian. Personal interview. 27 Nov. 2013.

Mills, C. Wright. *The Power Elite*. New York: Oxford University Press, 1956.

Montague, Louie. *I Never Knowed It Was Hard: Memoirs of a Labrador Trapper*. Edited by Elizabeth Dawson. Introduction by Robin McGrath. St. John's: ISER Books, 2013.

"MUN Physical Education Pioneer Dies." *The Telegram*, 10 Nov. 2007, 7.

Murphy, Capt. L.C. "How Ricketts Won the V.C." *Newfoundland Quarterly* 18, 4 (1919): 26.

Murphy, Dee. *Our Sports: The Games and Athletes of Newfoundland and Labrador*. St. John's: James Lane, 2010.

Murphy, Tony, and Paul Kenney. *The Trail of the Caribou: Newfoundland in the First World War, 1914–1918*. St. John's: Harry Cuff, 1991.

Myer, P.J. *Recollections of Cricket*. St. Johns: Evening Herald Print, 1915.

Neary, Peter, ed. *The Political Economy of Newfoundland, 1929–1972*. Vancouver: Copp Clark, 1973.

———. *Newfoundland in the North Atlantic World, 1929–1949*. Montreal and Kingston: McGill-Queen's University Press, 1988.

The Newfoundland Soccer Association 40th Anniversary Special Souvenir Edition: 1950–1990. St. John's: Newfoundland Soccer Association, 1990.

Newfoundland. *Report of the Examinations Conducted by the Council of Higher Education*. St. John's: Government of Newfoundland, 1920–1937.

———. *Report of the Public Schools of Newfoundland under Roman Catholic Boards for the Year Ended 31st December, 1918*. St. John's: Trade Review Publishing Company, 1919.

Newfoundland and Labrador. *Historical Statistics of Newfoundland and Labrador* 2, 1 (July 1977).

Newfoundland and Labrador Provincial Archives. *The Story of the Colonial Building*. St. John's: Government of Newfoundland and Labrador, 1972.

"Newfoundland Flavour to National Rugby Team." *The Telegram*, 15 June 1996, 23.

Newhook, Cle. *Mostly in Rodneys*. St. John's: Harry Cuff, 1985.

Nicholson, Colonel G.W.L. *The Fighting Newfoundlander: A History of the Royal Newfoundland Regiment*. St. John's: Government of Newfoundland, n.d. [1964?].

O'Brien, Dick. "Water Street Gets the New Look." *Atlantic Guardian* 7, 1 (1950): 36–42.

O'Dea, Shane. "Oration Honouring Edgar George House." *MUN Gazette*, 3 June 1993, 16.

O'Flaherty, Patrick. *Lost Country: The Rise and Fall of Newfoundland*. St. John's: Long Beach Press, 2005.

———. *Leaving the Past Behind: Newfoundland History from 1934*. St. John's: Long Beach Press, 2011.

"Old Colony Club Project Moving Ahead." *The Telegram*, 24 Aug. 2004, A3. Accessed online 9 May 2014.

O'Mara, John F. "Prominent Figures from Our Recent Past: Thomas McMurdo and Peter A. O'Mara." *Newfoundland Quarterly* 85, 3 (1990): 29.

O'Neill, Paul. *The Oldest City: The Story of St. John's, Newfoundland*. Erin, Ont.: Press Porcepic, 1975.

———. *A Seaport Legacy: The Story of St. John's, Newfoundland*. Erin, Ont.: Press Porcepic, 1976.

———.*The Oldest City: The Story of St. John's, Newfoundland*. St. John's: Boulder, 2003.

"Ottenheimer Dead at 63." *The Evening Telegram*, 19 Jan. 1998, 1.

Overton, James. *Making a World of Difference: Essays on Tourism, Culture and Development in Newfoundland*. St. John's: ISER Books, 1996.

"Parsons, Chesley Robert." *The Telegram*, 23 Jan. 2014, A7. Accessed online 9 May 2014.

Patey, Nina. *The Express*, 11 Mar. 1992, 23, 31.

"Pharmacy: One of the Oldest of the Established Professions . . ." Newfoundland Pharmaceutical Association, 1988, 8.

Philbrook, Tom. *Fisherman, Logger, Merchant, Miner: Social Change and Industrialism in Three Newfoundland Communities*. St. John's: ISER Books, 1966.

Pieroway, Kenneth G. *Rails across The Rock: A Then and Now Celebration of the Newfoundland Railway*. St. John's: Creative Publishers, 2013.

Pike, Denise. "Heart's Delight–Islington Residents Head Up SUF High Order." *The Compass*, 15 Jan. 2008, B1.

Pitt, Robert D. "Frederick Charles Alderdice." *The Canadian Encyclopedia*. Historica-Dominion Institute, 2012. Accessed online 10 Jan. 2012.

Poole, Cyril. *Mose Morgan: A Life in Action*. St. John's: Harry Cuff, 1998.

Poole, Cyril F., and Robert Cuff. *The Encyclopedia of Newfoundland and Labrador*, vol. 4. St. John's: Harry Cuff, 1993.

"Nangle, Thomas F."

"Neal, George Eric."

"Neyle, Richard."

"O'Leary, Francis Martin."

"Pharmacy."

"Prince of Wales College."

"Pulp and Paper Manufacture."

"Ryan, Daniel A."

"Ryan, Edmund."

"Ryan, James M."

"Ryan, Michael."

——— and ———. *The Encyclopedia of Newfoundland and Labrador*, vol. 5. St. John's: Harry Cuff, 1994.

"Scammell, Arthur Reginald."

"Sealing."

"Sports."

"Squires, Richard Anderson."

"Taverner, Benjamin."

"Tourism."

"United Church of Canada."

"Williams, Ralph Champneys."

"Winter, Marmaduke George."

"Wreck House."

Porter, Helen Fogwill. *Below the Bridge: Growing Up on the Southside*. Portugal Cove-St. Philip's: Boulder Publications, 2011.

Porter, John. *The Vertical Mosaic: An Analysis of Social Class and Power in Canada*. Toronto: University of Toronto Press, 1965.

Power, Don. "Frank Dyke and the Sports Shop: Both Are True Water Street Institutions." *The Express*, 22 May 1991, 12.

"Profile: Harold Goodridge." *The Newfoundland Herald*, 13 June 1979, 20–21.

Prowse, D.W. *A History of Newfoundland from the English, Colonial, and Foreign Records*. London: Macmillan, 1895.

"Reception to Ricketts, V.C." *The Evening Telegram*, 9 Feb. 1919, 9.

Red Indian Lake Development Association. *Khaki Dodgers: The History of Mining and the People of the Buchans Area*. Grand Falls–Windsor, Nfld.: Robinson Blackmore, n.d.[1993?].

Reflections of the Chinese Community on the Occasion of the 30th Anniversary of the Chinese Association of Newfoundland and Labrador 1976–2006. St. John's: Chinese Association of Newfoundland and Labrador, 2007.

Reid, John G. *Mount Allison University: A History, to 1963.* Toronto: University of Toronto Press, 1984.

Riggs, Bert. "A Newfoundlander to Be Proud of." *The Gazette,* 19 Feb. 1998. Accessed online 12 Aug. 2014.

———. "A Successful Fish Merchant." *The Telegram,* 21 Sept. 2005, A10.

———. "A Woman of Unswerving Loyalty." *The Telegram,* 14 Apr. 2003, 7.

Roberts, Terry. "Unwilling Hero." *The Telegram,* 11 Nov. 2008, A1. Accessed online 8 Sept. 2013.

Rompkey, Bill. "A Man Who Made a Difference." *The Telegram,* 13 Aug. 2006, 13.

———, ed. *St. John's and the Battle of the Atlantic.* St. John's: Flanker Press, 2009.

Rompkey, Ronald, ed. *The Diary of Bishop Feild in 1844.* St. John's: ISER Books, 2010.

The Rooms Provincial Archives Division, A 3-39, Water Street, St. John's [192-?], Provincial Archives photograph collection.

The Rooms Provincial Archives Division, VA 14–30, Water Street Looking East from Adelaide Street, St. John's, 1939, Gustav Anderson, Newfoundland Tourist Development Board fonds.

B 5-75, Memorial Day Parade, 1 July 1924/S.H. Parsons & Sons, family collection.

E 23-39, Float Representing Japan, Peace Celebration parade, 5 Aug. 1919, St. John's, Provincial Archives glass negative collection.

E 23-29, Official Inauguration Commission of Government, Newfoundland Hotel, St. John's, 16 February 1934, Elsie Holloway, Holloway family fonds.

VA 37-15.4, No. 2 Co., 2nd Contingent, 1915/S.H. Parsons & Sons [postcard: No. 34]. From The Royal Newfoundland Regiment in the Great War 1914–1918/The Provincial Command of the Canadian Legion, 7 June 1961 [photograph album].

Surgeon-Major Macpherson [photograph]. In Newfoundland Quarterly (vol. 16, Spring 1917, p. 7).

Roseman, Sharon R. "'How We Built the Road': The Politics of Memory in Rural Galicia." *American Ethnologist* 23, 4 (1996): 836–60.

———. "'Going Over to the Other Side': The Sociality of Remembrance in Galician Death Narrative." *Ethos* 30, 4 (2003): 433–64.

———. "Spaces of Production, Memories of Contention: An Account of Local Struggle in Late-20th Century Rural Galicia (Spain)." *Dialectical Anthropology* 27 (2003): 19–45.

———. "'Hai que entenderse' (We Have to Understand One Another): Fieldwork,

Migration and Storytelling Events." *Where Is the Field? The Experience of Migration Viewed through the Prism of Ethnographic Fieldwork.* Studia Fennica Ethnologica 14. Edited by Laura Hirvi and Hanna Snellman. Helsinki: Finnish Literature Society, 2012, 193–216.

Rowe, Frederick W. *The History of Education in Newfoundland.* Toronto: The Ryerson Press, 1952.

———. *Education and Culture in Newfoundland.* Scarborough, Ont.: McGraw-Hill Ryerson, 1976.

Rowe, Penelope M. *The Nonprofit and Voluntary Sector in Atlantic Canada: Regional Highlights of the National Survey of Nonprofit and Voluntary Organizations.* Toronto: Image Canada, 2006.

"The Royal Stores, Ltd., Was Established 1895." *Newfoundland Quarterly* 52, 2 (1953): 34–35.

"Royal Stores in Receivership." *The Evening Telegram,* 7 Jan. 1977.

Ryan, Shannon. *The Ice Hunters: A History of Newfoundland Sealing to 1914.* St. John's: Breakwater Books, 1994.

St. John's, Newfoundland. Newfoundland Tourist and Publicity Bureau, 1900.

"St. Paul's Anglican Church." Newfoundland and Labrador Heritage. Memorial University of Newfoundland and the C.R.B. Foundation, 1997. Accessed online 20 Mar. 2014.

St. Paul's Anglican Church Trinity, Newfoundland Index of Names, Baptisms, Marriages and Burials 1753–1867. St. John's: Newfoundland and Labrador Genealogical Society, 1995.

St. Paul's Anglican Church Trinity, Newfoundland Index of Names, Baptisms, Marriages and Burials 1867 to Early 1900's. St. John's: Newfoundland and Labrador Genealogical Society, 1996.

Scammell, Elizabeth L. "Bishop Spencer College 1845–1922." *The Spencer Letter* 6, 4 (2006). Accessed online 26 Mar. 2014.

"Shannie Duff Retires from St. John's City Council." CBC News Newfoundland and Labrador, 28 May 2013. Accessed online 5 Oct. 2013.

Sharpe, Christopher. *Preserving Inner City Residential Areas: The Planning Process in St. John's, Newfoundland 1983–1991.* ISER Report No. 7. St. John's: ISER, 1993.

———. "The Cape Cod Comes to the Avalon: Suburban House Design in St. John's." Paper presented to the annual meeting of the Canadian Association of Geographers, May 2002.

———. "'Mr. Dunfield's Folly': The Development of Churchill Park Garden Suburb in St. John's." *Four Centuries and the City — Perspectives on the Historical Geography of St. John's.* Edited by Alan G. MacPherson. St. John's: Memorial University Department of Geography, 2005, 83–123.

Short, Robin. "New Effort Underway to Replace Torbay Rec Centre." *The Tele-gram*, 15 Nov. 2004, C3.

Shuldham, Molineux. Grant of land to James Winter. 24 Oct. 1774. MS.

Sider, Gerald M. *Culture and Class in Anthropology and History: A Newfoundland Illustration*. Cambridge: Cambridge University Press, 1986.

Smallwood, Joey. *I Chose Canada*. Toronto: Macmillan, 1973.

——— and Robert D.W. Pitt. *The Encyclopedia of Newfoundland and Labrador*, vol. 1. St. John's: Newfoundland Book Publishers, 1981.

"Admirals, Fishing."

"Ayre Group of Companies."

"Benevolent Irish Society."

"Bowring Group of Companies."

"Caribou, S.S."

"Carriage Factories."

"Champneys."

"Cheeseman, John T."

"Chinese Community."

"Church Lads."

"Corner Brook."

"Crosbie, Chesley Arthur."

"Earle, Canon George Halden."

——— et al. *The Encyclopedia of Newfoundland and Labrador*, vol. 2. St. John's: Newfoundland Book Publishers, 1984.

"Garland, Samuel E."

"Goodyear, Roland."

"Government."

"Hebrew Congregation."

"Holloway School."

"Howse, Claude K."

———, Cyril F. Poole, and Robert Cuff. *The Encyclopedia of Newfoundland and Labrador*, vol. 3. St. John's: Harry Cuff, 1991.

"Job's Cove."

"Labrador Fishery."

"London, New York & Paris Association of Fashion Ltd."

"Macpherson, Cluny."

"McMurdo, Thomas."

"Meaney, Edward Benedict."

"Methodist College."

"Miller, Leonard Albert."

Souvenir Booklet: St. John's Memorial Stadium Official Opening Programme. 1954.

Sparrow, John Kenneth. "From Sojourning to Citizenship: The Chinese in St. John's Newfoundland, 1895–1967." Dissertation. Memorial University of Newfoundland, 2006.

Stacey, Jean Edwards. "Bridge to the Past." *The Evening Telegram*, 28 Sept. 1996, 17.

———. "Scout Master." *The Evening Telegram*, 20 Apr. 1996, 17.

———. "Theatre Icon Dead at 91." *The Telegram*, 19 June 2005, A4.

Stack, Carol B. *All Our Kin: Strategies for Survival in a Black Community*. New York: Harper Torchbooks, 1975.

Sterns, Maurice A., ed. *Perspectives on Newfoundland Society and Culture*. St. John's: Memorial University of Newfoundland, 1974.

Story, G.M., W.J. Kirwin, and J.D.A.Widdowson, eds. *Dictionary of Newfoundland English*. Toronto: University of Toronto Press, 1982.

"The Story of the Wesleyan Academy 1860–86 and the Methodist College 1886–1900." *The Collegian* (1960): 66–83.

Sullivan, J.M. "Stephen Rupert Morris." *The Globe and Mail*, 24 Feb. 2000, 20.

Sullivan, Joan. "Edna Ricketts, 97 / Widow of First World War Soldier." *The Globe and Mail*, 11 June 2010, S8.

Sweet, Barb. "Retired Teacher Moves Home after 40 Years Away." *The Telegram*, 27 Mar. 2010, A17. Accessed online 9 May 2014.

"The Ten Best Female Athletes of Newfoundland and Labrador: Soccer." *The Evening Telegram*, 6 July 1995, 19.

Teski, Marea C., and Jacob J. Climo, eds. *The Labyrinth of Memory: Ethnographic Journeys*. Westport, Conn.: Bergin and Garvey, 1995.

Thomas, A.H., ed. *Newfoundland Hockey Guide*. St. John's: A.H. Thomas, 1921.

"Thomas Edward Furlong Obituary." Obits for Life. Accessed online 21 Jan. 2014.

"Tireless Physician Dead at 78." *The Evening Telegram*, 31 Oct. 1992, 6.

"Under 20 Team." The Rock: Official Website of the Newfoundland Rugby Union. 2010. Accessed online 23 May 2014.

"Upper Fifth Form." *The Feildian* 27, 2 (1921): 49.

Vincent, John. "Bob Cole Talks Hockey." *Newfoundland Lifestyle* 2, 1 (1984): 24–27, 52.

"Violet Cherrington." Newfoundland and Labrador Heritage. Memorial University of Newfoundland and the C.R.B. Foundation, 1997. Accessed online 5 Jan. 2012.

Wadel, Cato. *Now, Whose Fault Is That? The Struggle for Self-Esteem in the Face of Chronic Unemployment*. St. John's: ISER Books, 1973.

Walsh, Bren. *More Than a Poor Majority: The Story of Newfoundland's Confederation with Canada*. St. John's: Breakwater Books, 1985.

"Wayfarer." "In the News." *The Daily News*, 28 May 1959.

"Ways to Screech." Newfoundland Liquor Corporation, 1990.

Webb, Jeff A. *The Voice of Newfoundland: A Social History of the Broadcasting Corporation of Newfoundland, 1939–1949.* Toronto: University of Toronto Press, 2008.

Weber, Max. *Economy and Society.* 3 vols. Totawa, N.J.: Bedminster Press, 1921/1968.

White, Gregory B. "Icing the Puck: The Origins, Rise and Decline of Newfoundland Senior Hockey, 1896–1996." Dissertation. Memorial University of Newfoundland, 1997. Accessed online 12 Dec. 2013.

White, Jack. "Fitzgibbon Everybody's Neighbour." *The Evening Telegram*, 14 Aug 1993, 7a.

White, Marion A. Frances. *A Woman's Almanac.* St. John's: Breakwater Books, 1991.

Whitehead, Kay, and Judith Peppard. "Placing the Grandy Sisters as Teachers in Pre-Confederation Newfoundland." *Historical Studies in Education* 17, 1 (2005): 81–105. Accessed online 29 Apr. 2014.

"William A. Neal Jr." *The Newfoundland Journal of Commerce* 30, 8 (1963): 21.

Williams, Ralph. *How I Became a Governor.* London: John Murray, 1913.

"W.J. Murphy's Is For Sale." CBC News, 22 June 2000. Accessed online 15 Jan. 2014.

Wright, Marie-Beth. *Grace Sparkes: Blazing a Trail to Independence.* St. John's: Flanker Press, 2014.

Yetman, Derek. *Riches of the Earth: The Story of Buchans.* St. John's: Tenax, 1986.

Name Index

Anderson, R.S., 242

Ayre, John, 268–69

Bartlett, Ern, 214–15, 221

Baxter, Lewis, 241

Bell, Charlie, 269

Best, Earl, 180

Bishop, Allan, 237–38

Blackall, William Walker, 104, 119,
189n, 191–92, 211, 244

Butler, Brenda (née Marshall), 36, 97,
180

Butler, Ches, 180

Butt, Charles, 52, 88–90

Butt, Dot (née Jardine), 36, 90

Butt, Gel, 36, 52, 90, 97, 149

Butt, Herb, 52, 90, 91, 97,

Butt, Maggie (née Taylor), 35, 52, 88,
89

Carnell, Andy, 99n17, 134n24, 136

Carnell, Geoff, 193, 230

Cashin, Peter, 96n14, 150

Chatwood, Ann, 241

Cherrington, Violet M., 189n, 192,
244–45

Coady, Sally, 266

Coates, Len, 156

Cole, Bob, 12–14, 23, 70, 236–37

Cole, Hughie, 272

Colley, Llewellyn, 110, 240

Collingwood, John, 233

Courage, Jack, 232

Crosbie, Ches, 253

Crosbie, John, 23, 70, 235–36

Currie, Chancey, 62, 101, 212, 253–54

Currie, Florence (née Hue), 36, 97, 101

Davis, Walter, 264

Day, Ben, 163, 177

Day, Bill, 76

Day, George, 76n, 162

Day, John, 162

Day, Nehemiah, 164

Dawe, Bill, 214

Dawe, Olive (neé Field), 214

Duff, Shannie, 196

Earle, Fred, 82

Earle, George, 82–83, 242

Eaton, J. Douglas, 256

Egan, Katie, 166

Egan, Paddy, 165–66

Elworthy, Clyde, 155

Emerson, Carla, 126

Emerson, Frederick R., 31n17,
125–26, 230

Feder, Herb, 158

Fitzgibbon, Joe, 265–66

Fitzgibbon, Rosemary, 265

Fitzpatrick, John, 275

Fowlow, Captain, 177

Fraser, Allan, 211, 268

Freeman, Mary, 163, 176

Furlong, Tom, 88

Furneaux, Edith: *see* House, Edith

Furneaux, Wilf, 36, 78, 243, 251

George V (King), 118

Godfrey, Ros, 177, 185, 254
Godfrey, Stuart, 36, 97, 177n15,
　185–86, 195, 249, 254
Goodridge, Harold, 228–30
Grenfell, Wilfred, 156
Hall, Claude, 157
Hefferton, Sam, 238–39
Hickman, Edgar, 269
Horwood, Harold, 28–30, 108n6,
　127n6
Hong, Kim, 231n8, 233
House, Aunt Hattie, 36, 183
House, Doug, 102, 113, 149n7, 183,
　208, 218, 222–23, 225, 267–68
House, Ed, 77, 157, 172
House, Edith (Mrs. Wilf Furneaux),
　33, 36, 43, 76, 78, 97, 113, 134,
　164, 168, 204, 210, 224, 235–36,
　243, 244, 246
House, George (Edgar's father), 12,
　24, 33–37, 38–41, 43, 47, 51, 65,
　75–78, 80–84, 86, 98–99, 103–13,
　119–21, 142, 148, 152–54,
　164–68, 172–75, 183, 186, 195,
　197, 204, 224–25, 237, 241, 245,
　248, 280
House, George (Edgar's grandfather),
　32–33, 51, 81
House, Hal, 77, 157–58, 172, 174
House, Jack, 76, 162, 166, 171, 174, 223
House, Jeannie, 5, 10, 54n55, 82n14
House, Mary (née Day), 33–35, 40,
　51, 54, 65, 75–80, 86–87, 105,
　107, 109, 113, 119, 126, 161–63,
　192, 210, 244–45, 280
House, Uncle Jake, 36, 181–84
Howse, Carl, 213
Howse, Claude, 138, 213, 263–64
Humber, Ish, 254
Hunt, Robert, 27–28

Jamieson, Don, 38, 125
Johnson, Arthur, 139, 142, 159
Johnson, Paul, 98, 142
Lane, Bill, 259–60
Lawlor, Mr. (cabman), 118, 129–30
Macpherson, Cluny, 85–86, 119,
　131n15
Manuel, Edith, 235, 243
Marshall, Kel, 173
Matthews, Rex, 265
Mattiford, Kay, 272
McMurdo, Thomas J., 121
McNamara brothers, 125
McNicholas, John, 275
Meaney, Ted, 283
Mercer, Isaac, 242
Milley, Walter, 219–20
Monroe, Walter, 194
Moore, Barbara, 33n20
Morgan, Mose, 255–56
Morris, Fred, 172–73
Morris, Rupert, 172, 180, 185
Murphy, Bliss, 36, 41, 70, 85, 117,
　127, 158, 180, 233, 265, 271–73,
　276–77
Murray, Neil, 134
Neal, Bill, 36
Nemec, Ada (neé Green), 168
O'Dea, Fabian, 38
O'Driscoll, Josh, 266
O'Flaherty, Patrick, 26
O'Leary, Frank, 257, 266, 270–71
O'Neill, Paul, 26–27
Outerbridge, Leonard, 153
Outerbridge, Neddie, 137
Parsons, Ches, 46n42, 227, 241,
Paton, John Lewis, 23, 53, 59, 70,
　95–96, 196–200, 241, 283
Perlin, Albert, 156
Perlin, Ted, 156

Pinsent, Doug, 158

Porter, Helen Fogwill, 29–31

Powell, Clarence, 180

Press, "Dim", 241–42

Ricketts, Edna, 122

Ricketts, Thomas (Tommy's son), 122

Ricketts, Tommy, 23, 35, 70, 78–79,
    85, 114n1, 116–22, 195

Rompkey, Bill, 283–84

Rusted, Ian, 256

Ryan, Daniel, 169, 171n10

Ryan, Edmund, 169, 171n10

Ryan, James M., 169

Ryan, Nora (neé Bourke), 171

Samson, Art, 36, 79, 114, 123,

Samson, Jerry (I.J.), 36, 38, 70, 79, 99,
    103–13, 209

Samson, Mildred, 113, 210

Scammell, Art, 70, 86

Shulman, Menjie, 235

Smallwood, Joey, 23, 29, 39n29,
    46n41, 63, 70, 167n5, 186,
    220–21, 238–39, 242, 250–55

Sparkes, Grace, 51n50, 96n13, 208

Squires, Jack, 138–39

Squires, Janet (née House), 35–36, 40,
    41n33, 47–48, 54n55, 66, 102,
    109, 113n10, 163, 181, 183, 185,
    225, 267

Squires, Jordy (George), 41n33,
    54n55, 66–67, 174, 280

Squires, Richard, 70, 202, 203n10,
    248–250,

Steed, Miss, 190

Steele, Dick, 269

Steele, Geoffrey, 38

Stephenson, Carl, 278

Stirling, Frank, 192

Stirling, Geoff, 38

Stirling, Gordon, 36, 97, 141

Tait, Bert, 144

Tanner, R.E., 12, 25, 212, 223n11, 226

Taverner, Capt., 171–72

Taylor, Stephen J.L., 255–56

Troake, Peter, 258–59

Trotters McCarthy, 135

Tulk, Davey, 202

Wells, Clyde, 278

Wells, Mark, 128, 162–63

Wells, Mid, 162–63

Wigh, Sylvia, 240

Winter, Gordon, 38, 105

Winter, Marmaduke, 88n3, 145

Winter, Tommy, 111, 158

Wilansky, Maurice, 40, 235, 273–74

Williams, Ralph Champneys, 75n2

Wood, Ralph R., 25, 212, 223

Woodley, Gwen, 241

Subject Index

A.A. (Associate of Arts), 33, 51, 103
Admiral's Island, 178–79
air force. *See* RAF
American military presence in New-
    foundland, 21, 23; in St. John's,
    127, 139–41, 158, 231–32; in
    Stephenville, 129, 263
Anglican Church, the, 45, 47–48, 59,
    60n60, 67, 82n15, 97–98, 165,
    198, 282
Anglican Cathedral, The (of St. John
    the Baptist), 47, 84, 105, 113,
    198, 229, 246
Armistice, the, 114–15, 195
Ayre & Sons Ltd. (Ayre's), 39, 76, 79,
    84, 100, 133, 144, 162, 268
bakeapples, 41, 79, 174
Bannerman Park, 61, 137–38
baseball, 89, 157–58
basketball, 52, 91, 95, 137, 154, 156,
    192, 245
Beaumont Hamel, Battle of, 20
bicycles and cycling, 84, 164, 200
B.I.S. (Benevolent Irish Society), 157
Bishop Feild College, 12–13, 17, 27,
    33–34, 43, 45–47, 51, 59, 62–63,
    76, 97, 105–6, 119, 121–22, 189–
    94, 209, 211–12, 223–26, 231–36,
    249, 254, 280, 283–84; sports at,
    144, 148–49, 154–55; teachers at,
    103–4, 227–30, 237–43
Bishop Spencer College: 43, 45–46n39,
    76, 189, 192–93, 210, 230, 235;

relationship with Bishop Feild,
    190–91; teachers at, 240, 243–46
blueberries, 41, 185; wine from:
    244–45
boats, 161, 163, 169, 171–73, 175, 178;
    boat building, 183; travel by, 109,
    163–64, 207–8, 246
Boer War, 118, 148
Bonaventure, 169, 173, 181, 183
Bonavista, 169, 170, 143n2
Bonavista Bay, 79, 107, 152, 172
bowling, 54, 101, 140, 152
Bowring Brothers, Ltd. (Bowring's),
    39, 133–34, 144, 195
Bowring Park, 133n20, 137–38, 152
bridge, 51, 54, 78, 101, 019, 216, 280
Brigus, 41, 98–100, 233
Britain. *See* England
Buchans, 12, 17, 37, 38, 41–42, 61,
    212–24, 251–52; economy, 213,
    217, 219; skiing, 214–16; social
    activities, 213, 217–18; weather,
    69, 214, 252
Burin Peninsula, 112n9, 138n29,
    146n5, 151, 266
businesses, 38–39; in Corner Brook,
    76–77, 158; in St. John's, 128,
    131–34, 144, 194, 234n12; in
    Trinity, 165–169, 172, 177, 181,
    187–88
Canada, 30, 46, 53, 253, 258
Canadian Military presence in New-
    foundland, 21, 23, 251

Carbonear, 38n27, 88, 144, 220n6

Caribou Group, 268, 271, 273–74

Carnell's: Carriage Factory, 134; Funeral Home, 134n24, 193n3

carpentry, 105, 162, 168, 177, 183, 219, 241

Catalina, 131n16, 147, 164, 172, 174

Catholic Church. *See* Roman Catholic Church

Caul's grocery (N.F. Caul's), 131

Champneys, 33, 40, 65, 75, 78–79, 86, 91, 161–63, 173, 175–77

Change Islands, 33, 76, 82

Chinese community, 231–33

Christmas Seal, the, 258–60, 264

Church Lads' Brigade (CLB), 59, 89, 119, 123, 151, 175, 190, 194–96, 210, 249, 273; camp in Topsail, 93, 110–11, 146, 195–96, 221; camp in Trinity, 180–81

Church of England. *See* Anglican Church

Churchill Falls, 37

Churchill Park, 40, 102n20

class (socioeconomic), 27–31, 39, 48–52, 65, 93n9, 108n6; in school, 45–47, 189n1; in Winter Place neighbourhood, 39–40, 107

coal. *See under* home heating

cobblestones (from Water Street), 99

Colonial Building riots (1932), 248–249

Colony Club, The Old, 127, 129, 142, 208

community involvement, 56–58, 71, 96n13, 196n8, 270–75, 280

Commission of Government, 19n1, 21, 60–62, 137; Edgar's feelings surrounding, 61; inauguration of, 249–50

company towns, 37

Confederation (Newfoundland's with Canada), 27, 29, 39n29, 111n8, 252–53; Edgar's views on, 62–64, 253

Congress, United States, act of, 141

Corner Brook, 37, 76–77, 90, 157–58, 162, 166, 223, 263, 267

Council of Higher Education, 82, 103, 268

crossing boys, 128–29

Daily News, The, 62, 96n13, 101

Dalhousie University, 53, 62, 154, 202–204, 248, 253

dancing and dances, 99n17, 270n4; in Buchans, 213, 218; at Feild and Spencer, 91, 152, 192–93; in Halifax, 205–7

denominational education system, 45–47, 229n5

Depression, the Great, 29–30, 52, 61, 93n9, 248n2

Doctor's Point, 184–85

dogs and dog sleds, 156, 162, 165, 222

driving and cars, 89n6, 98–99, 113, 127, 131, 140–41, 180–81

domestic work, 55, 78–80

downtown, 27, 39n29, 128, 130–34, 136, 137

economy, 37, 42, 57, 61, 187; ties between outport and city, 35, 80

education, 28, 33, 42, 43, 46–48, 50–53, 119, 156, 189–208

Ericson's store, 177, 181

Evening Telegram, The, 156

examinations, 82–83, 103, 183

family, 32–37, 52, 75–87, 181, 279–80

Feild Hall, 156, 157, 189n1, 240, 242–43, 251

Feildian Grounds, the, 13, 48, 151–54, 193, 216

Feildian Ladies' Association, 54, 78, 91, 230, 237

Feildians, Old, 145, 151–53, 155, 227, 241, 244, 284

fictive kin, 36

film, 40, 90, 217, 272

First World War. *See* World War I

fish and brewis, 195, 196n6

fishery, 37, 41, 76, 133n20, 169, 172, 179n18, 197; Labrador, 128, 184; at Quidi Vidi, 108–109; in Trinity, 161, 183

Football (soccer), 12–13, 146–52, 172, 202–3, 225; accidents playing, 146–48; Memorial jerseys for, 149–50; with Old Feildians, 153, 249

Fort Pepperrell, 140, 157, 231, 261, 273

Fundraising, 70, 152–53, 219, 257, 279

Furness Withy, 207

gardens and gardening, 105, 161

Garland's Bookstore, 131, 136

Girl Guides, 93–94, 243n25, 244n26

Glenridge Crescent, 39–40, 102, 132–24, 234

Glynmill Inn, 90, 263

Goodyear and House, 76–77, 166

Grand Falls, 37, 61, 76, 272n5

Guards, the Methodist, 143

Gun Hill, 147, 181

Halifax, 26, 38, 62, 109, 199, 201, 207

headmaster and principal, 47, 212–13, 223–24, 225–35, 246–47

Hercules bicycle, 84

history, oral, 22–23

hockey, 91, 123, 143–45; in Buchans, 216–17

holidays, 52, 60, 89, 258

Holloway School, 28, 30, 52, 53, 89, 96

home heating: coal, 79, 152, 178; firewood, 79–80, 165, 178

horses, 129–31, 134, 161, 169; racing of, 129

hunting, 175, 221

identity, 25, 30, 42, 48, 59; Canadian, 62–64; English 59–60; Newfoundland, 61–62; townie, 62

India, 97, 228

inuit, 263

Iris Kirby House, 275

Jewish community: at Bishop Feild, 234; on Glenridge Crescent, 234–35

Job's Cove, 88

Kerley's Harbour, 183

King's College, 59, 62, 199, 201–2, 253

King's Cove, 148, 169, 180

kinship, 32–37

knitting, 78, 107, 162, 245

Labrador City, 37, 263

Lions Club, 261–62, 263, 270

livestock, rearing of: in Champneys, 161–62; on experimental farm, 123; by Mary House, 78; by Smallwood, 251–52, 254–55

London, New York and Paris (store), 39, 131–33, 136, 149

London Players, the, 193

Lung Association of Newfoundland and Labrador, 63, 267, 278

mail delivery, 32, 76, 81–82, 156, 220

Manuels, 89, 146

marriage, 41, 53–54, 66, 93, 97–100, 176–77

marriage bar on female teachers. *See under* teachers

Masonic Terrace, 52, 88

McMurdo's Pharmacy, 121, 134

Memorial Stadium, 270

Memorial University College, 43, 52, 59, 90–93, 196, 200–201

Memorial University of Newfoundland: Board of Regents, 58; medical school, 255–56

memory, 25

Mercy Convent (Academy), 45; teaching chemistry to nuns from, 239

Methodist College, 90, 143–44, 154, 190, 212. *See also* Prince of Wales

Mi'kmaq, 222

mines and mining, 37, 42, 138n29, 213, 214, 216, 217

Model School, the, 210

Mount Allison University, 53, 62, 90, 94–95, 96, 208

movies. *See* film

mummering, 107–8

Murphy's (W.J., grocer), 131

National Convention, the, 21, 61–62

National Physical Fitness Council, 159

navigation, teaching of, 197

Newfoundland English, 64–65; Edgar's English, 64–65

Newfoundland Teachers' Association, 57, 238–39, 281

Newfoundland Tuberculosis Association, 57, 257

New Gower Street. *See under* poverty

New Perlican, 81–82, 200–201

New York (City), 109, 154, 176, 204, 227, 269

Neyle-Soper (hardware store), 134

outport Newfoundland, 27, 36, 40–41, 61, 234n12, 249; children from, in St. John's, 138, 154, 156n13, 190, 198, 200, 242, 245

partridgeberries, 79, 246

Pepperell, Fort, 140–41, 158, 231, 261, 273

physiology, teaching of, 94, 95–96

poverty, 28, 29, 30, 61, 157n15; on New Gower St. in St. John's, 136, 137; in outports, 136; in Trinity, 176

Prescott Street, 77, 84, 128, 130, 136; washing of, 139

Prince of Wales College, 45, 52, 53, 90, 95–96, 143, 154, 190, 225

Prince's Rink, the, 139, 142, 270n4

Queen's College, 82n15, 86–87, 229

railway and trains, 28, 81, 89, 122, 185, 208, 217, 265n8; close call on trestle bridge, 178; blasting for ballast for, 185

Rawlins Cross, 84, 115, 139

rehabilitation: of TB patients, 44–45, 57, 257–58, 260–62, 264–67; of Waterford Hospital patients, 58, 273–74

Rennie's River, 106; swimming pool, 138

resettlement, 31, 111n8, 183

Responsible Government, 21, 26, 61, 62, 96n13, 257n2

Riverdale Tennis Club, 158–59

Robinson's Hill, 39, 99, 152, 216

Roman Catholic Church, 30–31, 48, 60n60, 66, 98n15, 130n12, 165, 217, 222

Rotary International, 55, 57–58, 137, 254, 268–77. *See also* Caribou Group

Royal Air Force (RAF), 77, 114, 157

Royal Newfoundland Regiment, The, 20, 85n17, 116, 130, 144, 158, 194–95

Royal Stores, 128–29, 131, 214, 218, 221

rugby, 18, 154–56

Ryan Brothers Ltd., 169–70, 172, 177

St. Bon's (St. Bonaventure's College), 27, 45, 143–44, 154, 156, 190, 212, 225n, 238

St. Paul's Anglican Church, 168

St. Thomas' Anglican Church, 48, 162, 227, 240, 249, 279, 284

Salmon Cove (Champneys). See Champneys

sanatoriums, tuberculosis, 126, 184, 257, 258, 260, 266, 267

Screech, 139–40

Second World War. See World War II

skating, 142–43

Society of United Fishermen (SUF), The, 111–12

soccer. See football

S.O. Steele, 39

southside (of St. John's), 29–31

Sports Shop, The, 134, 260

Stephenville, 129, 263

story, life, 23–24

streetcars, 84, 99n17, 130, 137, 197

subjectivity , 20n2, 24–25

T. & M. Winter Co., 52, 88, 90, 145n4

Tannery Field, 105, 151–52

taxis and taxicabs, 129–30, 140, 172

teacher(s), 28, 43–44, 176, 192, 240–44, 246; art, 228–30; Edgar as, 13, 62, 209–12; Edith House as, 76; games, 226–27; George House as, 75; kindergarten, 230–31; Margie as, 95–96; marriage bar on female, 53, 96; music, 227; salaries of, 237–39; training, 67, 103, 109

teaching, 43–44, 183, 199, 204, 247, 264; discipline, 12–13, 211–12

tennis, 91, 138, 147

tool box, 83

Topsail, 93, 98, 146, 195

Torbay Rec Centre, 159–60

tourism, 128

Trapnell's Jewellers, 133

Trinity, 41, 65, 78, 164–65, 167, 172, 181, 187; blacksmith, 168; Garden Party, 175; tourism, 187; travelling to, 163–64, 180; Trinity Pageant, 188

Trinity Cabins, 180

trouting, 41, 121, 137, 163, 172–75, 214

tuberculosis, 57, 137, 258, 261, 283n1; from cow's milk, 161; drugs to treat, 266–67; testing for, 259

United Church of Canada, 53, 60n60, 98n15

Victoria Cross, the, 85, 116, 118, 119

Victorian Order of Nurses, 271–72

voluntary associations, 56–58

Waterford Hospital, 260, 272–73

Water Street, 38–39, 84, 226, 270; businesses on, 39n29, 131–34

Winter Estate, the, 99–100

Winter Place, 31, 38, 105, 107, 115, 123

women and gender relations, 52–56, 161–62, 260–61

World War I, 20–21, 109, 114, 194–95, 228; war stamps, 219

World War II, 21, 61, 100–101, 114, 157, 257n2

Wreckhouse, the, 264–65